On Whitcomb Hill

*Land, House, and History
in Rural Vermont*

E. J. Myers

On Whitcomb Hill

*Land, House, and History
in Rural Vermont*

E. J. Myers

Montemayor Press
Montpelier, Vermont

Copyright © 2019 E. J. Myers

Cover design Copyright © 2019 Montemayor Press

Cover photograph Copyright © 2019 Montemayor Press

Printed in the United States of America.

For information contact:

Montemayor Press
P. O. Box 546
Montpelier, VT 05601

Web site: www.MontemayorPress.com

1 3 5 7 9 10 8 6 4 2

All rights reserved, including, without limitation, the right of the publisher to sell directly to end users of this and other Montemayor Press books. No part of this book may be reproduced in any form or by any electronic or mechanical means, including information storage and retrieval systems, without permission in writing from the publisher or author, except by a reviewer who may quote brief passages in a review.

For Edith, Cory, and Robin—

fellow-travelers on the hillside

And in honor of

James C. Whitcomb (1819-1884)
and
Hannah Welch Whitcomb (1816-1873)

Robert Bohonon (1813-1892)
and
Betsey Smith Bohonon (1816-1869)

On Whitcomb Hill

Land, House, and History
in Rural Vermont

E. J. Myers

Contents

Forethoughts

    House, Meadow, Woods............................. 1
    Beyond House, Meadow, Woods?...................... 7

Part One - A Sense of Place

    1 - House History: Glimmerings..................... 15
    2 - Meadow 29
    3 - The Cheerful Reaper........................... 31

Part Two - Denizens

    4 - House History: One Hill, Three Families 45
    5 - Sound of Water................................ 51
    6 - Night Fliers 63
    7 - The Whiteness of the Weasel 81

Part Three - Planting, Growing, Harvesting

    8 - House History: Working the Land 99
    9 - A Stand of Wheat 113
    10 - Sugar(ing) 125
    11 - A Shed of His Own........................... 129
    12 - Scorecard 147

Part Four - Shadows and Light

    13 - House History: Changes and Calamities............ 151
    14 - What Would They Think? 165
    15 - Lunar Gravity 167

Part Five - What Lasts and What Doesn't

    16 - House History: Remnants and Ruins.............. 181
    17 - Heat 197
    18 - Past Present, Present Past 209

Afterthoughts

    Lovely, Dark and Deep............................. 221

Notes 253

Bibliography 269

I live in . . . the most quiet place in the whole world, I believe, with woods close at hand . . . I feel as if, for the first time in my life, I [am] awake. I have found a reality, though it looks very much like some of my old dreams.

> —Nathaniel Hawthorne, letter to Evert Duyckinck, November 26, 1843

[W]e often talk about love of place, by which we mean our love for places, but seldom of how the places love us back, of what they give us.

> —Rebecca Solnit, *The Faraway Nearby*

A man or woman who ventures outside the human bubble and pays attention to a given landscape season after season, year after year, may eventually become a true inhabitant of that place, taking it in through every doorway of the body, bearing it steadily in heart and mind.

Only those who achieve such bone-deep familiarity with a place are likely to care for it as they would care for their children or parents or lovers.

> —Scott Russell Sanders, *A Conservationist Manifesto*

Forethoughts

House, Meadow, Woods

An ordinary house, an ordinary hill. Built in 1840, the house seems old to us, but old houses in northern New England are as common as cows, so this one is nothing special, and the hill is just a minor rise on Vermont's rolling surface. The ten acres of meadow and woods are altogether typical for this central part of the state.

My wife and I don't care. The property on Whitcomb Hill drew us, charmed us, and struck us as remarkable for a long time before we ever stumbled into ownership of the house and its little plot of land. For a month each summer over a span of six years, Edith and I had rented a cottage just a mile down the road. That rental was a random bit of luck, a choice resulting from the Internet equivalent of throwing darts at a map on the wall. Casting about for a summer rental in Vermont, we had quickly ruled out tourist towns like Stowe, Waitsfield, and Killington; instead, we had chosen a less-chic but still beautiful part of Orange County southeast of Barre. This area is one in which most people either work the land, support themselves through the trades, or commute to jobs in nearby towns and cities. The towns look more or less as they must have in the 1950's. The landscape is dotted with dairy farms. Edith and I, along with our then-teenaged son, Cory, spent two or three weeks each summer from 2004 until 2010 in this quiet and unpretentious place.

One of our activities during those years was walking the local roads. Hilly and heavily forested, Orange County remains largely undeveloped. We would walk almost daily through the calm, sparsely populated farmlands. On our favorite route, we would always pass a yellow house near the crest of a hill. *That's the prettiest place in the area,* Edith and I would comment time and again to each other. Though clearly old, it was attractive and well maintained. The surrounding plot of land, the woods beyond the land, the farms beyond the woods, and the far ridge to the east gave an expansive mood to the entire property. Time after time we walked past this property, commented on its beauty, and continued down the road.

In June of 2010, Edith and I drove from New Jersey across the United States to drop off Cory at Deep Springs College, in the California desert, for the start of his first semester as an undergraduate. We flew back to the Northeast to conclude that cross-country errand. Then, in keeping with our routine summer schedule at the time, Edith and I drove up to Vermont for a few weeks at the rented cottage.

We had heard accounts over the years describing how difficult many couples find the empty-nest stage of life. When the last son or daughter leaves for college, people told us, everything changes. Hands-on parenting ends; domestic routines no longer focus on children's needs and routines; the house grows quiet. A relief, surely . . . but also a potential shock to the system. We had already observed the consequences among many friends, neighbors, and acquaintances. Sometimes the effects have been creative: marriages strengthened, career vistas broadened, physical and intellectual energies renewed. Sometimes the outcomes have been much less positive, especially in terms of marital side effects: several couples we know split up within a year or two of their kids' departures. Edith and I never felt concerned that we would experience an unpleasant outcome. We remain close, and we've felt confident that the empty nest would become a locus of much more positive than negative change. Yes, we would be wistful about Cory's absence, just as we feel the absence of our daughter, Robin, who had left home for college five years earlier. We also expected to feel some sadness about the end of day-to-day parenting; we would miss the opportunities to witness the constant and often astonishing mutability of children's development; and we would also miss the richness, complexity, humor, and "thusness" of family life. But there would be benefits as well: more time for each other, less manic activity, less pressure, more rest, more opportunities to pursue our own interests. Among other things, we would be able to devote renewed energy to artistic pursuits. So, when friends asked us, "How do you feel about the empty nest?" our answer was: "Just fine."

What we never expected was a change of venue. We intended to stay in Maplewood, New Jersey, less than twenty miles west of New York City, where we had lived for almost twenty-five years and had thrived in a vibrant multicultural town; we would spend a month or so each summer at the rental house in Vermont; we would travel elsewhere when opportunities arose; but we would basically remain in the same setting that had served us well for so long.

Then, just a couple of weeks into that year's stay in Vermont, which had started shortly after we returned to the Northeast from California, our landlady informed us that she couldn't rent the house to us the following year. Her thirty-something daughter and the daughter's husband would soon be moving there to live while building their own home on a nearby plot of land. End of story. So, unfortunately, our sixth stay in that old farmhouse would be the last.

This news prompted Edith and me to walk up the road right after the phone conversation with our landlady. More specifically, the news resulted in our passing the yellow house just a day after its owners had posted a little hand-written sign near the front garden: FOR SALE.

One thing led to another. Edith and I stopped by, we met the owners, and they showed us around. What we had assumed was a pretty house on a few acres of land turned out to be a larger property—the house, two large outbuildings, ten acres, and a pond. Initial conversations were cordial, respectful, and mutually enthusiastic. Doris and Paul, a retired couple in their early eighties, seemed to like us from the start. We liked them, too. Doris, petite and handsome, told us, "We want to sell to someone who really loves the house." Her tall, craggy husband, Paul, added: "We've owned this place for thirty years, and we've really put our hearts and souls into it."

Edith and I felt strongly drawn to the property. The old house was attractive and the right size for us, and the plot of land surrounding it was larger and more varied than we'd first assumed, fully half of it being woods. If we ever intended to make this kind of move, now seemed the perfect opportunity. On the other hand, purchasing a rural property felt daunting. Were we prepared to leave the urban environments where we had thrived personally and professionally throughout our lives? Were we capable of adjusting to country life? How could we do it? Yet how could we *not* do it? We debated the pros and cons for weeks; we considered all kinds of scenarios; and we made our decision. We wanted to buy the house on Whitcomb Hill. We made a bid on the property.

What followed was a best-case scenario for purchasing a house without benefit of real estate brokers. All the warnings we had heard about purchasing a FSBO property (For Sale By Owner) were pointless admonitions. Every aspect of the process turned out to be congenial, collegial, and often mutually attentive. Even our interactions with a local bank to obtain a mortgage became a pleasant experience. The only hitch occurred when the bank's appraiser, a local resident who apparently harbors a deep resentment of "flatlanders"—non-Vermonters—low-balled his estimate so absurdly that the valuation nearly scuttled the deal. Edith and I then negotiated with Paul and Doris in person, we asked them to lower their asking price a little, we raised the amount of our down payment to keep the bank's "loan-to-value" ratio in line, and by this gambit we succeeded in outfoxing the appraiser. As a result, Edith and I secured our mortgage after all. Paul and Doris netted over 95% of their asking price. Both couples amiably signed all the documents at the closing a few weeks later.

What could be more trite than a writer moving to Vermont? Worse yet, moving into an old farmhouse? I get it. I'm aware that the north woods host almost as many writers as white-tailed deer. What, then, should I do? Should I stay clear of this state simply because so many other novelists, poets, visual artists, and musicians have found Vermont inspiring? Should I recoil from the risible aspects of a city boy finding this state's landscape remarkable, its history intriguing, its mix of solitude and social engagement congenial? I don't think so. Or, more to the point: no. I need this place. I want it. I feel no need to ignore it. All the better that Edith, too—herself a writer and musician—finds the place at once reassuring, uplifting, and delightful.

In mid-October of 2010, we took possession of the house and its acreage on Whitcomb Hill.

Beyond House, Meadow, Woods?

Almost every time I step outside this house I'm struck by the realization that Whitcomb Hill is the most beautiful plot of land on earth. The English Lake District, the Serengeti Plain, the Hawaiian archipelago, the Torres del Paine, the Amazonian rainforest—none of these places could possibly possess more beauty than our ten acres.

An absurd thought, of course. Whitcomb Hill is an attractive but unremarkable thread in Vermont's tapestry. It's a useful illusion, however, for me to believe that the place is extraordinary. This state of mind bears some resemblance to the standard parental delusion that one's own children are the most handsome, the most talented, the most brilliant ever to grace the earth. What's wrong with this fiction? Parenthood is hard enough without the belief that one's daughters and sons are special. It's easier, more productive, and more consoling to tackle the task of raising kids while convinced that they're remarkable. So much the better, too, that Edith and I might tend these few acres—might nurture and protect them, might value the fabric in which they're interwoven—while regarding them as exemplary.

What does it mean to love a place? Is it simply a matter of delighting in a specific parcel of land—for Edith and me, these ten acres in rural Vermont? Or does loving a place require a commitment that goes deeper than delight? Living now in the 1840's-era farmhouse surrounded by the meadow and the woods, I'm intent on grasping the thread of this specific place and, by pulling it, attempting to find out what Whitcomb Hill is connected to. By "connected," I mean more than just in a geographical sense. Our hillside is part of central Vermont, which in turn is part of northern New England, which in turn is part of the North American continent, which in turn is part of the earth. This sense of connection is only the start of what interests me. Even if I intend to value one particular place above all others—and, especially, if I wish to value this place during a time of environmental crisis—I have to value what it's connected *to*. I also have to go beyond valuing and cherishing Whitcomb Hill in merely aesthetic ways. I have to perceive the historical, ethical, and spiritual aspects of owning the place, of living here, of having stewardship of these ten acres. I have to go beyond perception to intervention.

There's another issue on my mind, another aspect of place.

Can Whitcomb Hill serve as a gateway to somewhere else? Can this hillside, though stationary, become a vehicle for certain kinds of travel? Time travel, perhaps, at least in a metaphorical sense? Perhaps other kinds of travel as well? Here again I use "gateway" and "vehicle" in more than literal senses of the words, though not in ways that imply something transcendental or hocus-pocussy; rather, I mean transitions into, or ways of delving into, states of insight that the privacy and serenity of this meadow and these woods may foster more fully and easily than might be possible for me elsewhere. Is it possible, in short, that living on Whitcomb Hill may be conducive to change, perhaps radical change, during the late stage of life that Edith and I have entered?

I started meditating in 1974, when I was twenty-four years old. I had known about meditation much earlier—first during my 1950s boyhood, when I heard vague, dismissive references to "navel gazing" and "the mysterious knowledge of the Mystic East'"; and then again during my adolescence, when I read about the Beats and their interest in Buddhism, about the Beatles and their dalliance with Maharishi Mahesh Yogi, and about other trendsetters and their obsessions with this or that meditative practice. Although I fancied myself a teenaged bohemian, I dismissed these inward-looking disciplines as chicanery. My being the son of a philosophy professor explains this attitude to some degree. I admired and emulated my father for his intellectual rigor and his resistance to cant. By my early twenties, I considered myself well armed with the shield of skepticism and the sword of reason. My perception of myself as wielding these weapons against fatuity, delusion, and faddish practices was grandiose, but it served me well on many occasions. A legion of gurus, sadhus, swamis, roshis, rinpoches, and perfect masters invaded America during the Sixties and Seventies. So much the better, then, to be well prepared for resistance. My overall attitude: if meditation was so popular and, worse yet, so universally accessible, then it surely must be nonsense. Two years later, though, my rigid dismissal of all meditative practices started to ease. I began to perceive differences between the Central Casting swamis and some of the extensively trained, less pretentious teachers. I decided to give meditation a try. In the more than forty years since then, I have explored three meditative techniques.

What I've practiced for fifteen years now is the *vipassana* approach. This method, drawn from the *Satipatthana Sutta* and attributed to Gautama Buddha, is the oldest of many Buddhist meditation practices. Focusing on breath awareness, the *vipassana* discipline emphasizes full experience of the present moment and closely examination of perceptions, experiences, and thought processes. The goal isn't transcendence but immanence: not escaping the here-and-now for a lofty "higher reality" but, rather, inhabiting the present moment. You sit. You follow the breath—inhalation, exhalation. You let thoughts and feelings arise, you observe them, and you let them go. This process sounds absurdly simple, but in practice it's remarkably difficult. Both the body and the mind quickly grow restless; the welling up of thoughts and emotions can become distracting, annoying, unsettling, even alarming; and there's a constant temptation to flee from the "confinement" of meditation—a confinement that is unsettling and alarming precisely because your mind often confronts you with unpleasant emotions, memories, and insights. It can even challenge your fundamental assumptions about who you are. In the longer term, however, meditation can lead to a greater awareness of yourself and of the world. What I've found most appealing about *vipassana* meditation is that precisely because it emphasizes being present rather than attempting to withdraw, you can practice it anywhere and in the midst of any activity. You can meditate while sitting on a bench or *zafu*, certainly, but also while sweeping the floor, petting the dog, fixing dinner, shopping for groceries, helping a child do homework, performing your job, or experiencing whatever else makes up the substance of your life.

In any case, it's clear to me that over the years I've been meditating, I've become less driven overall, less haunted by the past, less anxious about the future, less prone to compulsive striving, and less concerned about external accomplishments; and I'm more patient, more compassionate, more open to other people, and more willing to let life unfold at its own pace rather than to make it conform to my preconceived expectations. Are these changes the direct result of meditation? Have forty-five years of meditative practice prompted or simply coincided with these changes in my previously driven, often obsessive, frequently impatient, sometimes selfish personality? Is it possible that over the span of four-plus decades, the real evolution (if that's the right term) has resulted simply from a diminishment of energy? From an aging male's normal decline of testosterone? From the inevitable process of slowing down as the years pass? I can't say I know the answer. Even if proving or disproving a cause-effect relationship were feasible, I don't know if I would make the effort. What seems more important is that meditation feels intrinsically worthwhile. The practice of "non-doing" is one of the most important things I do. It prompts me both to accept the world more patiently and to engage with it more energetically.

Beyond these benefits, however, has this practice moved me toward a more substantial outcome? Perhaps even toward the Big E? Probably not. First of all, the various Buddhist lineages all warn against seeing Enlightenment as a goal: sought as an end point, it becomes just another object of craving, thus confounding the effort to relinquish desires and preconceived assumptions. Second, I'm not sure if my practice is sufficiently consistent, persistent, or clear-headed enough to add up in the long term. Practitioners of Zen often meditate for decades to master the discipline of *zazen,* or sitting meditation. Vajrayana (Tibetan) meditation can involve retreats lasting months, years, even decades. My most earnest efforts have amounted to little more than twice-daily sessions of about thirty minutes apiece. What are the odds that this desultory approach will add up to much?

My answer at this time: I don't know. Yet even if my uncertainty and doubts are valid, I intend to proceed with this approach. Living on this hillside seems the perfect time and place to try. Whitcomb Hill is Whitcomb Hill, but maybe it's more than that. Although it may or may not turn out to be a gateway, perhaps it's something as good or better: a window.

Part One

A Sense of Place

1

House History— Glimmerings

"Every house is a ship carrying its own cargo of loneliness," according to Arundhati Roy. Maybe so—but not just loneliness. Every house also carries a cargo of joys, sorrows, longings, hopes, frustrations, and delights. Above all, every house carries a cargo of stories.

Our house on Whitcomb Hill, built in 1840, is now almost a hundred eighty years old. Parcels of this property have changed hands twenty-two times. Deeds of ownership indicate thirty-eight owners and co-owners. This house has sailed through Time carrying at least two dozen families, their belongings, their relationships, and their inner lives. What is the history of this house? To what degree can I identify our predecessors, determine the basic facts of their lives here, and conjure at least some notion of the experiences that left them feeling content, frustrated, enriched, or bereft? To what degree will knowing about their past alter what Edith and I experience in the present?

When we first took possession of our property on Whitcomb Hill, Edith and I knew only the general outlines of its history. Our immediate predecessors, Paul and Doris, told us that the land had been a working farm for many generations, and that the house had gone through several cycles of deterioration, salvage, and renovation. We also learned that Doris and Paul had rescued the place from dereliction when they purchased it in 1983. Beyond that, we knew almost nothing. The nature of the house itself told us little. This isn't a property that the National Register of Historic Places would even consider listing. It's just an old farmhouse. Most of the owners lived humble lives. Even humble folk leave traces, however, so Edith and I grew curious about these people. We wanted to find out whatever we could about them. By visiting our local town hall to search the municipal records, we traced the transfer of the property over the nearly eighteen decades of its existence, an effort that revealed the sellers' and buyers' names and the dates of transfer. Unfortunately, this process didn't reveal much about the owners themselves. The next few years of desultory research provided only glimpses of our predecessors' time here. Lacking more information, we could only guess about the lives they lived, the work they performed, the families they raised, the joys they felt, the sorrows they suffered. The quotidian but often rich details seemed forever lost.

Here's what little we could reconstruct during our early efforts. Public records showed that around 1840, a man named James Whitcomb inherited land in Orange County, Vermont, and built a house. Eleven years later, James and his wife, Hannah, sold a parcel of land to one B. W. Bartholomew. The town's logbooks reveal that during the next few decades, a complex and sometimes confusing series of transfers took place. "Clark Cheney sells to Robert Bohonon" in 1853, for instance, but "Robert Bohonon leases to Moses Ring" on the same date of the same year. Just a year later, "Moses Ring and wife sell to Levi Jr. and James Whitcomb." Do these transfers mean that owners sold the house itself? Or, more likely, that the properties in question were parcels of farmland? Edith and I couldn't fully clarify what happened. Neither could we learn much about the participants in these transactions. Were Levi Jr. and James brothers, cousins, or father and son? Who were the other people that the town logbooks mention as buyers or sellers—Darius Whitcomb, J. D. Eastman, Mary C. Whitcomb, Laura Flint, Albert E. Whitcomb, and Patrick Moran, among others? We assembled a list of owners, but the sequence of names didn't add up to form a narrative.[1] All we could determine was that the property, or at least portions of it, had changed hands with surprising frequency: fifteen times in the nineteenth century alone. The pace slowed in the twentieth, with just eight transfers. Our immediate predecessors, Paul and Doris, hold the record for the longest period of unaltered ownership: almost thirty years.

Could the local cemeteries tell us more about these people? To gain a better sense of the past owners' lives, Edith and I started visiting each of the seven graveyards scattered among the nearby hills. Some of these had started out as family plots that grew with the community. One is more or less the official town cemetery now. In each of them, Edith and I wandered among the cordilleras of gravestones and attempted to locate any evidence of our predecessors. Maple Hill Cemetery is the largest, beautifully maintained and flanked by old-growth hardwood trees. Cheney Cemetery is even prettier, with a view in all directions across fields and woods. In these and in three smaller local graveyards we found some of the names we searched for: James Whitcomb (died 1884, age 67) and his first wife, Hannah (died 1873, age 57); Betsey Bohonon (died 1869, age 53); Leonard Flint (died 1901, age 87); and Albert E. Whitcomb (died 1912, age 51). What did these names and dates tell us? Not much. Only that some of our predecessors had been buried here, and that by today's standards, most of them had died fairly young.

Some clustered stones told appalling stories. Bethyah Ring, first wife of Moses Ring Sr., bore many children, among them Infant Ring (1819), Infant Ring (1824), and Infant Ring (1827). All of these children died well before Moses and Bethyah acquired property on Whitcomb Hill, but surely the little ghosts accompanied the parents, if only in their dreams.

A cliché uttered at funerals and memorial services is that the dead "will live on in our memories." True enough—for a while. But the persons holding those memories will die too, and their memories will then die with them. I remember a lot about my parents, little about my grandparents, nothing at all about my great-grandparents. The stories that Edith and I have told our daughter and son about their forebears are the merest distillation of the lives the tales describe. With the passing of each generation, the distilled memories vanish. This evanescence is appalling, but *c'est la vie*. Reassuring ourselves with clichés about the durability of the departed does nothing to make them linger.

Who remembers anything about James or Hannah Whitcomb, about Robert or Betsey Bohonon, about Moses Jr. and Lucinda Ring? Our predecessors have diminished to a few lines of ink in the town hall's ledgers and a few chiseled names on local gravestones. The only other remnant is the house on Whitcomb Hill. James Whitcomb built it, he and his wife lived in it, and subsequent owners enlarged and maintained it. They kept it roofed and painted. They protected it from storms. They managed to avoid burning it down. Given the hardships of rural life throughout the nineteenth century and during much of the twentieth, I find it astonishing that the house exists at all. Harsh winters, the Great Depression, the hurricane of 1938, the constant risk of fire, and the cumulative wear and tear that can ruin any house over time: somehow these forces proved insufficient to defeat our predecessors. The house remains. Yet with just one exception, Edith and I have detected no personal artifacts left by the people who lived here. (The exception is a cluster of names etched in a concrete hearthstone: "PAT and JOE"—Patricia and Joseph Rafferty, who owned the house from 1979-1983—as well as "JIM, BILLY, BRIAN, and F.J."—presumably Pat and Joe's children.) We have found no box of old letters stashed in the attic, no hatpin stuck between the floorboards, no initials—J.C.W., 1840— carved into the foundation stones. Neither have we sensed any disembodied presences of the kinds that some people claim to detect in old houses. We hear no odd noises and see no strange sights suggesting the presence of a ghost. We feel no uncanny sensations in the middle of the night. We sense no auras. The house isn't the haunting ground for its former inhabitants' souls. The house is simply the artifact of its past owners' lives. The house is the house.

It is architecturally unremarkable. The oldest structure, what James Whitcomb built back in 1840, is just a one-and-a-half-story rectangular box with a peaked roof. A centered front door opens onto a small foyer with a staircase to the second floor. The kitchen lies to the right, the living room to the left. The living room is one of the few areas anywhere in the house that shows signs of elegance, and then only in the moldings above and around the windows: intricate leaves and vines carved above and below the sashes. This room is currently large, but an alignment of the wide-plank floorboards shows that a wall once stood two-thirds of the way back. What was the room beyond this now-absent wall? A local historian speculated during a recent visit about what she called a "birthing room"—a common feature in old New England houses—since pregnancy was a frequent, recurrent aspect of nineteenth-century women's lives. Extending from the living room at the right-rear is the current dining room, its door opening up to the back of the kitchen. This kitchen is nondescript and utilitarian, probably dating originally from the 1890's or later, then upgraded with 1990's-era appliances. Off the kitchen is our bathroom. (A woman who once spent her childhood summers here during the 1970's mentioned that this house lacked indoor plumbing even in that recent decade.) In any case, it's likely that James and Hannah Whitcomb, or else one of the subsequent owners, added a room off the kitchen to connect the main house with what must have been a small barn. This would have been a variant of the so-called "ell," the house-to-barn passageway common in old New England houses.

Upstairs are the living quarters—three bedrooms and a large multipurpose room. Originally, the biggest of these rooms was probably just a loft for a small barn. A late-nineteenth-century owner must have converted the barn's loft to a large, habitable room. The current result is the most spacious, striking area in the house, big enough to accommodate separate his-and-hers work areas, two double futon beds, several bookshelves, a cast-iron woodstove, and a living room-like area near the stove. Adjacent to this big room is a small bathroom. Beyond that there's a small bedroom on the right (we use it as a study) and a second small bedroom on the left. The master bedroom lies beyond the upstairs landing.

What's clear is that this house has gone through almost continuous changes over the years. Other than the massive granite foundation stones, the sill beams, the hand-hewn joists anchored to the beams, and perhaps the studs inside the walls, little of the present-day house resembles what James Whitcomb built in 1840. Generations of owners have replaced most of the walls, have added new layers of flooring atop the old, have changed the original barn into habitable rooms, have reshaped the interior spaces, have swapped out lath and plaster for sheetrock. Like a living organism, the house has grown into something far different from how it began.

A few years ago, Edith and I decided to contact some neighbors whose surname was identical to that of several past owners. The situation seemed auspicious. The couple's presence a few hundred yards up the road suggested a family connection to the area. Surely these neighbors would know something about former residents of Whitcomb Hill. For this reason, I wrote a note asking if we could discuss the family who once owned our property. After introducing ourselves and explaining that Edith and I lived a short distance away, I raised the issue of my research. "We're writing now partly to say hello," I wrote, "and also to ask if you are related to the people who built our house back in 1840. Our research at the town hall indicates a number of past owners with your family name." I then listed some of the nineteenth-century owners of the house. "Edith and I would be interested in understanding more about previous owners of our property. If any of the people listed above are among your ancestors, could you please contact us?"

Days passed, then weeks. We received no response, not even a scribbled note saying "Sorry, wrong family." Even a clear rebuff—"I really don't have anything to say about those people"—would have been a relief by comparison. We received no comment at all.

What did their silence mean? Did this couple view our note as the opening gambit in a scam? Did they suspect a hidden agenda—thieves casing the joint, perhaps, or evangelists preparing to lay siege on their souls? Was it possible instead that their reluctance to respond hinted at shame about one or more of their ancestors? Or did they simply not want to get involved? The last of these possibilities seemed the most likely. Either these neighbors weren't related despite the shared surname, or else the notion of commenting on their ancestors simply held no appeal. I found the last of these possibilities implausible: most people like talking about their families. In any case, nothing came of our inquiry.

A year later, I wrote a similar note to another couple who may share roots with our predecessors. They run a long-established, well-regarded local business in a nearby town. No response. I considered making a follow-up phone call but held off. Perhaps these people weren't related to prior residents of our house. Or perhaps there was a family connection after all, but once again a connection that descendants preferred not to reveal or discuss. Fair enough. Still, I couldn't help but feel disappointed.

Why do some houses exert such power over the imagination? Is it chiefly because of their beauty? Their location? What they make possible? Of the latter, my experiences include a shabby refurbished garage in Denver, a little cottage that was physically insignificant yet personally important for providing a haven when I launched my career as a writer. Another is the six-room brick-and-concrete house that I helped a Mexican family build in the state of Guanajuato early in the 1970s. Still another is the 1790s-era mansion that Edith's family once owned in western Maine: the largest, most complex house I had ever explored during an extended visit.

Houses appear in many people's dreams, my own included. I dream occasionally of my childhood home, an unremarkable 1900-vintage farmhouse that stood at the southeast edge of Denver during the 1950s but was soon engulfed by the sprawling Front Range suburbs. Now that Edith and I live in Vermont, I also dream now and then about the two-story colonial in Maplewood, New Jersey, where we lived for twenty-five years and raised our children. Other houses make unpredictable appearances: real houses, including those I mentioned earlier, as well as a variety of half-recalled or altogether imaginary dwellings that range from the mundane to the fantastical—rustic cottages, Tudor mansions, foreboding woodsy huts, and infinite-roomed, maze-like castles.

Why so many houses? C. G. Jung regarded the house as more than just a house; it was the House, an archetype symbolizing a fundamental dimension of the human personality. Jung himself dreamed about a house that he regarded as personally salient and crucial to his theories about the Unconscious and the Collective Unconscious.[2]

In his dream, Jung found himself in an unfamiliar two-story house that he perceived as his own. Entering the upper story revealed "a kind of salon furnished with fine old pieces in rococo style." Fine paintings hung from the walls. Jung found the décor admirable but grew curious about other areas of the house. Descending a staircase, he reached the ground floor. Here the architecture and the decorations were much older, prompting Jung to realize that this part of the house must have dated from the fifteenth or sixteenth century. "The furnishings were medieval," he noted, and "the floors were of red brick. Everywhere it was rather dark." Intrigued, he proceeded from one room to another and decided to explore further. Soon he encountered a heavy door and opened it. Beyond were layers of brick among the ordinary stone blocks, as well as chips of brick in the mortar, indications that the walls dated from Roman times. "My interest was by now intense. I looked more closely at the floor. It was of stone slabs, and in one of these I discovered a ring." When Jung pulled this ring, the stone slab lifted, and once again he saw a stairway—this time narrow stone steps leading down into the depths. He descended and found himself inside a low cave cut into the rock. There he discovered a bizarre sight: "Thick dust lay on the floor, and in the dust were scattered bones and broken pottery, like remains of a primitive culture. I discovered two broken skulls, obviously very old and half disintegrated. Then I awoke."

Analyzing what he had experienced that night, Jung considered the house in his dream to be an image or map of the psyche—of his state of consciousness at the time "with hitherto unconscious additions." The second-floor salon represented normal waking consciousness; the ground floor, the first level of the unconscious. "The deeper I went," Jung wrote, "the more alien and the darker the scene became. In the cave, I discovered remains of a primitive culture, that is, the world of the primitive man within myself—a world which can scarcely be reached or illuminated by consciousness." Proceeding into lower levels of the house, Jung encountered the long uninhabited ground floor in medieval style, then the Roman cellar, and finally the prehistoric cave, all of which signified past times and passed stages of consciousness." Viewing this house as a whole, Jung considered it "a kind of structural diagram of the human psyche" that "postulated something of an altogether impersonal nature underlying that psyche." This, he wrote, "was my first inkling of a collective *a priori* beneath the personal psyche."

And Freud? It's common knowledge now that in the psychoanalytic schema for interpreting dreams, hollow objects—a box, a room, a cave—often represent the female reproductive organs. In *A General Introduction to Psychoanalysis*, Freud generalized about the nature of dream symbols representing aspects of Woman or womanhood: "The female genital is symbolically represented by all those objects which share its peculiarity of enclosing a space capable of being filled by something—viz., by *pits, caves*, and *hollows*, by *pitchers* and *bottles*, by boxes and *trunks, jars, cases, pockets*, etc. The ship, too, belongs in this category. Many symbols represent the womb of the mother rather than the female genital, as *wardrobes, stoves*, and primarily a *room*. The room-symbolism is related to the house-symbol."[3] Many commentators have criticized this and other aspects of Freudian symbolism as simplistic, not to mention sexist. I find these criticisms generally persuasive. Viewing all interior spaces as uterine/maternal symbols seems reductive and limited. This reductiveness holds true even regarding spaces like houses that appear in dreams as embracing, generative, and nurturing. Yet despite my skepticism, I had a nightmare many decades ago that sidestepped or demolished my doubts in at least this one instance.

In June of 1981, my mother suffered a massive cerebral hemorrhage. She survived the initial stroke but suffered extensive neurological deficits—expressive aphasia (inability to speak), bilateral loss of motor function, and diminished consciousness. Following initial assessment, however, the doctors treating her expressed optimism that immediate surgery might lead to substantial recovery and perhaps a resumption of fairly normal functioning. The key intervention: a craniotomy that would remove the blood pooling in her brain, locate the source of the hemorrhage, and clip the leaking artery or vein. I approved the plan. The surgeons performed the surgery.

Initially, the post-op outcome was positive. My mother began to improve. The worst phase of the crisis appeared to be over. Soon, however, her condition deteriorated. The doctors speculated that surgical intervention had been insufficient: despite their best efforts, they must have missed locating one or more leaky blood vessels, thus leading to further hemorrhage. The only recourse was a second craniotomy. This "succeeded" by stopping the hemorrhage, but it prompted further complications, including a generalized intracranial infection, severe cerebral edema, and, as a consequence, further neurological deficits.

A few nights after the second surgery, I dreamed a terrible dream. A fire had swept through my childhood home, severely damaging it. Worse yet, the firefighters' desperate, well-intentioned efforts to quench the flames had caused even more damage. The house hadn't burned to the ground but was essentially destroyed. In the dream's final scene, I wandered outside and viewed the now-wrecked house—the roof charred and breached in several places, the walls upright but with huge gaps visible, the windows shattered, the floors flooded and buckled. On awakening, I realized for the first time that my mother's severe disabilities were permanent, that she would survive but only in a damaged, diminished, rudimentary state of being.

The house on Whitcomb Hill is no dream. Edith and I find it fully present, vivid, and richly tangible. At the same time, it is—to use a word that recurs in my comments to friends about the property—resonant. It's a place where we can explore this stage of our life together. Simultaneously, it's a locus for exploring our inner lives: whatever we can discover during this late phase of our lives. We read, we write, we play our musical instruments. We welcome our adult children, Robin and Cory, whenever they come to visit us, and we deepen our relationships with them as peers. We host our friends both from the local community and from the wider world. We use the house as a springboard into our volunteer commitments—Edith's within the restorative justice system, mine at a regional medical center. This house is vivid in the here-and-now. At the same time, we can't help but wonder about the people who lived here throughout its more than one hundred and seventy-five years of its existence.

How did James Whitcomb build this house? In the 1840's, as during earlier periods of American history, a farmer with limited financial resources generally would have performed much of his own labor to construct his family's home. James, born in 1819, would have been twenty-one years old when he acquired the property on Whitcomb Hill. I've found no information or photos that might suggest anything about his size; but given his lifelong work as a farmer and his eventual survival to age 67, he was probably strong and healthy. Even so, building a house would have required assistance from his father, brothers, male cousins, friends, or hired assistants. These men would have dug the thirty-foot-long, twenty-foot-wide cellar by hand. Setting the foundation would have required teams of oxen and block-and-tackle equipment to lower hand-hewn granite blocks into place. (The granite probably came from boulders that the men located in the nearby woods, then split and transported. Some of these foundation stones measure 3x2x2 feet, which, given the weight of granite—around 165 pounds per cubic foot—would have added up to over a ton apiece.) Having set the foundation, James and his collaborators would have installed long wooden sill beams, eight inches tall and eight thick, along the tops of the granite blocks, then would have set hand-hewn joists on top of the beams. These joists are pine logs measuring ten to twelve inches in diameter and twelve feet in length. Two narrow granite pillars support a pair of transverse joists near the center of the cellar. Overall, the resulting appearance is one of great solidity. However, as a local carpenter-friend once warned us, "Joists are only as strong as the mortised end of the log"—the trimmed-down end that rests on the sill beam—and, consequently, "most old houses are significantly under-framed." The translation into lay persons' language: the beams aren't as sturdy as they look. Another contractor we know, noting the two skinny, six-foot-tall granite pillars that support the transverse beams near the cellar's midline, commented, "Wow!—a couple of blows with a sledgehammer and you'd bring down the whole place." In any case, James Whitcomb and his team built a home consistent with that era's construction principles. The house is solid enough to have survived almost eighteen decades.

In structure and style, it's what historians and architects call a Cape Cod house. It probably wasn't the first home on the property. James's father, Levi Sr., or James's grandfather, Reuben, had most likely constructed at least one other house on the hillside during the process of homesteading. As Jan Albers describes in *Hands on the Land: A History of the Vermont Landscape,* "Many settlers and their families went through a three-house progression: rustic shelter (used only for a year or two) to snug log house to more elegant frame house."[4] The Cape Cod-style house was familiar to many of these immigrants from their earlier years in southern New England. "The form was (and remains) very adaptable," Albers notes, "appearing in larger and smaller versions according to a family's means and space requirements."[5] The Cape's typical features included a height of one and a half stories, a width of five bays, a steeply pitched roof, a large central chimney, and a plain façade. All of these attributes are present in our house on Whitcomb Hill.

James used the so-called "balloon frame" method to construct the place. This approach, which became popular starting in the 1830's, revolutionized housing for middle- and low-income families throughout the United States. Ed Lehmann, writing about house construction, notes that before the advent of balloon framing, "Home construction previously was arduous and expensive. Houses were built using stout pieces of lumber fitted together with heavy joints. For example, the traditional New England frame house was built using hardwood beams connected with mortise-and-tenon joints fastened by hand-cut dowels or hand-wrought nails." These homes were solid but expensive, labor-intensive, and dependent on the expertise of skilled craftsmen. Starting in the 1830's, however, house construction became easier and cheaper. "[T]he balloon frame was based on much lighter precut two-by-four-inch studs positioned sixteen inches apart and held together by factory-produced nails," Lehmann writes. "Although light, the frame was very strong and able to withstand heavy winds, since the stress was spread over a large number of studs. The factory production of nails and mill cutting of standardized lumber reduced costs and increased availability of materials to individual builders."[6] Cheaper and more adaptable than earlier methods, balloon-frame construction required only two workers using basic carpentry techniques. A local sawmill would have provided studs for the walls, floorboards for the floors, clapboards for the exterior, lath for the interior, steps for the staircase, trim for the windows and doors, and wood for other areas throughout the house. James and his brothers, cousins, and neighbors would then have installed windows, plastered the walls, and made other improvements.

    The result: an ordinary but livable two-story cottage typical of the era. It's not a dream house in either the Jungian or real estate uses of the phrase. The house itself is spatially small but temporally big. Big enough, anyway, stretching back far enough in time, that Edith and I needed several years to start understanding our predecessors' lives.

2

Meadow

When Edith and I first moved to Whitcomb Hill, the meadow was essentially a five-acre lawn. Our immediate predecessors, Paul and Doris, had groomed the hillside from May through October, a task that apparently kept Paul in the seat of his Husqvarna mower for many hours day after day. The result was a beautiful expanse of green surrounding the house and rolling down toward the woods and the pond. Edith and I loved the appearance of the mown hillside; however, we considered this expanse of grass too much of a good thing. We didn't look forward to spending so much time riding the Husqvarna. In addition, we weren't eager to pay for all the gasoline necessary to mow five acres week after week all summer long. Neither did we want to inject more carbon into the atmosphere for this discretionary purpose. While it's true that many rural homeowners favor huge lawns—two, three, or more acres aren't uncommon—we saw no reason to maintain one so large.

We chose instead to let the lower lawn revert to meadow. Over the years of our living here, we've kept a fifty-foot-wide border of mown grass around most of the house, somewhat more at the upper edge, to serve as a buffer from disease-bearing ticks. The rest of the open area has now grown out. The result is shaggy, even messy-looking, throughout the warm months. It isn't always attractive. It's true that the wildflowers are lovely in the late spring, and a profusion of wild strawberries appears briefly in the early weeks of summer. Later, though, when the goldenrod, Queen Anne's lace, and milkweed plants mature, the meadow takes on a disheveled look. Some areas are grassy; others show a hodge-podge of plants. Yet we delight in the unpredictability of what grows there. The variety of plants provides a habitat for many animals. Butterflies materialize in great numbers and flit among the blossoms. Dragonflies zip to and fro. Bees make their rounds in search of nectar. Birds dart among the plants to feast on bugs. A family of woodchucks lives halfway down the slope, and we often see the big rodents, as plump and dark as pumpernickel loaves, feasting on the smorgasbord of grasses and wildflowers spread out around them. Edith and I have spotted fox and coyotes loping across the hillside. Deer wander in during all seasons: grazing on the vegetation, eating the apples from the trees, and bedding down in a patch of soft grass we call the Deer B&B.

One late-summer evening I notice critters of another kind. Looking out over the hillside, I see thousands of tiny insects—gnats or midges—suspended over the meadow. I say "suspended" because they seem to hover, not swarm. Each stays within its own sector of a few cubic feet of air. So vast is their number, and so reflective are their tiny wings, that the end-of-day sunlight illuminates them like a sparse snowfall. Each bug is an autonomous creature. Each patrols its own little zone. The insects are so profuse and so evenly distributed that they somehow transform the air itself into a huge three-dimensional object that rises over the meadow as high as I can see. It's as if each bug is a cell in the tissues of a vast, quivering organism. They create a single mega-bug, a diffuse giant, that fills our entire meadow yet is visible only in a certain slant of sunlight.

3

The Cheerful Reaper

> There was never a sound beside the wood but one,
> And that was my long scythe whispering to the ground.
>
> —Robert Frost, "Mowing" [1]

Of our ten acres, five are forest, land that flies on its own woodsy autopilot. The other five are a meadow left over from the original farm's fields, and these require more attention. The question is what *kind* of attention. Even meadows need occasional grooming. Neighbors warn Edith and me early on that if we don't mow once a year, saplings will spring up, trees will grow, and our open land will gradually revert to forest. During our first autumn on Whitcomb Hill we hire a local contractor to "bush hog" the hillside. This task involves a tractor towing an agricultural mower. The cost: $300. The result: grass, weeds, saplings, and wildflowers laid low.

The following summer, my brother-in-law Geoff notices a rusty old scythe hanging in the front shed—one of many tools that Doris and Paul left us when they moved out. "That's an American scythe," Geoff tells me, and he points out the dull blade and the ungainly aluminum handle (which I later learn is called a *snath*). Geoff goes on to say: "Someone told me that these American scythes are almost useless. They're heavy and tiring to use, and the blades aren't very sharp. The good ones are Austrian—lighter and much sharper." These comments catch my attention but prompt no action at the time. A few weeks later, though, an article about scythes appears in (of all places) *The Wall Street Journal*. This piece—"Who Needs a WeedWacker When You Can Use a Scythe?"—describes the ancient tool and its contemporary renaissance. "While Americans persist in cutting grass with labor-saving devices," Barry Newman writes, "faithful scythers believe their old tool has plenty of life left in it. U.S. scythe sales are nearing 10,000 a year now. . . . Predictably, scythe buyers are small, green farmers; unpredictably, they are also city folk and suburbanites."[2] Intrigued, I visit the Web site for the Marugg Company, a Tennessee-based husband-and-wife enterprise that Newman has mentioned in his article. This firm, founded by Swiss immigrants in 1873, is one of three main American sources for scythes. Most of the products they feature are made by Schrockenfux, an Austrian manufacturer founded in 1540. A helpful conversation with one of the Marugg Company's owners, Amy Wilson, leads to my ordering the first of two scythes that I purchase that summer. On receiving my order, I try out the tool in our meadow. I am instantly thrilled with the experience—both the "feel" of the scythe and its elegant efficiency in cutting grass and weeds. Edith is skeptical at first but soon feels a similar delight. Within a few days we start working in the fields together—good outdoor exercise that becomes our equivalent of a daily run.

The scythe is essentially a sabre on a stick. Excepting the chain saw and the axe, no tool I've used seems more dangerous. It has a dark reputation, too, since most people know the scythe only as the Grim Reaper's deathly implement.
    The bad rep is unfortunate. Just about any tool is dangerous if misused. Surely the most lethal device in our midst is the most utilized, most beloved, and most romanticized—the auto. Given the statistics on how we die in the modern era, the up-to-date icon for Death should be the Grim Driver: a skeleton behind the wheel of an SUV. Yes, the scythe is dangerous. But its nature, its modus, and its consequences aren't negative; on the contrary, civilization almost literally sprang from its blade.

With a pedigree dating back to the pre-Neolithic sickle, the scythe made agriculture so much more efficient that it transformed the pre-industrial world from the Fertile Crescent outward. Never mind the Grim Reaper's harvest: the scythe in human hands was the giver of life.

Something else is positive about the scythe. Unlike the chain saw, the SkilSaw, the Sawzall, the WeedWacker, the hedge trimmer, the push mower, the ride-on mower, the leaf blower, the snow thrower, the lawn edger, and all the other strident gas- and electric-powered machines that have replaced so many traditional hand tools, the scythe needs no fuel and makes no awful noise. It has an ancient, venerable feel to it, and not just because this implement is nearly silent. The scythe runs on human energy and certainly requires some effort, but it's surprisingly easy to use and repays the user with productivity, satisfaction, and a sense of wellbeing. Now, having acquired our scythes, Edith and I must learn to use them. There's no one around to train us—no relatives or neighbors to demonstrate the basics, as would have been true throughout much of the world over the past two thousand years, or to coach us as we refine our skills. Paintings from the medieval and renaissance eras show men, women, and children working together in the fields. Knowledge of using these tools, passed down through the generations, must have been almost universal. But Edith and I have no savvy elders, siblings, or neighbors to show us the way. How are we going to learn?

Typical for us as writers, our first recourse is to buy some books. The best of the lot is David Tresemer's *The Scythe Book: Mowing Hay, Cutting Weeds, and Harvesting Small Grains with Hand Tools.*[3] This manual provides exactly what the title and subtitle promise. Particularly helpful are several chapters on the proper technique for mowing. Tresemer is reassuring from the start. "Mowing should be comfortable, not too strenuous, not . . . tiring. If it is exhausting, it is wrongly done. . . . At its best, the stroke does not have to be stopped. It is initiated with just enough energy that the last of the grass is cut and thrown to the windrow [that is, a row of mowed-down stalks] as the momentum of the stroke is reduced to zero; the leftover energy is comfortably stored in the tendons to power the recovery back to the right." But instructions like these, even if precise, can be difficult to translate into action out in the meadow.

Soon I resort to a standard contemporary gambit for learning a new skill: watching YouTube videos. I'm not surprised that scything videos are available, since videos about anything and everything are present on the Web, but the number and variety strike me as bizarre. Options include "Scything," "Scything with Susan," "Lawn Scything," "Scything and Wind-rowing Hay in Scotland," "West Country Scythe Festival 2010," and "Polish Peat Bog Scything Competition." The list goes on and on. Typical of YouTube, many of these clips are amusing but short on substance—the scything equivalent of cute-cat videos. Some, however, prove to be useful. "How to Scythe," for instance, demonstrates and describes basic techniques so well that I acquire my first really effective "feel" for the tool. "Scything and Wind-rowing Hay in Scotland" helps me refine my stance and stroke (and, while I'm at it, my Scottish brogue as well). "Martin Kebblewhite Teaching Scything" presents an expert's useful tips on multiple issues, among them the proper approach to peening, the tricky technique for periodically hammering the blade before honing it with a whetstone.

Edith and I experiment with the techniques we acquire, and soon each of us develops an individual style for how to use the tool. Edith's preference for mowing hay with a grass scythe leads to a graceful, rhythmic sweep. My task—trimming weeds and saplings with the brush scythe—requires shorter, more aggressive strokes. Over the next few months we hone our skills as well as the blades.

A question keeps nagging at me: who are our fellow scythers? Given the mechanization of agriculture in Vermont and throughout most of the world, who else is mowing with these ancient tools? To find out, I call Amy Wilson, co-owner of the

Marugg Company. "I used to be able to pinpoint exactly who our customers are," she tells me, "but in the past four years or so, our typical customer has changed a lot. We used to get mostly people in the homesteading movement—people who want to go back to the land. We also get a lot of Amish or Mennonites. But around the end of 2007 and the beginning of 2008, things started to change. We got a lot more calls from people who lived in urban areas, people with community gardens. We had people who didn't want to use their mowers in urban areas because of higher gas prices, or else they wanted to use scything as a form of exercise. So it's changed to being just about anybody and everybody. But we still have a stronger following among the green communities—the back-to-the-land folks." The traditional customers, she says, are generally in places like Bucks County, Pennsylvania; in Amish and Mennonite regions of Ohio; and in other parts of the Midwest. The newer customers, including the urban gardeners, "could be anywhere."

After some further discussion, Amy mentions another kind of customer. "I don't know any other way to say this," she says, "but we get a lot of end-of-the-worlders—your doomsday preppers. I have no problem with that at all. Those people can live their life as they want. And they want a lot of references for other tools—'Do you know where I can get this? Do you know where I can get that?' Anything manual. There are some who don't want just one type of blade; they want just about every type of blade that we have. I know when they call I'm going to be on the phone for a very long time."

Where do Edith and I fit into this picture? We aren't Amish or Old Order Mennonites. Nor are we back-to-the-landers, homesteaders, urban gardeners, or doomsday preppers. We're just a couple of artsy former urbanites who love our meadow and want to keep it healthy.

Being such a crucial and common tool, the scythe and its ancestor, the sickle, have shown up frequently in poetry throughout the world. Among the surviving instances are many verses in the Bible, such as Joel 3:13—"Swing the sickle, for the harvest is ripe" and Revelation 14:18—"And another angel came out from the altar, which had power over fire; and cried with a loud cry to him that had the sharp sickle, saying, Thrust in thy sharp sickle, and gather the clusters of the vine of the earth; for her grapes are fully ripe." However, more recent literature includes not just the sickle but also the scythe as a subject. One example is "Sláttuvísa," ("Mowing Song,") by an Icelandic poet, Jónas Hallgrímsson, published in 1844.[4]

> Mowing Song
>
> Swishing, stripping, slashing,
> slowly he goes mowing,
> scythe-blade lashing lithely,
> lethally beneath him.
> Gallant flowers are falling,
> fate betrays the daisies.
> Iron edge is tireless;
> under him, earth thunders.
> "Let's be glad!" the little
> lamb bleats out and gambols,
> "glad that when the winter
> wakens, and they take me
> from its dread and deadly
> dangers to the manger,
> loads of luscious fodder
> lie there sweet and drying!"
> Slashing, stripping, swashing,
> sweeping, he goes reaping,
> scythe is swishing blithely.
> Slow, behind the mower,
> walks a woman raking—
> watch your distance, mistress!
> not too near me, darling—

> near my vicious whishing!
> All the flowers have fallen,
> fairest grasses perish:
> life is brief, aborted
> by the ripper's stripping.
> Haft is humming softly,
> hefted firmly, deftly;
> iron edge is tireless;
> under him, earth thunders.

With its heavily accented alliterations and its unblinking acceptance of mortality, "Mowing Song" sounds as if it could have been composed by the author of *Beowulf,* the Scandanavian epic that marked the start of Old English poetry. A strong Norse vigor, a barely constrained Viking harshness, powers this poem. The grass and the flowers fall before the mower's blade; the woman raking hay nearby is in peril; the earth itself resonates to his powerful strokes. Even the lamb, which would seem to be a symbol of life, will surely suffer harsh consequences from the scythe's work, since the "luscious fodder" he craves will leave him fattened for autumn slaughter. Hallgrímsson's mower may be a strong, vibrant farmer, but he bears a disquieting resemblance to the Grim Reaper himself.

By contrast, Robert Frost's "Mowing," presents someone wielding a far subtler, far less aggressive implement.[5]

Mowing

> There was never a sound beside the wood but one,
> And that was my long scythe whispering to the ground.
> What was it it whispered? I knew not well myself;
> Perhaps it was something about the heat of the sun,
> Something, perhaps, about the lack of sound—
> And that was why it whispered and did not speak.
> It was no dream of the gift of idle hours,

Or easy gold at the hand of fay or elf:
Anything more than the truth would have seemed too weak
To the earnest love that laid the swale in rows,
Not without feeble-pointed spikes of flowers
(Pale orchises), and scared a bright green snake.
The fact is the sweetest dream that labor knows.
My long scythe whispered and left the hay to make.

In addition to its dense beauty, this sonnet is not only one of Frost's finest meditations on work—a recurrent subject—but also a richly considered statement about what the late scholar Richard Poirier calls "the work of knowing." The mower, scything his meadow, listens to the sound the blade makes and ponders what it says. He rejects out of hand the notion that the scythe speaks of something dreamy ("the gift of idle hours") or supernatural ("easy gold at the hand of fay or elf"); instead, the substance of work itself—as well as the imaginative engagement with the ordinary world that work implies—is sufficient reward. Poirier writes:

> By laboring in the field, where he meets with feeble flowers and bright snakes, he has shown what it means to "make hay while the sun shines"; he has shown, also, that the very process of knowing what he is up to constitutes the "making" of the poem; and he can leave the "hay" to "make" what it will of whatever it can. . . .
> When the sonnet arrives at the conviction that "Anything more than the truth would seem too weak," it arrives at an oxymoron. And this is one evidence that the "truth" . . . which is promised for the sestet, far from being denuded of poetic and intellectual tradition to which the whole poem responds, will instead transcend these. . . . The speaker has the satisfaction not in the results of his labor but in the labor itself, and his earnestness, in every sense of the

word just mentioned, is communicated both in the grammatical simplicity of his declaration and in its open-ended myths. "The fact is the sweetest dream that labor knows."[6]

What does "Mowing" tell me about the task of scything? Essentially it says what I've already sensed during my early efforts with the tool, though Frost always puts the matter more subtly than I can grasp: that the "thusness" of such work offers deep, though often intangible, even imperceptible, satisfactions.

One summer day a neighbor drives by and, spotting Edith and me in our front yard, backs up his truck and pulls over. We chat about the weather, our gardens, and his hunting trips. Then, as we discuss some changes Edith and I are making to the property, he suddenly grows animated, almost giddy. "And weren't you guys actually—?" He interrupts himself, then blurts, "The other day I said to my wife: 'I drove past Edith and Ed's place, and you know what? They were actually *scything!*'" He couldn't have sounded more astonished if he'd said, *"They were dancing naked on the roof!"* This comment confirms what Edith and I have suspected: that our use of scythes will make us the laughing stock of the area. *What will those crazy flatlanders do next!* I respond to our neighbor's remarks by explaining that we like to try out these traditional farm tools because they give us a glimpse of our ancestors' lives. Surely James and Hannah Whitcomb hand-mowed their hay. What was their experience back in the nineteen century? Our friend smiles patiently. I could say more, of course—could explain how easy a good scythe is to use, how graceful in cutting the grass, how efficient in grooming the meadow, how pleasurable in making hard work easy, how exhilarating, how entrancing, how meditative. I hold back. Explanations will get us nowhere. At a time when people consider the noisy, smelly, gas-wasting WeedWacker to be a sensible device, waxing poetical about our Austrian scythes won't work in our favor.

Oddly enough, it's Leo Tolstoy who teaches Edith and me what we need to know. In Part III of *Anna Karenina,* Tolstoy describes how the wealthy landowner Konstantin Dmitrievich Levin participates in the autumn harvest. Just as Tolstoy himself labored among the peasants at Yasnaya Polyana, his family estate, Levin joins the peasants mowing hay on his own property; and during that days-long communal effort, he finds himself working with an older, experienced mower and a younger, less experienced one. The harvest passages from *Anna Karenina* provide the fullest, richest description of scything as a sensory experience.[7]

> After lunch Levin was not in the same place in the string of mowers as before, but stood between the old man who had accosted him jocosely, and now invited him to be his neighbor, and a young peasant, who had only been married in the autumn, and who was mowing this summer for the first time.

Levin immediately notices the older peasant's efficiency and economy of motion:

> The old man, holding himself erect, moved in front, with his feet turned out, taking long, regular strides, and with a precise and regular action which seemed to cost him no more effort than swinging one's arms in walking, as though it were in play, he laid down the high, even row of grass. It was as though it were not he but the sharp scythe of itself swishing through the juicy grass.

By contrast, the younger peasant works harder but less effectively:

> Behind Levin came the lad Mishka. His pretty, boyish face, with a twist of fresh grass bound round his hair, was working with effort; but whenever anyone looked at him he smiled. He would clearly have died sooner than own it was hard work for him.

Somehow Levin reaches a compromise between these two states of skill and grace; and as the work proceeds, he manages to attain a rhythm that makes the work easy and almost automatic.

> Levin kept between them. In the very heat of the day the mowing did not seem such hard work to him. The perspiration with which he was drenched cooled him, while the sun, that burned his back, his head, and his arms, bare to the elbow, gave a vigor and dogged energy to his labor; and more and more often now came those moments of unconsciousness, when it was possible not to think what one was doing. The scythe cut of itself. These were happy moments. The longer Levin mowed, the oftener he felt the moments of unconsciousness in which it seemed not his hands that swung the scythe, but the scythe mowing of itself, a body full of life and consciousness of its own, and as though by magic, without thinking of it, the work turned out regular and well-finished of itself. These were the most blissful moments.

This state of being—familiar to athletes, artists, meditators, and lovers—is *flow*. The doer and deed are one and the same. It's a state not just of efficient work but also of *sati*, of bare attention, of mindfulness, of fully and deeply inhabiting the present moment. "Levin did not notice how time was passing. If he had been asked how long he had been working he would have said half an hour—and it was getting on for dinner time."

The sun sank behind the forest. The dew was falling by now; the mowers were in the sun only on the hillside, but below, where a mist was rising, and on the opposite side, they mowed into the fresh, dewy shade. The work went rapidly. The grass cut with a juicy sound, and was at once laid in high, fragrant rows. The mowers from all sides, brought closer together in the short row, kept urging one another on to the sound of jingling dipper and clanging scythes, and the hiss of the whetstones sharpening them, and good-humored shouts.

So there you have it. Wielding the scythe properly, you get a good full-body workout, a flow state, a bonding experience with your fellows, hours of sensory delight, and communion with nature. You get hay or wheat, too, while you're at it. You aren't grim at all as you reap, you're cheerful, and rightly so.

The scythe bestows not death but life.

Edith and I have no peasants toiling on our property, so we can't partake of the communal experience that Levin enjoys in the fields. We are our own serfs. Unlike our predecessors on Whitcomb Hill, we have no grown children present or collaborative neighbors nearby to share in the farm labor. We have, in fact, no farm. We enjoy the work, however, and we revel in collaborating on this task. In September of that first year of scything, we hand-mow our entire meadow. We then wheel many barrows piled high with cut grass into our big vegetable garden to use as mulch. The rest of the hay lies mounded across the hillside where, once the heavy frosts arrive in October, the windrows look as white and as glittery as snowdrifts. All winter the old grass withers and deteriorates beneath the real snow—so much the better to nurture the new grass that will spring forth in April.

Part Two

Denizens

4

House History—
One Hill, Three Families

Long before this hillside became a patchwork of ten- and twenty-acre properties, it was a much larger farm owned by the Whitcomb clan. Two other families lived on the slopes of Whitcomb Hill. The Bohonons, the Rings, and the Whitcombs appear to have been close friends, and they assisted one another in working the land.

These facts and many others are what Edith and I found as we dug deeper into the local, regional, and online archives.

Here's what we discovered.

At some point between 1794 and 1800, a couple named Reuben and Dinah Whitcomb moved to the new town of Washington, Vermont. I've found almost no information about Dinah beyond the facts that she grew up in Marlboro, Massachusetts; that her maiden name was Howe; and that she married Reuben on December 6, 1770. Reuben, born in 1747 or 1748 in Stow, Massachusetts, lived for a number of years in Henniker, New Hampshire. In 1778, he joined a Revolutionary War militia and served in Capt. Jonas Bowman's Company (Col. Moses Kelly's Regiment) in the Rhode Island Expedition. Following the war, Reuben and Dinah joined the exodus out of Massachusetts, Connecticut, and New Hampshire into northern New England.[1] They acquired land in Orange County, Vermont, and called it Whitcomb Hill Farm. The couple raised a large family: eight sons and a daughter. One of the sons was named Levi.[2]

Levi, born in 1789, married a somewhat younger woman named Sarah Parret. This couple's seven surviving children included sons named Levi Jr. (born in 1817) and James (probably born in 1819). I have located very little information about Levi Sr., Sarah, and their years on Whitcomb Hill. Sarah appears to have died in 1858, Levi Sr. in 1867. As Levi Jr. and James grew up, however, the historical data become more ample. Public records suggest that when Reuben, the paterfamilias, died in 1840, his grandsons either inherited the farm, co-owned it with Levi Sr., or purchased it from their father. Levi Sr. doesn't appear to be the primary owner. Perhaps issues of health or disability limited Levi Sr.'s willingness to take over. Another possibility is that James and Levi Jr.'s parents had "assigned" them the tasks of running the farm. As Lynn A. Bonfield and Mary C. Morrison write regarding this New England tradition in *Roxana's Children: The Biography of a Nineteenth-Century Vermont Family*, a particular son (not necessarily the oldest) might be "designated to continue the farm" on behalf of the family.[3] James and Levi Jr. appear to have jointly assumed this role, whether by their own preference or by assignment, and then began running the family property. A map of the Whitcomb Hill area dated 1853 shows a property marked "L. and J. Whitcomb." Census data from the same era show James as the primary owner of a large farm, with Levi Jr. owning either an adjacent farm or else co-owning his brother's property. In 1850, the first year in which public records show the brothers owning the farm (or farms), James was 30 years old; Levi Jr., 33.

A separate but related issue warrants some attention. The U. S. Census for that year also shows that Levi Jr.'s household, which is listed separately from James's family, included a man named Moses Ring, age 79; a woman named Sarah Ring, age 60; and a youth named Joseph Bohonon, age 13. The mention of these non-Whitcomb residents on the hillside farms is significant. Why? Because the older adults' presence, as well as the teenager's, show the interweaving of two other families with the Whitcombs. The issue of this multi-family fabric requires a digression.

The Bohonons, like the Whitcombs, had settled in Vermont several decades earlier. The *paterfamilias* of the Bohonon family was Joseph Sr., an Irish or Irish-Canadian immigrant to the United States. Born in 1789, Joseph Sr., along with his wife, Sally, raised at least one child, a son named Robert, born in 1813. Robert grew up in the same area as the Whitcombs and married a local woman, Betsey Smith, three years younger than Robert. The couple settled down to farm the land and raise a family. By twenty-first-century standards, Robert and Betsey's brood was huge—twelve children—but that size wasn't unusual in their own era. The public records show that Betsey gave birth to a child almost every other year between 1837 and 1863. Betsey was 21 at the time of the first birth, 47 at the time of the last. Three of the children died before reaching age six. (A high rate of infant mortality, too, was routine during the nineteenth century.) Nine of the twelve Bohonon offspring—four sons and five daughters—reached adulthood. Betsey herself died in 1869 at age 53. Robert lived much longer, dying in 1892 at age 79. In any case, Robert and Betsey were a vigorous couple during their time together, fertile and energetic in many ways.

Two other players in this drama are two men named Moses Ring, *pere et fils*. (Father-and-son namesakes were common in that era.) Moses Sr., an Irishman (born in 1771) who lived in New Hampshire for some years, emigrated to Vermont at around the same time that Reuben Whitcomb and his family moved northwest from Henniker. Perhaps Moses was a long-time friend of the Whitcombs. Perhaps the two families' arrivals in Vermont were coincidental. In any case, Moses married a woman named Bethyah, who apparently gave birth to many children, most or all of whom died in infancy. Bethyah herself died in 1834. Later, Moses married again—this time to Sarah Bohonon, widow of Robert Bohonon's father, Joseph Sr. In the meantime, Moses Jr., born right at the close of the eighteenth century, grew up in the area and married a woman named Lucinda. Moses Jr. and Lucinda acquired property from the Whitcombs and appear to have maintained a close relationship with them, as well as with the Bohonons.

(An intriguing issue is that both Moses Sr. and Jr. seem to have been opinionated, perhaps controversial members of the community. Two annotations in the local records suggest strong personalities. The first, dated 1807, states: "I do not agree on religious opinion with the majority of the inhabitants of this parrish [sic] as the case may be. Moses Ring." Was this statement a reflection of Catholic-Protestant tensions typical of that era, or of other theological issues? Unclear. The second annotation is a clause present in the document that leases land from Robert Bohannon to Moses Jr. in 1853. Robert stipulates that "Said Ring is to carry on said farm in a good farmer-like manner." What does this requirement suggest about the younger Moses's skill or attitude as a farmer? And what would it mean to "carry on" in a way that was not "a good farmer-like manner"—or that was a bad farmer-like manner?)

What seems clear and relevant regarding the relationships on Whitcomb Hill is that the Whitcombs, the Bohonons, and the Rings were closely interwoven families. The 1850 data, as noted earlier, show that Levi Jr., age 33 and still unmarried at the time, shared his household with the elder Moses Ring, with Sarah Ring—widow of Joseph Bohonon Sr. and now Moses's second wife—and with the teenage Joseph Bohanon, Robert and Betsey Bohonon's oldest son. Later records indicate that this close interweaving continued among the three families. The Whitcombs, Rings, and Bohonons lived in close proximity; they appear to have collaborated on agricultural and domestic tasks; and at least two marriages occurred over the years between members of the three clans.

Back to the main point, however: James and Hannah owned a significant parcel of the land on Whitcomb Hill, but their ownership and their use of the property was complex and dynamic. James almost certainly grew up on "the old Whitcomb farm," as one historical document calls it, along with his brother Levi Jr. and other siblings. In 1840, the year of the elder Levi's death, the brothers either inherited separate parcels of land or else jointly inherited the property. James and Levi Jr. then collaborated closely to work the land. They sold a parcel to someone named B. W. Bartholomew in 1851; then another part of the property changed hands in 1853, this time to Robert Bohannon. Other transfers of property included sales of land from Moses Ring (the elder or the younger?!) to Levi Jr. and James jointly, and later (during the 1860's) from Levi Jr. and his wife, Louisa, to James. Still more transfers occurred between other members of the Whitcomb clan and between the Whitcombs and other families. It's clear that over the years, the Whitcombs, the Bohonons, and the Rings remained closely intertwined.

5
Sound of Water

The pond rests in a hollow halfway down the slope right where the meadow meets the woods. A spring keeps it filled; an outlet notched into the opposite rim empties the overflow through a narrow trench and down the steep hillside. Eighty feet in diameter, this man-made pond is so well landscaped that it looks completely natural. The water and the setting are lovely in their own right, and this tiny ecosystem is congenial to wildlife that wouldn't be present otherwise—minnows, peepers, newts, dragonflies, and frogs. The pond seems to have been here forever. Its presence out of sight from the house makes it feel separate and mysterious, a realm distinct from both the meadow and the forest.

There's one other aspect of this place that draws me. When Edith and I took the ramble that first sparked our desire to purchase this property, I immediately perceived the pond as a splendid spot for a meditation shack. I could go down there daily during good weather to sit in stillness. I could meditate in a quintessential Buddhist setting. Of an evening, I could contemplate the moon.

ཀྵ ཀྵ ཀྵ

> The old pond —
> a frog jumps in,
> sound of water.
>
> —Matsuo Basho
> (tr. Robert Hass)[1]

❧ ❧ ❧

Even during our first summer of living on Whitcomb Hill, Edith and I conclude that the pond is sick. The water has grown turbid; the smell is heavy. A few feet below the surface, wispy aquatic plants have bloomed in great profusion. Wild irises mass along the far shore like tourists waiting on the dock for the Nantucket ferry. Frogs are clearly thriving in that environment, but I see no signs of the trout and perch that our predecessors stocked during their years of ownership. When autumn arrives, maple and ash leaves stream down from the nearby trees, float on the surface for a week, then sink out of sight. I gradually begin to grasp what I'm witnessing. These changes are all part of eutrophication, a natural sequence of changes that will gradually fill in, dry out, and convert the pond into merely another part of the meadow. The pond isn't really sick at all; it's just . . . *changing*. From Edith's and my standpoint, however—the standpoint of human beings intent on maintaining an attractive pond on their property—the process amounts to a terminal disease. It's advancing rapidly. By our second summer on Whitcomb Hill, the water has grown dense with aquatic plants and smells more and more fetid.

The issue quickly moves beyond diagnosis to treatment. We consider the options. Chemicals are one possibility. Algaecides would quickly wipe out the bloom, but they would also sterilize the water, poison most other plants, sicken or kill many animals present, and potentially endanger people and creatures downstream from the outflow. The State of Vermont has rightly banned this type of treatment. What, then, are the alternatives? I pose this question to our neighbor Jeff, the local excavation contractor who dug the pond for a previous owner back in the 1970's. "Well, you could always muck it out," he tells me. What would that involve? "You'd pump out the pond and get an excavator down there to scrape out the plants. Then you'd let the rain fill it up again." The cost? "Oh, maybe a couple thousand dollars."

Other projects surely take precedence. Edith and I have at least three dozen tasks on our list that are more urgent than upgrading the pond.

Yet the situation continues to deteriorate. By late summer, the water has turned a hazy green-brown. Worse, it looks less like water than algae in aspic—a vastly intricate mass of vegetation, soft and filigreed, with a transparent substance encasing it. To call this a dying place would be inaccurate. It's very much alive. Mosquitoes, water striders, dragonflies, and other insects clearly thrive here. Minnows dart about in the shallows. Frogs reveal their presence by their calls—*cut cut cut cut*—and by their abrupt leaps into the pond when I approach the shore. But these critters are clear signs of a transformation that we still hope to forestall and, if possible, to reverse.

That summer is the hottest ever recorded in the United States and a time of severe drought in most of the country. Although the temperatures are lower in Vermont than elsewhere, the weather is still unpleasant. Edith and I find the heat stressful despite knowing how much worse the situation is nearly everywhere else. Late in August, however, the dry warmth gives me an idea. Why not simply drain the pond and leave it empty for a while? The water weeds would die in the dry heat. That in turn would solve most of the problem—or would at least slow the process of eutrophication. When I cross paths with Jeff again, I ask him about this scenario. "Yeah, you could do that," he states in his gravelly baritone. He even offers an approach that would be simpler and cheaper than using the rented pump I've proposed for managing the task. "Just put a one-inch hose into the pond, start a gravity feed, and siphon the water over the edge and down the hillside."

That's what I set out to do. At the local hardware store I purchase three twenty-foot lengths of flexible plastic hose and some coupling devices to link the pieces. My plan: immerse the hose in the pond to fill it, drag one end up the bank, and throw that end over the down-hill side to get the water flowing. In practice, the task isn't quite so simple. The pond's shore is steep and slippery. Just reaching the water's edge is much trickier than I've expected. I could easily slide into the pond and have trouble getting out. Rather than risk a potentially dangerous situation, I find a long branch, tie it to one end of the hose, throw the rest of the coil into the pond, and use the branch as a handle to help me dip the open end. By repeatedly scooping water, I plan to fill the hose until it sinks altogether. Then I'll cap the open end with one hand, drag it up the hillside, fling it over the edge, and start the flow. But this approach turns out to be much harder than I've expected. Filling the hose is difficult. Dragging it up the slope lets most of the water drain back into the pond. I never succeed in starting the flow.

After brooding over this initial fiasco, I abandon the effort and go to bed. An insight dawns as I fall asleep: I'll run a garden hose down to the pond. Using it to fill the exhaust hose will be quick work. How quick? The next morning, all I have to do is pirate every length of every garden hose from every part of the property, purchase another hundred feet of hose from the local hardware store, connect all these separate segments, and run the assemblage downhill from the house to the pond. Not so quick after all. My initial experiments are promising, however, since filling the siphon hose takes only about two or three minutes. The problem is what happens next: getting one end of the hose up and over the pond's rim without letting the water inside it drain back into the pond. Trying this on my own isn't effective, so Edith and I attempt a two-person gambit.

"Okay, here's the plan," I explain. "I'd like you to stand right there by the edge of the pond. Hold your end of the hose pointing upward."

"Got it."

"I'll stand up here by the rim and fill my end of the big hose with the garden hose. When I say *Go,* drop your end into the pond."

Edith nods.

As we hold our respective ends of the big hose to form a large U, I proceed to pour in water from the garden hose.

"Go!"

Edith throws her end into the pond at exactly the same moment that I throw my end over the pond's rim onto the hillside.

Water gushes out of the outlet and down the hill. *Eureka!* Sort of. After a minute or two, the flow diminishes to a trickle and then stops.

We try the sequence again. No go. We try again. No go.

Plans A and B have now achieved the same result: nothing. The pond continues to fill from the spring and to drain from the outlet. A few minnows dart about near the shore. Now and then a frog belches in its lair of irises. Insects skim above the water.

        ❧   ❧   ❧

> Cold, wet leaves
> Floating on moss-coloured water
> And the croaking of frogs—
> Cracked bell-notes in the twilight.
>
> —Amy Lowell, "The Pond"[2]

        ❧   ❧   ❧

A book I acquire—Tim Matson's *Earth Ponds: The Country Pond Maker's Guide to Building, Maintenance, and Restoration*—confirms that my concern about eutrophication is valid and that attempting to slow the process is worthwhile. "Taking the water out of a pond can be an effective vegetation control method," Matson writes. "Algae and aquatic weeds cannot live without water, and when the pond is dried out, much of the vegetation dies." Even a partial drawdown can make a difference. But Matson goes on to state that algae and weeds "are more effectively eradicated after complete drainage during both warm and cold weather."[3]

These comments inspire a further gambit. Mid-November, during an unusual dry spell, I decide to roll out the artillery. From a local rental service I acquire an industrial-strength pump for the weekend before Thanksgiving. It's a Wacker Neuson—a gasoline-powered diaphragm pump that, in the words of the manufacturer, "can move anything that flows." Most often used for draining construction sites, this machine is probably underpowered for drawing down an entire pond, but running it for a few days seems a worthwhile experiment. I tow it down the hillside in a little wagon hitched to our Husqvarna lawnmower. I set it up with the twelve-foot "hard hose" immersed in the pond and the thirty-foot canvas outlet hose draped over the pond's southern rim. Starting the pump without difficulty, I watch with satisfaction as it begins to work. The black rubber intake hose jolts from the force of the pump's suction. The outlet hose quivers and pulses as water heads uphill and over the edge. I walk up to the rim and see the nozzle gushing onto the slope. Surely this device will make quick work of the task.

Edith comes down the hillside somewhat later to inspect my handiwork. After watching the pump gush tan water for a minute or two, she asks, "Is it—*working?*"

"See for yourself."

"Looks like quite a ways to go."

"We have to start somewhere, right?"

She spares me a response.

Six hours later, I can tell that my optimism has been foolish. The surface of the pond has dropped by only five or six inches. While it's true that the circumference of the pond will narrow as the water level drops, accelerating the decline, it's also true that the process is taking much longer than I've anticipated. I have a belated impulse to estimate the pond's volume. I find some calculators on the Internet and quickly run the numbers. The answer: about half a million gallons. An old pump like the Wacker Neuson can move about eighty gallons per minute. Running twenty-four hours a day, the machine would take more than four days to eject five hundred thousand gallons. But I can't run the pump 'round the clock; limited daylight in November will curtail the time available. Sixteen days of pumping is more like what I'll face. The pump's rental fee is forty-eight dollars per day. This is ridiculous. I conclude that the experiment has been worthwhile, but less to remove the water from the pond than to drain the delusions from my own mind.

Plans A, B, and C have now failed. I execute Plan D: I give up.

Buddhism includes a long tradition of imagery about ponds. Zen poems, especially, include frequent references to the pond as a locus of meditation and as a metaphor for consciousness. In his collection of Chan (Chinese Zen) poems, Charles Egan describes the origins and nature of this approach to imagery: "Chinese poetic images appeal to the senses, primarily the visual, and are most often drawn from the natural world. The poems reveal a heightened sensitivity to the meanings of ordinary objects, for since the *dharmadhātu* [the fundamental ground of consciousness] is present and complete in everything, virtually anything can be a trigger to enlightenment." Egan then offers a Tang-era poem by Hanshan as exemplary of the Chan use of metaphor:

> My mind is like the autumn moon,
> As fresh and pure as a jade pond.
> But nothing really compares with it—
> Tell me, how can I explain?

Egan provides this commentary:

> The moon and pond each carry both general and Buddhist associations. . . . The moon and pond form a polarity with the multivalent enlightenment message. On one level, the bright round moon obviously

alludes to the light of *prajñā* wisdom that dispels ignorance. . . . The shining jade pond is a combination metaphor: as the *Awakening of Faith* has it, still water is the enlightened mind, revealed when the wind (of ignorance) dies and the waves (modes of mind) cease . . . ; the water then becomes a bright mirror, reflecting things as they really are. . . .[4]

Does this commentary, or the poetry behind the commentary, or the sutras behind the poetry, suggest that I will benefit more fully from meditating at a pond's edge, or by meditating upon the pond itself, rather than somewhere else? Am I more likely to gain wisdom while meditating there than, say, in front of the compost heap . . . or perhaps down in our messy basement? Is a locus of beauty and calm inherently more spiritual than a plain, uninteresting place? Is it possible, even, that the compost heap or the basement would be more effective in helping me disengage from preconceptions?

On the other hand, who am I to dismiss the notion that meditating beside a pond can offer inspiration, even some sort of grace? Surely legions of Buddhist monks can't be mistaken.

The body of water on Whitcomb Hill is an ordinary pond. It is, however, what Edith and I now find entrusted to our care, and it deserves its own share of attention. Having never owned a pond before, I decide that no matter how small and humble, this is the one I should focus on. I start spending time there several times each week, so much the better to perceive it, observe it, value it, and start to understand it.

The pond in autumn: the water full of fallen leaves—first a wide swath of yellow-orange-red fabric on the surface; then a three-dimensional cloud of more muted color that gradually sinks over a period of several days; then a layer of detritus fading to a uniform muddy hue on the bottom. The surface then clarifies and fills once more with sky.

The pond in early winter: frozen perfectly flat, the surface pure white with fresh snow, this expanse marred only by a single set of animal tracks—fox? fisher cat?—perfectly bisecting the circle.

The pond in late winter: frozen hard now following the January thaw and a subsequent drop into subzero temperatures. The surface is so intricately crazed that in the evening light, patterns there mimic the complex angles of Marcel Duchamp's "Nude Descending a Staircase"—or should that be "Nude Falling Down an Icy Staircase"?

The pond in early springtime: open water again, devoid of weeds and allowing a view six or eight feet into its depths. The floor is brown-gray with matted leaves. I see no signs of fish or other wildlife. A few water bugs veer about like tiny speedboats.

The pond in late spring: blooming anew with intricate water plants. Most striking isn't what I see, however, but what I hear. This is the season of peepers—*Pseudacris crucifer*—the small forest-dwelling frogs nicknamed for the males' mating call. One nature guide describes the call in this manner: ". . . [T]he spring peeper has a high-pitched call similar to that of a young chicken, only much louder and rising slightly in tone. They are among the first frogs in the regions to call in the spring. As a chorus, they resemble the sounds of sleigh bells."[5] To my ears, the chorus sounds more like a one-note *stretto* fugue, a high B-flat entering and exiting in countless voices.

᪣   ᪣   ᪣

The old pond,
A frog jumps in:
Plop!

—Matsuo Basho
(tr. Alan Watts)[6]

❧   ❧   ❧

In May the pond reveals itself in a way that Edith and I hadn't noticed before. Odd, wispy skeins of an unknown substance—shimmery and narrow, like discarded lengths of nylon hosiery—float near the irises that are now resurgent along the shore. Nearby are blobs of a different substance, silvery gray-green, at once granular and gelatinous. We have no idea what we're looking at. Algae of some sort? Rotten leaves? Then, looking closer, I see that both masses contain hundreds of pea-sized, bubble-like chambers. "These are *eggs!*" I shout, startling Edith. The pond, we now realize, is a frog incubator.

We do some research that week and learn that the substances we've spotted are frogspawn—masses of eggs that the females have laid in the water. Each mass contains between five hundred and two thousand eggs. The visibly distinct globs indicate that two separate species are reproducing here. Given the several adult frogs we've spotted along the shore, one species appears to be the mink frog (*Rana septentrionalis*). The other species—which we haven't seen but have heard in profusion at dusk each evening—is almost certainly the spring peeper. What will be the "yield" from so many eggs? We have no idea. One thing seems certain: if last year's efforts to drain the pond had succeeded, we would have killed the adults that are now propagating. Since frog population are rapidly declining throughout the world, drawing down sor fully draining this pond would have contributed to an environmental problem.

After making this discovery, Edith and I walk down to the pond each day to monitor the developing brood. Both types of frogspawn—the wispy skeins and the gelatinous blobs—look different with each successive visit. The skeins elongate and thicken. The blobs expand, grow rough in texture, and shift in hue from gray to a repulsive, snotty green. When we look closely, we can see a tiny black squiggle at the center of each pea-sized egg. Some of the squiggles are moving. Embryonic tadpoles! The water will soon teem with hatchling frogs.

The pond in summer: the green water dark and hazy, the irises dense on the far side, the surface almost granular with leaf debris. Despite the buggy, dank nature of this environment, I continue to go there almost daily. I take a one-quart plastic jar with me one afternoon, fill it with water, and return to the house. Having purchased an inexpensive microscope at a toy store, I examine a drop of this broth under magnification. I'm surprised by how little I see in the field of vision: a few ciliated micro-critters, a couple of shimmering paramecia, and many brownish flecks of deteriorated leaf matter. I feel immediate and intense disappointment. Is this all? Shouldn't there be more microscopic—*action?*

Then, pulling away from the viewfinder and looking at the liquid in the jar, I realize that there's plenty going on here . . . but not on the microscopic level. What's happening is visible with the naked eye. Half a dozen water bugs the size and shape of wheat berries race around underwater, as urgent and reckless as bicycle messengers in New York City. A dozen quarter-inch-long crawdads crawl about on the bottom of the jar. Most startling are hundreds upon hundreds of mystery creatures, each no larger than the dot on the letter *i*, hovering throughout the liquid. Collectively they resemble a cloud of gnats, only aquatic and far smaller. It's impossible for me to guess how many animals are going about their business in this jar. I wouldn't be surprised if the number exceeded a thousand. If a thousand of these creatures inhabit a single quart of water, and if the pond contains half a million gallons . . .

I watch them for a long time. Then I carry the jar back down the hillside and pour the contents back into the pond.

Should Edith and I attempt to forestall the drift toward eutrophication? Is this process something we can slow, stop, or even reverse? Or is it like our own aging—a normal sequence of events that takes place regardless of our efforts, resentment, or lamentation? Perhaps resistance is futile. Perhaps the pond is destined to change. The shore will contract and the water will evaporate; the fish will die, the frogs will die, the newts will die; the water bugs, the crawdads, and the aquatic gnats will die; the algae and the irises will die; but voles, beetles, worms, grass, ferns, wild strawberries, and maple saplings will move in and take over until the once-aquatic ecosystem will become just another part of the forest. Why should I struggle against this transition? Simply because I have a preconceived notion of what the pond should be? Because I want to build a meditation shack beside the pond? Maybe it's best to relent.

So be it.

Then, abruptly, this decision leads to an insight. Whatever comes of my project to construct a meditation shack—which, I decide, I should delay at least until next spring—there's nothing to prevent me from meditating here and now. Isn't that the point? Start where you are. Inhabit the moment. Face the world without preconceptions. Forget about the shack: the flat boulder near the west bank is flat enough to serve as a good meditation spot. The pond is still the pond. The irises are the irises. The trees and birds and frogs are the trees and birds and frogs.

I'll make this boulder my bench. I'll settle in. I'll wait for the sound of water.

6
Night Fliers

Just now,
Out of the strange
Still dusk . . . as strange, as still . . .
A white moth flew . . . Why am I grown
So cold?

—Adelaide Crapsey [1]

Dumping the garbage one summer night, I find my attention drawn to the spotlight mounted on the front shed. The lamp casts a big cone of light outward from that structure. Illuminated in the beam, a cloud of moths billows in the air—hundreds upon hundreds of them, individually small but collectively as thick as a snow flurry. Their wings, though insubstantial, are so numerous as to create a faint yet easily audible hiss. What impresses me even more than the multitude in flight, however, is the smaller but visible array of moths on the wooden doors. The boards are speckled with them. They are so abundant and so varied that no two appear to be of the same species. Some are little wedges. One, triangular and white, looks like a corner snipped off a piece of paper. One resembles an inch-long model airplane, narrow wings jutting straight out from the fuselage, a little tail at the rear end. One appears to be the world's smallest space shuttle. Several are unimaginably delicate, almost angelic: ghostly pale, nearly transparent, like a shred of a woman's negligee. Their beauty is obvious, shocking, and almost totally unfamiliar.

Minutes pass. The tumult of their light-drawn flight continues. I watch them, amazed and appalled, for a long time.

Butterflies generally fly in the daytime, while moths usually fly at night. There are exceptions to this pattern, but the day/night distinction is a significant feature differentiating one order of lepidopteran insects from the other. It's also part of what makes moths less familiar than butterflies: they're harder to see in dark settings, and few people are around (or even awake) to notice them. The nocturnal nature of moths also gives them an air of mystery. As a boy prowling about my yard each summer, I was frequently startled by the sensation of almost intangible wings brushing against my face and by the sight of nearly invisible wisps flitting by. Most eerie was the tapping of moths at the windows, the unsettling arrival of unbidden presences—messengers, it seemed, intent on delivering bad news. I also felt unnerved by the strangeness of moths' legendary obsession: seeking out lights even at the peril of incineration.

During my boyhood I noticed moths in the same places where most people do: circling light bulbs, swarming under streetlamps, tapping at the screens in summertime. I wasn't afraid of bugs—I collected them, examined them under a magnifying glass, and observed them mating or eating one another—but I found moths more mysterious than other insects because of their nocturnal ways. They always seemed beyond reach, longing for light but otherwise going about their business in the dark. When I was ten or so, my mother found a Cecropia moth, and the creature's great size—the wings easily four inches across—amazed and alarmed me.

My interactions with moths intensified when I was twelve. That summer, thousands of inch-long, slate-gray caterpillars swarmed over the trees in our yard. The plum and apple trees, especially, suffered great damage: caterpillars stripped many branches bare of foliage. The plague grew so severe that my father paid my brother and me to collect and destroy as many of the invaders as possible. We shook them out of the trees and stomped on them, picked them off one by one, and sprayed them off the branches with the garden hose. The infestation and the resulting damage continued. Then summer ended; the caterpillars simply disappeared. We had won the war.

Except that we hadn't. During the cool Colorado autumn, I saw moths that I knew had metamorphosed from caterpillars and that now emerged from the air vent in my bedroom: dark little inch-long triangles crawling out through the grate and launching themselves into the air, then fluttering about, seeking and orbiting my table lamp. They seemed harmless enough, so I swatted a few but otherwise ignored them. Then the number increased. What had begun as the occasional arrival of insects became more frequent—two or three at once, then five or more, then a steady launching of moths into the air, soon a stream, one after another, until dozens of tiny winged creatures flitted about the room.

I decided to fight back. Rummaging through our family's cleaning closet, I found a can of aerosol insecticide; now properly armed, I retreated to my bedroom to repel the assault. I stood on a chair, raised my weapon to the air vent, and sprayed the moths as they emerged into my bedroom. They would fly for a few seconds before falling to the floor and flopping there like beached fish. Hundreds came out; I sprayed them; they fell; they died. I would stand there all night, I decided, if that were what's required. I would wipe out the entire swarm. Soon, however, I felt so dizzy and sick from inhaling clouds of insecticide that I abandoned the fight, descended from my strategic roost, opened all the windows, and let the cool autumn air wash in.

I needed a different approach to avoid a Pyrrhic victory. On cleaning up the dead and dying moths with a vacuum cleaner, I realized that the ideal armament would be mechanical, not chemical. The vacuum itself would be my secret weapon. Removing the head from the stainless steel wand, I turned on the machine, returned to my chair, raised the wand, and suctioned the insects right out of the air. Dozens of them emerged from the duct but instantly disappeared into the wand with a bizarre slurping sound: *Thlup! Thlup! Thlup thlup thlup!*

        ઝ   ઝ   ઝ

> A Moth the hue of this
> Haunts Candles in Brazil.
>
> —Emily Dickinson[2]

        ઝ   ઝ   ઝ

Why are moths drawn to light? What accounts for their insistent, counterproductive, often fatal attraction to lamps, candles, and other open flames? This behavior is *phototaxis*, an organism's automatic movement toward or away from light. Cockroaches, for example, are negatively phototactic, while moths are positively phototactic. Scientists currently have no definitive explanation for why moths seek out lights, but there are a number of intriguing theories. One concerns migration. Since some moth species are migratory insects, perhaps lights in the night sky, especially the moon, provide navigational cues during their travels. Alternatively, positive phototaxis may figure in moths' escape reflexes: flying toward the light (usually in the sky, or at least upward) tends to be a more advantageous response to danger than flying toward darkness (which is usually downward). In any case, the phototactic response probably served moths well up to the modern era, but the proliferation of artificial lights over the past century has presented challenges far beyond what their evolutionary development can accommodate.[3]

If nothing else, these insects' intense attraction to light—especially light in its pre-industrial forms as candles, oil lamps, and other open flames—has given rise to one of the most persistent and widespread metaphors present across human cultures. *Drawn like a moth to the flame* . . . But moths and butterflies turn up in other images and other myths as well. One of the most prevalent is the notion that conflates these insects with souls or spirits. The Greek word *psyche*, for instance, means soul, but it can also designate a butterfly or moth. The Latin word *anima* can have the same dual meaning. This *double entendre* may derive from these insects' evanescent lives. In addition, a fundamental aspect of moths' and butterflies' nature—metamorphosis—provides such a powerful, undeniable image of transformation that human beings feel compelled to extrapolate from this natural phenomenon to the supernatural. To observe a lowly worm or caterpillar disappear into a cocoon, then emerge a short while later transformed into a completely different, ethereal, often beautiful creature—one capable of flight, no less—is an irresistible inducement to images of human transformation.

> I can give not what men call love;
> But wilt thou accept not
> The worship the heart lifts above
> And the Heavens reject not,—
> The desire of the moth for the star,
> Of the night for the morrow,
> The devotion of something afar
> From the sphere of our sorrow?
>
> —Percy Bysshe Shelley [4]

Poetry is aflutter with moths. (One could easily assemble *Of Wings and Flames: The Singed Moth Anthology*.) By contrast, moths flit only now and then into novels and stories. The American humorist James Thurber, writing in his *Fables for Our Time* (1939), offers this revisionist tale. [5]

> A young and impressionable moth once set his heart on a certain star. He told his mother about this and

she counseled him to set his heart on a bridge lamp instead. "Stars aren't the thing to hang around," she said; "lamps are the thing to hang around." "You get somewhere that way," said the moth's father. "You don't get anywhere chasing stars." But the moth would not heed the words of either parent. Every evening at dusk when the star came out he would start flying toward it and every morning at dawn he would crawl back home worn out with his vain endeavor.

The moth's parents criticize him for his lack of practical ambition: "You haven't burned a wing in months, boy, and it looks to me as if you were never going to. . . . Come on, now, get out of here and get yourself scorched! A big strapping moth like you without a mark on him!" Instead of responding to these imprecations, however, the moth continued to pursue his absurd ambition.

He went right on trying to reach the star, which was four and one-third light years, or twenty-five trillion miles, away. The moth thought it was just caught up in the top branches of an elm. He never did reach the star, but he went right on trying, night after night, and when he was a very, very old moth he began to think that he really had reached the star and he went around saying so. This gave him a deep and lasting pleasure, and he lived to a great old age. His parents and his brothers and his sisters had all been burned to death when they were quite young.

The moral of the story (perhaps riffing on Shelley): *Who flies afar from the sphere of our sorrow is here today and here tomorrow.*

The most butterfly- and moth-obsessed writer in all of literature is, of course, Vladimir Nabokov. His first publication in English was an article titled "A Few Notes on Crimean Lepidoptera"; he published many technical papers on moths and butterflies; he became an expert in the group of small, brightly colored butterflies known as blues; and he spent six years as a professional lepidopterist at Harvard's Museum of Comparative Zoology—a period that he described later as "the most delightful and thrilling in all my adult life." He became so engrossed in his meticulous work on the taxonomy of butterflies that his wife, Vera, had to prod him at one point to resume work on an unfinished novel. Nabokov felt intensely torn between literature and lepidopterology. In 1967, Nabokov commented: "The pleasures and rewards of literary inspiration are nothing beside the rapture of discovering a new organ under the microscope or an undescribed species on a mountainside in Iran or Peru. It is not improbable that had there been no revolution in Russia, I would have devoted myself entirely to lepidopterology and never written any novels at all."[6]

His books contain multiple references to butterflies. In *Pnin* he writes a passage that describes the Karner Blue species that obsessed him: "A score of small butterflies, all of one kind, were settled on a damp patch of sand, their wings erect and closed, showing their pale undersides with dark dots and tiny orange-rimmed peacock spots along the hindwing margins; one of Pnin's shed rubbers disturbed some of them and, revealing the celestial hue of their upper surface, they fluttered around like blue snowflakes before settling again." What about moths? Nabokov's letters include references to moths, including one from August of 1942 in which he instructs the literary critic Edmund Wilson, of all people, on how to attract these insects. "[Y]ou mix: a bottle of stale beer, two pounds of brown sugar (or treacle) and a little rum (added just before applying); then just before dusk you smear . . . a score of tree trunks . . . with the concoction and wait. They will come from nowhere, settling on the glistening bark and showing their crimson underwings. . . ."[7] Addressing Wilson by his nickname, Nabokov adds this exhortation: "Try, Bunny, it is the noblest sport in the world." (Whether Wilson followed these suggestions and dipped into his ample supply of liquor isn't evident in the literary record.) Despite Nabokov's clear interest in moths, I've found no description of them anywhere in his fiction; even this most lepidoptera-obsessed of authors allowed only butterflies into the pages of his novels.

Virginia Woolf, writing in "The Death of the Moth" (published in 1942, one year after her suicide), created a dark, fable-like essay.[8] Woolf begins by describing the autumnal vitality beyond her window—the plowman tilling the fields, the crows soaring above the treetops, the light shining on the downs—and then, in this idyllic setting, she notes her awareness of a moth on the windowpane.

> One could not help watching him. . . . The possibilities of pleasure seemed that morning so enormous and so various that to have only a moth's part in life . . . appeared a hard fate, and his zest in enjoying his meager opportunities to the full, pathetic. He flew vigorously to one corner of his compartment, and, after waiting there a second, flew across to the other. What remained for him but to fly to a third corner and then to a fourth?

But pity isn't her only response:

> Watching him, it seemed as if a fiber, very thin but pure, of the enormous energy of the world had been thrust into his frail and diminutive body. . . . He was little or nothing but life. Yet, because he was so small, and so simple a form of the energy that was rolling in at the open window and driving its way through so many narrow and intricate corridors in my own brain and in those of other human beings, there was

something marvelous as well as pathetic about him. It was as if someone had taken a tiny bead of pure life and decking it as lightly as possible with down and feathers, had set it dancing and zigzagging to show us the true nature of life.

Soon, however, something intervenes to quench this spark.

He was trying to resume his dancing, but seemed either so stiff or so awkward that he could only flutter to the bottom of the window pane; and when he tried to fly across it he failed. . . . After perhaps a seventh attempt he slipped from the wooden ledge and fell, fluttering his wings, onto his back on the window sill. . . . It flashed upon me that he was in difficulties; he could no longer raise himself; his legs struggled vainly. But, as I stretched out a pencil, meaning to help him to right himself, it came over me that the failure and the awkwardness were the approach of death. I laid down the pencil again.

Woolf realizes that the life force so evident everywhere beyond the window has somehow abandoned the small creature.

[T]he power was there all the same, massed outside, indifferent, impersonal, not attending to anything in particular. Somehow it was opposed to the little hay-colored moth. It was useless to try to do anything. One could only watch the extraordinary efforts made by those tiny legs against an oncoming doom which could, had it chosen, have submerged an entire city, not merely a city, but masses of human beings; nothing, I knew had any chance against death. . . . The unmistakable tokens of death showed themselves. The body relaxed, and instantly grew stiff. The struggle was over. The insignificant little creature now knew death. As I looked at the dead moth, this minute wayside triumph of so great a force over so mean and antagonist filled me with wonder. Just as life had been strange a few minutes before, so death was now is strange. The moth having righted himself now lay most decently and uncomplainingly composed. O yes, he seemed to say, death is stronger than I am.

The moral of the story? It is simply *Mors vincit omnia*? Or perhaps merely a novelist's compassion for a tiny creature? At the time of her writing "The Death of the Moth," Woolf surely also let her mind roam beyond the idyllic English countryside to occupied Europe, where Hitler had unleashed "an oncoming doom which [had] submerged an entire city, not merely a city, but masses of human beings." As her long struggle with madness continued—she probably suffered from what would now be diagnosed as bipolar disorder—a severe depressive episode, allied with "so great a force over so mean an antagonist," soon compelled her to fill her coat pockets with stones and wade into the River Ouse.

ҩ   ҩ   ҩ

The Moth

Isled in the midnight air,
Musked with the dark's faint bloom,
Out into glooming and secret haunts
The flame cries, "Come!"

Lovely in dye and fan,
A-tremble in shimmering grace,
A moth from her winter swoon
Uplifts her face:

Stares from her glamorous eyes;
Wafts her on plumes like mist;

> In ecstasy swirls and sways
> To her strange tryst.
>
> —Walter de la Mare [9]

❧ ❧ ❧

How remarkable that we pay attention to moths almost exclusively because of their strange, disturbing, inadvertently suicidal attraction to flames and other lights. Never mind that somewhere between 150,000 and 250,000 moth species exist, ten times the number of butterfly species.[10] Never mind that among these species are innumerable creatures of great beauty, grace, and ecological benefit. It's analogous to regarding dogs as remarkable and fascinating simply because of their tendency to run into the road and get struck by cars. On the other hand: if moths didn't exist, we would have to invent them. By what other means would we have such a powerful, readily available metaphor to describe fatal attraction resulting from sexual, political, financial, artistic, or spiritual impulses?

The other element that makes butterflies and moths so mysterious and so transfixing to humans is, as I noted earlier, metamorphosis. That a meager and often repulsive caterpillar can emerge as a completely different being is bizarre and compelling in its own right; in addition, it also hints at the possibility of transformation beyond the natural phenomenon itself. Christians throughout the ages have extrapolated readily from metamorphosis. As described in a Catholic website: "The butterfly [as a] Christian symbol represents and symbolizes the Resurrection. . . . The caterpillar symbolizes normal earthly life, where people are preoccupied with taking care of their physical needs. The chrysalis or cocoon resembles the tomb. The butterfly represents the resurrection into a glorious new life free of material restrictions." Small wonder that butterflies decorate many American Christians' homes and yards, as well as elsewhere throughout the world.[11] But what about moths? Moths are fully as subject to the resurrection-like process of metamorphosis, yet I've never seen Christians festoon their walls with representations of dun-colored moths. Are moths too shadowy in appearance? Too suspicious because of their fly-by-night activities? Too symbolic of the Dark?

One exception to this leeriness is the American writer Annie Dillard, who, as a youthful, heterodox Christian, stoked a moth's death into something almost literally incandescent. Moving beyond the standard images of metamorphosis, Dillard describes a bizarre incident in her book *Holy the Firm*. While camping alone in the Blue Ridge Mountains of Virginia, she read all day at her campsite and then each night by candlelight. "Moth kept flying into the candle," she writes. But after a series of these deaths—the moths singed and destroyed—a more remarkable incident took place.[12]

> One night a moth flew into the candle, was caught, burnt dry, and held. I must have been staring at the candle, or maybe I looked up on a shadow crossed my page; at any rate, I saw it all. A golden female moth, a biggish one with a two-inch wingspan, flapped into the fire, dropped her abdomen into the wet wax, stuck, flamed, frazzled and fried in a second. Her moving wings ignited like tissue paper, enlarging the circle of light in the clearing and creating out of the darkness sudden blue sleeves of my sweater, the green leaves of jewelweed by my side, the ragged red trunk of a pine. At once the light contracted again and the moth's wings vanished in a fine, foul smoke. At the same time her six legs clawed, curled, blackened, and ceased, disappearing utterly. And her head jerked in spasms, making a spattering noise; her antennae crisped and burned away and her heaving mouthparts crackled like pistol fire. When it was all over, her head was gone, so far as I could determine, gone, gone the long way of her wings and legs.... All

that was left was the glowing horn shell of her abdomen and thorax—a fraying, partially collapsed gold tube jammed up right in the candle's round pool.

As if the moth's death weren't sufficiently appalling and remarkable, her transfiguration continued:

> And then this moth-essence, this spectacular skeleton, began to act as a wick. She kept burning. The wax rose in the moth's body from her soaking abdomen to her thorax to the jagged hole where her head should be, and widened into flame, a saffron-yellow flame that robed her to the ground like any immolating monk. The candle had two wicks, two flames of identical height, side-by-side. The moth's head was fire. She burned for two hours, until I blew her out.
>
> She burned for two hours without changing, without bending or leaning—only glowing within, like a building fire glimpsed through silhouetted walls, like a hollow saint, like a flame-faced virgin gone to God, while I read by her light . . .

But this tale of the flame-filled moth, this extension of the quintessential moth schema, is only the start of Dillard's narrative. In the second section of *Holy the Firm*, the author tells of an even more calamitous immolation:

> Into this world falls a plane. . . . There was no reason: the plane's engine simply stilled after takeoff, and the light plane failed to clear the firs. It fell easily; one wing snagged on a fir top; the metal fell down and smashed in the tin woods where cattle browse; the fuel exploded; and Julie Norwich seven years old burnt off her face. . . .

What follows her description of the child's tragedy are several dozen pages of eloquent, wrenching, ultimately white-hot ruminations on life, knowledge, God, and suffering:

> Of faith I have nothing, only of truth: that this one God is a brute and traitor, abandoning us to time, to necessity and the engines of matter unhinged. This is no leap; this is evidence of things seen: one Julie, one sorrow, one sensation bewildering the heart, and enraging the mind . . . Has God a hand in this? Then it is a good hand. But has he a hand at all? Or is he a holy fire burning self-contained for power's sake alone? Then he knows himself blissfully as flame unconsuming, as all brilliance and beauty and power, and the rest of us can go hang. Then the accidental universe spins mute, obedient only to its own gross terms, meaningless, out of mind, and alone.

What, then, should we make of human suffering? Dillard quotes John 9:1-3, in which Jesus, healing a blind beggar at the roadside, proclaims that "Neither has this man sinned, nor his parents: but that the works of God should be made manifest in him." Dillard is appalled: "The works of God made manifest? Do we really need more victims to remind us that we're all victims? . . . Do we need blind men stumbling about, and little flamefaced children, to remind us what God can—and will—do?" Yet she calls herself down immediately for expressing her own outrage. "Yes, in fact, we do. We do need reminding, not of what God can do, but of what he cannot do, or will not, which is to catch time in its free fall and stick a nickel's worth of sense into our days." Then she scolds herself and other doubters much as Yahweh scolded Job: "Who are we to demand explanations of God?"

Holy the Firm ends with a flaming, inflamed, inflammatory passage in which Julie Norwich ends up as totally transformed as the moth Annie Dillard observed at her Virginia campsite:

> There is Julie Norwich. Julie Norwich is salted with fire. She is preserved like a salted fillet from all evil, baptized at birth into time and now into eternity, into the bladelike arms of God. For who will love her now, without a face, when women with faces abound, and people are so? People are reasoned, while God is mad. They love only beauty; who knows what God loves? . . . You might as well be a nun. You might as well be God's chaste bride, chased by plunderers to the high caves of solitude, to the hearthless rooms empty of voices, and of warm limbs hooking your heart to the world. Look how he loves you! Are you bandaged now, or loose in a sterilized room? Wait till they hand you a mirror, if you can hold one, and know what it means. . . . You cry, My father, my father, the chariots of Israel, and the horsemen thereof! Held, held fast by love in the world like the moth in wax, your life a wick, your head on fire with prayer, held utterly, outside and in, you sleep alone, if you call that alone, you cry God.

It's a heavy burden we place on moths: the weight of our metaphors.

Metamorphosis may be common, but perhaps only for insects and amphibians.

A better bet for humans: being. Just being.

> On the one-ton temple bell
> a moon-moth, folded into sleep,
> sits still.
>
> —Buson[13]

One afternoon, during a visit from our friend Dianne, Edith and I show her the front flowerbeds. The previous owners of the house had operated a commercial flower nursery on Long Island for many decades, and they had lavished great skill and attention on their own property as well, so the gardens delighted us from the outset with their size and the variety and splendor of their plantings. Now Edith and I want to show them off to Dianne, herself an accomplished gardener. The front bed is especially lush at that point of the summer.

Dianne is impressed. At one point, however, as she comments on the various flowers and their proper care, she suddenly interrupts herself and exclaims, "Look, a baby hummingbird!"

What she points out is so small—just a little over an inch long—that I can't see it at first. Soon it is unmistakable. Flitting, hovering, darting about, this little bird pokes its needle-narrow beak into the tiniest flowers, then withdraws, then angles about to probe the next bloom.

A stirring sight! I have long delighted in these tiny, unimaginably agile creatures. Here now is one even smaller than the miniscule birds I've observed in Mexico, Colorado, Peru, Singapore, and elsewhere. It doesn't seem possible that something so delicate, so beautiful, so perfect can exist.

The three of us watch in silence for a long time.

Something soon puzzles me. Yes, the wings beat so fast as to be almost invisible. Somehow they seem different, though, not quite as rapid as what I've seen on hummers in the past. A consequence of this one's size, perhaps? Or of its youth? I can't even guess. Yes, the tiny creature pokes its beak into the flowers . . . but somehow with a slightly different motion, or in a slightly different way, from what I've observed in the past. Intrigued, I edge closer to get a better look. The bird may or may not notice me, but in any case it keeps moving from flower to flower. I expect it to zip away at a moment, but it allows me to draw near.

I then see something I would never have expected: antennae. Stepping closer still, I spot another feature out of keeping with a hummingbird's: legs that dangle from the tiny body. Two legs . . . No, four legs . . . No, six.

The hummingbird isn't a hummingbird at all—it's a moth. As I learn later, it's *Hemaris thysbe,* the so-called hummingbird clearwing moth. First identified in 1775 by Johan Christian Fabricius, a Danish naturalist, members of this species are common throughout the entire eastern half of the United States and in much of Europe; and, according to several articles I've read, they are frequently mistaken for hummingbirds because of their coloration and fast-moving wings.[14] They may also have contributed to the legend of faeries in England and elsewhere. Our perceptual error in the garden is understandable. But at that moment, the moth itself—delicate, gentle, languid in its motions—transfixes all three of us simply for existing, simply for being there.

I am not a mystic who feels drawn to see the moth, whether immolated or merely airborne, as a promise of Reality beyond reality, of Life beyond life. Moths are intriguing in the moment, of the moment, for the moment. I'm not convinced that there is transfiguration or metamorphosis of what lies right before us. There is no fleshly transcendence, only immanence. There is perfection in the here-and-now: the day warm and bright, the air still, the flowers resplendent, the hummingbird-impostor moth beautiful and beguiling as she makes her rounds among the blossoms.

7
The Whiteness of the Weasel

We are not alone. I've known since boyhood that houses often have critters—that the structures we humans perceive as *ours* often contain other denizens who don't happen to share this proprietary attitude. The resulting interspecies disagreement often leads to conflict. During twenty-five years of residence in suburban New Jersey, for instance, I fought a low-intensity war against squirrels on the property that my wife and I owned there. These cute troublemakers persistently invaded and nested in our attic, and I resolutely set traps to catch and relocate them to a nearby nature preserve. The result: nearly three hundred squirrels deported over the course of a quarter century. Following this and other experiences, I'm not surprised that our house on Whitcomb Hill would appeal to wildlife, nor am I shocked to hear scratchy sounds above the ceiling and inside the walls.

Neither am I astonished one January morning when Edith announces: "There's a rat in the bathroom!" She utters these words emphatically but without alarm.

"A rat? Are you sure?"

"It's big and white and has huge black eyes." Having closed the door, she has trapped this critter in the room.

I'm puzzled by her description. It's true that a large rodent might well be a rat, but I'm surprised by the color. Most wild rats are gray, brown, or black. I've never heard of one that's white. I tell Edith I'll investigate; I ease into the bathroom; I look around. I sit on the closed toilet for a while and wait in silence. There's neither sight nor sound of an intruding animal. I don't doubt that she has spotted *something*, but whatever she saw has somehow escaped.

A day later, after Edith has left Vermont for a work assignment, I prepare the house for my own week out of town. One of my chores is to move firewood from the attached garage into the house and then stock two racks near the wood stoves. I make multiple trips into the garage. On my third or fourth trip, something catches my attention: a rustling sound in the far right corner. I can't see what's making it. Then, after fifteen or twenty seconds, I catch sight of the intruder. A small creature, long and lithe and altogether white except for two huge black eyes and a black tip at the end of its tail, emerges from beneath the ride-on mower, slinks into plain view, rears up on its hind legs, and stares at me. It's a weasel of some sort. I'm struck at once by its beauty. This animal is agile, supple, and alert. Despite my total ignorance of weasels, I decide that this one is female. She stares at me with interest but without any sign of alarm. I realize just then what has drawn her out: a bag of frozen garbage that I carelessly left on the garage floor the previous night. One corner has been chewed open. This little beast has clearly been exploring the trash. Even as I watch, she scampers over to the bag, pokes her head inside, and returns to pilfering whatever she can extract. I step closer. She startles at once and darts under the mower. There's no sign of her for several minutes. Impatient, I return to my task of stocking firewood. Each time I return to the garage, however, I find her exploring the garbage, so I walk over, surprise her with my approach, pick up the bag, and remove it. My later visits to the garage show her still present as she attempts to figure out what happened to her *smörgasbord*.

It's clear to me that I can't let this animal remain here. For all I know, she is the source of the scratching sounds that Edith and I heard on the second floor. Spotting one such creature probably means that others are present—an entire family, even.

Very well, then: they have to go. But I decide on the spot that there's no way I'll set a spring trap. I don't have a non-lethal trap small enough to catch such a little creature, though, so I'll have to obtain one. Since I'll be leaving Vermont in just a few hours, I realize there's nothing to be done until I return.

I have always hated killing animals, including rodents. This aversion has been a longtime city-dweller's luxury and hypocritical as well: although I was completely vegetarian for twelve years during my twenties and early thirties, I now eat meat two or three times per week. Rodents aren't on the menu in our household, but during my almost three years of living in Peru during the 1960s and 70s, I periodically sampled *picante de cuy*—spicy grilled guinea pig—standard fare in the Andes. Regardless, I can recall feeling deep sadness from the age of five and older when I found dead mice in the spring traps that my parents had set in our family home. The sleek, glossy fur and slim tails . . . The tiny paws with those perfectly formed, finger-like claws . . . The shiny, midnight-black eyes . . . Killing these animals seemed an injustice.

During the mid-1970s, after graduating from college, I shared a thin-walled, drafty little bungalow with my girlfriend at the time. Judith and I were avid yogis. One of the precepts we followed was *ahimsa*, the practice of nonviolence. In addition to being strict vegetarians, we expressed our commitment to ahimsic principles by avoiding any actions that might result in the death of another sentient being. Even flies venturing into our little house benefited from our pacific attitudes: we caught them in jars and released them outside. The notion of setting snap traps to kill mice was unacceptable. How, then, could we cope with the vermin that raided our pantry, scattered droppings throughout the house, skittered across the floor at night, and at one point even scampered over us in our bed? The infestation was intolerable—but so was slaughtering the creatures that caused it. Nowadays it's not difficult to purchase a non-lethal mousetrap, but no one had marketed anything of the sort back then. Even the Havahart company, well known for making traps designed to catch raccoons, squirrels, and other animals, produced nothing at the time small enough for catching mice. Undeterred, I purchased the smallest Havahart trap available, constructed of steel wires too widely spaced to constrain a mouse, and I used surgical sutures to stitch pieces of window screen around the whole device. Judith and I then proceeded to catch a shocking number of mice, sometimes two or three per day, a total of eighteen in a week, which we deported to a park five or six blocks from our cottage. Problem solved; karma unsullied.

The modus I employed decades later as a family man battling squirrels and mice in suburban New Jersey riffed on the earlier methodology. Squirrels proved to be manageable invaders—easy to catch, easy to deport. The result was a war of attrition, not of victory, but I prevailed against my foes. Attempting to spare mice through the use of nonlethal mousetraps, however, often produced frustrating outcomes. Tiny creatures don't last long without food and water. More than once I found my quarry alive but debilitated inside the trap: terrified, hungry, thirsty, exhausted, fur spiky and damp with urine. Sometimes I would forget about the traps altogether, which led now and then to my discovering a dead mouse that had surely died a slow, painful death rather than a quick, painless one.

And this new critter? How, I wondered, should I respond to her arrival in our midst?

A few days after spotting the white rodent in the garage, I learned from a little Internet research that I'd seen an ermine. This species, also known as the short-tailed weasel, is *Mustela erminea* and, according to one guide I consulted, "is distinguished from the least weasel (*Mustela nivalis*) by its larger size and longer tail [and its] prominent black tip." (Is there a *most weasel*, too?) Dark and two-toned in warm weather—sandy brown on the back and head, creamy tan on the chest and belly—the ermine's fur turns pure white in winter. This snowy coat makes the animal's large, round eyes even more striking than they would look otherwise. The species inhabits territory spanning most of the North American continent. "As with the least weasel, mouse-like rodents predominate in the stoat's diet," the guide's author notes, using the British name for the same creature. "However, unlike the least weasel, which almost exclusively feeds on small voles, the stoat regularly preys on larger rodent species." Was it possible, then, that because of the ermine's dietary preferences, any effort I might make to trap and deport ours (I have already started to regard her as "ours") would be counterproductive? Far from infesting the house, she might be a useful ally in holding down other rodents. Some members of the weasel family will even attack and kill rats. These aspects of the situation argue that peaceful co-existence may serve both the human and mustelan species residing on our property. On the other hand, weasels burrowing through the walls could easily damage the expensive insulation that we've installed to keep the house warm in winter. How, then, should Edith and I proceed?

Winter fades. Spring bursts forth. Summer arrives and flourishes. Throughout the warm months, Edith and I spot signs of many rodents: voles nibbling at the vegetables in the garden, moles forcing up piles of dirt as they tunnel under the lawn, chipmunks exploring the flowerbeds, squirrels nesting near the front shed, and a large, pumpernickel-hued woodchuck grazing in the lower meadow. Not once during the summer months, however, do I catch sight of the ermine. I'm aware that she will have changed color by now, but I spot no creature of either cold- or warm-weather hue on our hillside. Still, I think about her constantly; and, like a lover pining for his beloved during a long separation, I imagine her not as she is now but as she was when I first cast eyes on her. I want to see her once again in her pure-white guise.

Which brings me to the remarkable Chapter XLII of *Moby-Dick*, "The Whiteness of the Whale."[1] In that chapter, Melville surveys the strange nature of the color that is no color yet is all colors; he explores how "in many natural objects, whiteness refiningly enhances beauty, as if imparting some special virtue of its own, as in marbles, Japonicas, and pearls"; and he enumerates a long list of objects, animals, and artistic attributes that are rendered attractive, noble, or admirable by virtue of being white. The white charger on the Hanoverian flag . . . The white robes of a magistrate . . . The Greek god Jove incarnated as a snow-white bull . . . The white banner hung in Roman Catholic churches to mark the Passion of Christ . . . The American Indian's white belt of wampum as a pledge of honor . . . Melville notes, however, that "for all these accumulated associations with whatever is sweet, and honorable, and sublime, there yet lurks an elusive something in the innermost idea of this hue, which strikes more panic to the soul than that redness which affrights in blood." Melville then describes a series of disturbing creatures—"the white bear of the poles[,] . . . the white shark of the tropics[,] . . . " and even "the Albino man [who] so peculiarly repels and often shocks the eye"—all of which lead him to a disturbing conclusion: "That ghastly whiteness it is which imparts such an abhorrent mildness, even more loathsome than terrific, to the dumb gloating of their aspect." Further meditations on alarming natural phenomena, such as fog and ocean whitecaps, lead Melville to plumb the depths of whiteness and find within it an existential emptiness:

> Is it that by its indefiniteness it shadows forth the heartless voids and immensity of the universe, and thus stabs us from behind with the thought of annihilation, when beholding the white depths of the milky way? Or is it, that in essence whiteness is not so much a color as the visible absence of color, and at the same time the concrete of all colors; is it for these reasons

that there is such a dumb blankness, full of meaning, in a wide landscape of snow was—a colorless, all-color of atheism from which we shrink?

The implications for Captain Ahab and for the obsession overtaking his mind and soul become clear to Ishmael as well. "It was the whiteness of the whale that above all things appalled me," Ishmael states early in this chapter; and then, after pondering all the implications of the color-that-is-all-colors-and-no-color, he concludes: "[Of] all these things the Albino whale was the symbol. Wonder ye then at the fiery hunt?"

My hunt is not fiery. My quarry, though reputed to be fierce, is small and not the least appalling. She doesn't stab me from behind with the thought of annihilation. The memory of her doesn't prompt me to shrink from a dumb blankness. At the same time, I am aware that the ermine's snowy fur and some aspect of this creature's resultant pure white appearance contribute to my obsession. Would I feel so fascinated if she were ash-gray? No. Would I feel the same intensity of interest if she retained her brown-and-tan summer coat all year long? Not likely. Am I therefore subject to the same bias that seems to affect some people as they campaign to save the white, very cute harp seal while generally ignoring other species, such as the dun-colored, wrinkled, hideously snouted elephant seal? Probably. Perhaps that's no surprise, and surely it's not shameful that I should find the ermine's beauty so beguiling. Bird fanciers may go a lifetime on the lookout for a lovely species—the ivory-billed woodpecker, perhaps, or the Asian crested ibis—and nobody regards these obsessions as worse than quirky. The short-tailed weasel has become my equivalent. But is there something else in play here, too, something more archetypal, something more akin to what Melville describes in his chapter about the Whiteness of the Whale? I can't shake the feeling that the answer is Yes. It would appear that I've become an Ahab of sorts: confined to dry land rather than roaming the seven seas, walking normally rather than thumping about with one leg and an ivory peg, motivated not by revenge but by curiosity, and not fully monomaniacal but still intent on encountering the object of my obsession.

Autumn arrives; the weather cools. November and December are less snowy and less cold than the same months a year before, which had provided the snowiest winter in Vermont since at least the 1970's, but January brings a series of weak snowstorms, then a mid-month descent into sub-zero temperatures. It's enough to set a man's mind to trapping ermine.

How, though? Snap traps are out of the question. The mouse-sized Havaharts I own are too small for weasels. The squirrel-sized traps would let an ermine slink out effortlessly. Thus I have no recourse but to exercise a hunting skill that we *Homo sapiens* has mastered only after eons of our species' evolution as a hunter: I order goods through the Internet. Specifically, I acquire a mesh-walled "live trap" suitable for my quarry. I pay $40 and receive my order less than a week later. Then, baiting the trap with a piece of steak—the first beef I've bought in four decades, a purchase that feels illicit after all these years—I smear the meat against the outside of a narrow wooden box I've constructed to house the trap. This box will protect any animal from the elements if I succeed in catching one. Then I place both the box and the trap where a stone wall meets the northwest corner of our garage.

I wait. More days pass. Snow falls—an inch of light, fine powder that creates the ideal surface for spotting animal tracks. Stepping outside, I find tiny paw prints all around the trap. Courtesy of the ermine? Perhaps. But I've seen chipmunks in the area, too, and a rodent of that species would leave tracks similar to a weasel's. Consulting a field guide provides no clarity about what kind of critter has visited the box. In any case, none has entered the trap itself. A warm front moves in, drenching the area in unseasonable rain. Now as before the bait remains untouched, the trap not yet sprung.

Meanwhile, the war of attrition against mice continues. Edith and I had first heard scritchy-scratchy sounds in the second-floor walls starting in October, and shortly after that we spotted mice in the basement. Setting mini-Havaharts early on, I started catching mice immediately, and I soon felt so frustrated by the task of deporting them—especially as the weather turned cold and a daily drive down the road grew less and less appealing—that I now resort to snap traps. (I purchase a widely available brand whose logo melds the V for Victor into a mouse's head and pointy nose.) This gambit presents a moral line that I would prefer not to cross. Even when I plug holes in the basement walls, however, mice keep finding their way in, and I sometimes catch half a dozen in a week. The slaughter of the innocents, I call it . . . But what is the alternative?

Then I see the grisly consequences of my decision snap shut like a trap. Descending the basement steps one morning, I find a big male mouse caught in a Victor but not yet defeated. The wire bar has descended on the critter's hindquarters, smashing his pelvis flat but somehow leaving him still alive. Now, clawing his way across the floor with his front paws, he drags the tormenting device along with him. The sight couldn't be more pathetic. At once I grasp my dilemma. I have undoubtedly caused this animal to suffer a mortal injury, yet he shows no signs of acknowledging death's approach; on the contrary, he appears almost vigorous in his efforts to soldier on. I can free him—but doing so will release a dying mouse into the basement. Freed, he may also take far longer to expire than if he remains in the trap's jaws, and he may even crawl off and die in a remote cranny, thus stinking up the house. I can, of course, resort to the *coup de grace* that ranchers and farmers routinely deliver—stomping—but I can't bring myself to take this step (literally). For a moment I wonder if I might emulate veterinarians and somehow euthanize this two-inch-long rodent . . . But how? Shall I start a tiny IV? Hang a miniscule bag of saline? Administer a lethal microdose of pentobarbital or sodium thiopental? Ultimately, the only thought I can tolerate is to put the mouse out in the meadow, trap and all, in hopes that the sub-freezing temperatures will rapidly hasten the inevitable.

This incident leaves me unnerved. The situation is clear: snap traps aren't necessarily humane, and even under the best circumstances I've been snuffing out a remarkable number of lives. Let my farmer-neighbors dismiss me as a sentimental city slicker who can't grasp the realities of the rural life. True enough. In the meantime, here's how I see the situation. The crime: serial murder of sentient beings. The verdict: guilty as charged. The penalty: community service by using Havahart traps only—forever more.

A day after having caught the injured mouse, I find him exactly where I had placed him near the meadow's edge. He is still caught in the trap. Despite rigor mortis and the incipient smell of death—mild because of the low late-December temperatures—he looks merely asleep. I pick up the trap and carry it into the garage, where I set it on the Husqvarna mower's seat. There I can get a closer view of this creature whose fate has intersected with my own.

He rests his pointy nose on the coiled spring that powered the trap's spine-crushing wire. His back and sides are gray-brown; his belly is white. In spite of the massive injuries he has suffered—the wire has completely creased his body sideways at the pelvis—I see no sign of blood. This absence of gore is a relief, yet the ordinary features of this animal are what most surprise me. His eyes remain open, pure black, large, and still shiny. Two perfect cones of whiskers radiate outward from the slightly ridged, pointy snout. Some of these filaments are almost an inch in length, much longer than the head itself, and so abundant as to form a beautiful, complex sensory apparatus. He has perfect, scoop-like ears, the tissue of the scoops as thin as paper but softer than suede and arrayed with hundreds of subtle, almost imperceptible hairs lining their interior. What I find most remarkable is that his tiny paws have digits as narrow as fine wire, and yet-narrower claws extend from these digits, the aggregate forming what I can only perceive as *fingers* on what I can only call *hands*—hands once capable of what I imagine was great agility—and the right one now grasps the trap's coiled wire with an appearance of calm much like that of a sleeping toddler who finds comfort in holding the padded bumper that lines his crib.

I examine the mouse for a long time.

It occurs to me at some point that I have never truly *looked* at a mouse until now.

If ermine were infesting this house; if my sleep were troubled by their scuttling through the walls at night; if I were catching half a dozen short-tailed weasels each week; and if only a single, elusive mouse had appeared a full year ago but not since, foiling my best efforts to catch him month after month—that is, if *Mustela erminia* and *Mus musculus* had somehow swapped the roles they play on this property—would I then regard the ermine as a mere nuisance while longing for even a glimpse of the mouse? Maybe so. Maybe rarity is a factor that distorts my perceptions and intensifies my desire to attain the unattainable. This is plausible. However, I doubt that rarity and frequency tell the entire story. Few creatures enter my awareness as often as moths, yet I always find them mysterious and intriguing. Few objects in my life have been as absurdly numerous as snowflakes, yet I am always astonished and impressed, if not always delighted, when they materialize out of the winter sky. Rarity alone, or at least the absence of rarity, doesn't fully explain my responses to mice and weasels. The fact remains that ermine are creatures of intrinsic beauty;

they are agile; they have an air about them suggesting that they know exactly who they are.

Thus the hunt continues. Mice remain a problem to be solved. And the ermine? The ermine appears only in my dreams at night.

In June of 1999, Rudolph W. Giuliani, then Mayor of New York, pushed the city council to ban the ownership of ferrets. Owners of these pets were incensed; pushback was immediate and fierce. Giuliani gave no personal leeway on the issue of these pets, however, and as the citywide discussion of the topic ensued, he famously attacked a caller on his weekly radio program:[2]

> **David Guthartz:** Let me introduce myself again, David Guthartz, executive president of New York Ferrets' Rights Advocacy. Last week when we spoke, you said a very disparaging remark to me, that I should get a life. That was very unprofessional of you. . . . We're trying to get an important issue taken care of where the city is violating state law, and I asked you last week if you care about the law.
>
> **Mayor Rudolph W. Giuliani:** Yes, I do care about the law. I think you have totally and absolutely misinterpreted the law, because there's something deranged about you.
>
> **Guthartz:** No, there isn't, sir.
>
> **Giuliani:** The excessive concern that you have for ferrets is something you should examine with a therapist. Not with me.
>
> **Guthartz:** Don't go insulting me again!
>
> **Giuliani:** I'm not insulting you. I'm being honest with you.

Guthartz: I happen to be more sane than you.

Giuliani: This conversation is over, David. Thank you. There is something really, really, very sad about you. You need help. You need somebody to help you. I know you feel insulted by that, but I'm being honest with you. This excessive concern with little weasels is a sickness. But you should go consult a psychologist or a psychiatrist, and have him help you with this excessive concern, how you are devoting your life to weasels. Your . . . excessive concern with it is a sign that there is something wrong in your personality. You have a sickness, and I know it's hard for you to accept that, because you hang on to this sickness, and it's your shield. . . . You need help! And please get it!

Fifteen months later, the Humane Society of New York sued Mayor Giuliani and the Department of Health to prevent the enforcement of the ban. The City Council revoked the ban in May of 2001. This story was big news in New York that spring. Eleven days into September, though, residents of the city shifted their attention from ferrets to other issues.

I followed these events while living in the New York City area at the time; I shared David Guthartz's outrage at the arrogant mayoral response to him; yet I also agreed with Rudy Giuliani that something seemed a little off, a little *cuckoo,* about the caller's monomania. One could only hope that Guthartz followed the free mental health advice he had received from the mayor and sought psychological counseling. No doubt there's a therapeutic modality to address this specific pathology, or at least a support group. In any case, I thank God every morning that I am not obsessed with ferrets.

"Hast seen the white whale?"
  "Aye, yesterday. Have ye seen a whale-boat adrift?"
  Ahab, questioning Captain Gardiner of the *Rachel* when this

ship crosses paths with the *Pequod* late in the novel, learns that his quest is almost over—and that Moby-Dick has dragged away one of the *Rachel*'s whale-boats when its crew succeeded in harpooning and fastening a line to their quarry. Now both Moby-Dick and the crew have vanished.

A few days later, when the *Pequod* encounters another ship, the *Delight*, Ahab poses his urgent question: "Hast seen the white whale?"

> "Look!" replied the hollow-cheeked captain from his taffrail, and with his trumpet he pointed to the wreck [of a whale-boat on the deck of his ship].
> "Hast killed him?"
> "The harpoon is not yet forged that ever will do that," answered the other, sadly glancing upon a rounded hammock on the deck, whose gathered sides some noiseless sailors were busy sewing together.

It transpires that the captain of the *Delight*, having battled Moby-Dick, has suffered the loss of five crewmembers, four of them drowned and their bodies sunken, the fourth now stitched into his shroud for burial at sea.[3]

My situation is different. I never cross paths with fellow ermine questers in my corner of Vermont. I will never inquire, "Hast seen the white weasel?" If at long last I encounter the object of my search, I will never end up with my boats stove, my crew dead, my harpoon anchored in the beast as the line tangles and my nemesis drags me away.

This snowy landscape is a *tabula rasa* for critters to write upon. All winter I find scribblings near the house. These marks are unmistakably the footprints of a rodent... but of what species? I'm not experienced enough to read these hieroglyphics. Too large for a mouse's tracks and too small for a squirrel's, however, they clearly belong to a creature of intermediate size. One set shows that the animal in question has circumnavigated the house, has stopped every five or six feet to burrow into the snow against the foundation stones, and, as nearly as I can tell, has attempted to gain entry into the basement. Yet so far he or she has avoided the traps I've generously baited with fresh meat and have left fully accessible.

Our second Vermont winter, far milder than the first, sputters to a close. A warm, dry early spring follows. Weeks of near-drought then shift into a rainy transition. Green emerges in a welter of hues and shades. The summer turns hot enough to break records set since the 1890s.

One day in late July, after months of leaving the outdoor trap idle and empty, I bait it with meat just to see what happens. Two days later I find it sprung. Inside is my long-awaited, long-sought, long-pursued, long-longed-for prey. She waits inside the trap looking neither tense nor hostile. There's no clawing at the wire mesh, no dashing back and forth in hopes of escape. She looks calm but perplexed: *What took you so long?*

I carry the trap to our picnic table to view her more easily and, I suppose, to let her view me in turn. I have no idea what she sees, but what I find before me is a compact creature of great beauty. The sleek body, the pert tail, the teddy bear ears, and above all the big obsidian eyes—all of these features delight and transfix me. So too does her complete attentiveness. Never in my life have I seen any animal more fully, more unceasingly alert. Rearing up on her hind legs into the same position I've observed in black bears standing over six feet tall, she stares at me with altogether focused curiosity.

We gaze at each other for a long time.

I want to regard this moment as the fulfillment of my quest. Against all expectation, however, my disappointment is immediate, intense, and visceral. The ermine lacks her winter coat; she is brown-and-tan, not snowy white; and thus she isn't an ermine at all, only a short-tailed weasel. This outcome falls far short of what I've hoped to accomplish.

Is my response peculiar, even ridiculous, following so much effort over a period of twenty months? I can't help but scold myself for what I'm feeling. Here she is at last. She is present, beautiful, perfect. Yet perhaps my reaction makes sense. If whales, like weasels, could change color from one season to another, and if Ahab had encountered, battled, and vanquished Moby-Dick at a time when the White Whale was no longer white, would the captain have felt victorious? Not likely. His foe wasn't just the whale; it was the very whiteness of the whale. It was both the "whiteness refiningly enhances beauty, as if imparting some special virtue of its own, as in marbles, Japonicas, and pearls" and the "indefiniteness [that] shadows forth the heartless voids and immensity of the universe." Have I been searching for a pint-sized personification of these attributes—of the positive ones, at least? At the moment of capturing my quarry, am I now dissatisfied because the critter has evaded me even as I attain the goal of my quest?

I realize at this moment that I haven't been hunting weasels at all. I've been stalking a *concept*. And the trap is not yet forged that ever will catch a *concept*.

Then I grasp a solution to my quandary. I pick up the Havahart and carry it across the meadow to the woods. I crouch to set the trap on the ground. I pull open the spring-mounted door. At once my quarry escapes—shooting out quicker than seems possible—and disappears into the foliage.

Time is on my side. In just four months the seasons will change, the temperature will drop, and this creature—my friend, my nemesis, my companion animal—will once again turn the color of the winter landscape, which, like her, will be the color that is all colors and no color at all.

Part Three

Planting, Growing, Harvesting

8

House History—
Working the Land

What was our predecessors' work, and what were the fruits of their labors? Unlike some nineteenth-century American families, the Whitcombs, Bohonons, and Rings seem not to have left any diaries or letters describing their daily lives. (Many documents of both kinds exist for thousands of Vermonters, especially dating from the mid-century exodus to "the West"—what we now called the Midwestern states—and from the Civil War years.) I've found useful information in other sources. Raw data from the U. S. Census documents are abundant and invaluable. In addition, the State of Vermont undertook a series of agricultural censuses in 1850, '60, '70, and '80 that provide a remarkable level of detail about rural families and their activities. The Vermont Agricultural Census documents list every farm in the state and inventory its output down to the last cow, pig, horse, bushel of oats, and pound of butter.

Here's how the U.S. and Vermont census data portray James and Hannah's farm in 1850.

First, the *dramatis personae*. It appears that three male members of the Whitcomb clan owned adjacent plots on or near Whitcomb Hill. Levi Sr., age 65 in 1850, still lived on "the old Whitcomb farm." His household consisted of Levi himself; Levi Sr.'s wife, Sarah Whitcomb, 63; their son, Nathaniel, 26; and Sally Welch, 25. As mentioned earlier, Levi Jr., 33, maintained his own household nearby in the company of the now-elderly

Moses Ring; Moses's second, much younger wife, Sarah; the teenage Joseph Bohonon; and Amanda Welch, 23, Sally Welch's younger sister. Also present on a nearby property were James and Hannah Whitcomb (*née* Welch, the oldest of the three sisters), both spouses being in their thirties and childless at that point in their married life. James appears to have owned the largest acreage. Levi Sr. isn't listed as owning property in 1850, yet he's clearly present in the immediate area.[1]

In 1850, James Whitcomb's farm was larger than average for that part of Vermont at the time. The Vermont Agricultural Census for that year specifies that James owned 145 acres of "improved land" as well as 15 acres of "unimproved land." ("Improved" was cleared, arable land; "unimproved," probably woodlands.) The family's livestock included 14 milch cows, four working oxen, nine sheep, two swine, and a single horse. The implications: James and Hannah were running a family farm that produced most or all of their own food plus a variety of cash crops and other products. James worked the land with oxen, grew hay (35 tons in 1850), kept cows, and produced butter (800 pounds that year) and cheese (200 pounds). In addition, the Whitcombs harvested 50 bushels of wheat, 75 of "Indian corn," 100 of oats, three of peas and beans, and 400 of Irish potatoes. James and Hannah probably sold much of this output for cash but used some of the products themselves.[2]

The mid-nineteenth century was a transitional period for Vermont agriculture: the subsistence farming typical of the Early American period and the next several decades was giving way to market-driven agriculture. Farmers often produced far more than they could use themselves. Christopher McGrory Klyza and Stephen C. Trombulak describe these changes in *The Story of Vermont: A Natural and Cultural History*. "During this revolution [of cultural and economic changes], which lasted roughly from 1800 to 1860 in Vermont and much of northern New England, production became oriented toward profit rather than subsistence."[3] The Whitcombs' production of maple sugar, for instance—450 pounds in 1850—would have been an important source of cash for the family. So was meat from James and Hannah's slaughtered animals. The nine sheep produced 24 pounds of wool. Hannah, in a role typical of the times, almost surely spun some of this wool into yarn, then sold the yarn on the local market.

This portrait of what James and Hannah owned, along with what they produced, is consistent with Vermont family farms of that era. If anything, however, this couple seems unusually productive. Klyza and Trombulak note that according to early nineteenth-century statutes in the State of Vermont, certain possessions and goods were exempted from collection for payment of debts. "These exemptions," they write, "are a good indication of the basic level of subsistence at the time: one cow, one or two swine, 6 to 10 sheep and their wool, a pair of oxen or horses, hay to sustain livestock through the winter, all standing crops, 20 to 30 bushels of corn and grain, and 10 to 12 cords of firewood. This subsistence would probably be achieved on 45 to 65 acres."[4] Since James and Hannah produced considerably more than what the State of Vermont exempted, they appear to have been well above average in productivity.

How even a vigorous young couple could perform all the work involved in this endeavor defies comprehension—or at least my own comprehension. Constant hard work was a farmer's lot, and a farmwife's as well, during that era. To accomplish so much, James and Levi Jr. almost certainly collaborated on all aspects of agricultural labor, probably aided by the young Joseph Bohonon and perhaps by the younger Moses Ring (who, in fact, owned and worked his own 50 acres nearby). It seems likely as well that Hannah and the other two Welch sisters benefited from mutual assistance. Even so, the amount of work involved, as well as the resulting output, is astonishing. Meanwhile, Robert and Betsey Bohonon, in their mid-thirties in 1850), lived a short distance to the south of the Whitcomb brothers' farms, worked their smaller plot (26 "improved" acres, 10 "unimproved"), and raised a brood of five children younger than eleven years old. (Six or seven more kids would join the family over the next fourteen years.) The younger Moses Ring settled a short distance to the northwest with his wife, Lucinda, to raise their own family and tend their farm.

Although I haven't located any documents in which the early residents of Whitcomb Hill describe their experiences, other Vermonters of that era wrote letters and kept diaries that chronicle the nature of mid-nineteenth century farm life. Roxana Brown Walbridge Watts (1802-1862), a resident of Peacham, Vermont, provided an especially detailed record this topic. The mother of twelve children and stepchildren, Roxana corresponded with her offspring over a period of many years, and other Watts family members described their tasks, experiences, and concerns in their own letters and journals. Since Peacham lies only thirty miles from Whitcomb Hill, life there must have been nearly identical to what the Whitcombs, Bohonons, and Rings experienced.

Roxana's letters, as well as many other historical documents, make it clear that all the men and women living in nineteenth-century rural Vermont worked almost constantly. Tilling the fields; planting, tending, and hand-harvesting crops; raising pigs, chickens, and cattle; milking cows several times a day; growing, scything, and stockpiling hay; keeping and maintaining draft animals—these were the tasks that had faced Vermont farmers since colonial times and that continued well into the modern era. (More sophisticated and powerful machinery has gradually eased the burden, but even twenty-first-century farmers work harder than just about anyone I've ever met in the contemporary United States.) Horse-drawn mowers didn't come into use until after the Civil War. Gasoline-powered tractors weren't invented until the 1890's and weren't affordable or practical until the 1920's and '30's.

Even the most rudimentary milking machines didn't arrive on the scene until the turn of the century. Safe, reliable chain saws weren't available until the 1940's. Lacking these and other modern machines, nineteenth-century farm families, assisted by oxen and horses, did all their work by hand. Bonfield and Morrison, writing in *Roxana's Children,* describe these tasks in detail. Consistent with that era's gender roles, men and boys performed most of the farm labor. "The men were responsible for the farm animals, the farm machinery and tools," Bonfield and Morrison write, as well as "the care of the land including roads and fences, the upkeep of the barn, the privy, and other buildings, and the unending maintenance of the wood pile." Boys' assistance was crucial: "'The Boys all grow and have got to be a good deal of help,' Roxana wrote in one letter, noting her sons Charles and Augustus chopping wood 'at the door.'" Boys "tended the calves and lambs, fed the hogs, helped with the milking, 'laid up' the apples, and dried potatoes. They boiled sap in the sugarhouse in March and April and hoed the garden in June and July; they helped with the haying and harvesting, too, as they grew older." Although nineteenth-century division of labor generally allotted gardening to women and girls, "it was the custom within the Watts family for the men and boys to do all the outside chores, including gardening."[5]

Women faced unending work as they maintained the household, contributed to the farm labor, raised the children, and cooked for the family. Bonfield and Morrison write that "although concentrating their work in the house, [women and girls] connected closely with the produce of the barn and field, and they were familiar with all the tasks handled by their husbands, sons, and hired hands."[6] Constant tasks included "spinning and weaving, cooking and sewing, bearing children and rearing them, feeding hungry men and sending them out into the fields . . ."[7] At night she sat by the fire and mended by the light of a tallow candle—the closest she came to relaxation."[8]

Bonfield and Morrison note that

To ease her daily burdens, Roxana assigned tasks to each of her children and directed them as they did their work. Her daughters helped with the laundry and other household tasks. As she reported to her married daughter, Martha: "Sally has done almost all of my spinning and she has wove one web for fulld [sic] cloth and has another in the loom," while Clara does "some spinning" and "takes care of Baby." She added: "[W]e have made between 4 and 5 hundred pounds of butter and a hundred and 50 of Chese from 6 Cows." Yet for the most part, Roxana took the daily housework of her daughters so for granted that she seldom mentioned it in her letters.[9]

In addition, women faced labor of another kind: recurrent pregnancies and childbirth. "Large families were common," Bonfield and Morrison write, "with many households numbering a dozen or so members. Roxana's family occupied a Cape-style cottage, twenty-eight by thirty-six feet, with an unfinished chamber on the second floor that was most likely used as a sleeping quarters for the children, the boys on one side and the girls on the other."[10] James and Hannah Whitcomb must have maintained similar quarters in their house as Roxana's in Peacham. Roxana, like Betsey Bohonon, gave birth almost every other year for most of two decades. (Small wonder that old New England houses often had a separate area set aside as a "birthing room.") Of Roxana's brood, all twelve of her children and grandchildren reached adulthood—an unusual achievement in that era. Betsey and Robert Bohonon weren't so lucky: they suffered a particularly appalling series of losses in 1864. Daughter Armina, age five years old, died of "brain fever" that January; Lucy Ann, just five months old, died of "lung fever" two months later; then late that same year, Joseph, age 25, died of scurvy, and Harris, age 20, succumbed to typhoid fever. Childhood and childbirth-related deaths were appallingly common; the rate of child mortality by age ten in 1860 was around 23%.[11] "Women often died in childbirth or of childbed infections," Bonfield and Morrison note, "and their new babies with them. . . ."[12] Maternal mortality, as well as the rate of infant deaths at childbirth remained high until the twentieth century."[13] Bonfield and, Morrison add that "Infections . . . took many lives. Diphtheria killed many, especially children, and whole families could be wiped out in the course of a single week."[14]

Adults, too, faced frequent, often fatal threats to health and wellbeing. The average life expectancy for white males born in nearby Massachusetts during 1850 was 38.3 years; for females, 40.5 years. Even by 1900, life expectancy was only 48.23 years for males, 51.08 years for females.[15] The situation was perilous for mothers as well: even at the close of the nineteenth century, 850 women died in childbirth per 100,000 live births.[16]

The many causes of death included ailments now easily preventable or treatable, as well as relatively minor injuries, such as ordinary cuts and minor accidents. In an era preceding the development of anesthetics and antibiotics, surgery was a brutal nightmare, pneumonia was often fatal, and even trivial wounds could progress quickly from infection to gangrene, septicemia, and death. Infectious diseases now all but eradicated by vaccinations were common and deadly. The ledgers at our local town hall specify causes of death that remain common in our own day—heart disease, cancer, diabetes, and "apoplexy" (stroke)—but also many other problems now easily preventable or treatable, especially in the young, such as diphtheria, typhoid, measles, dysentery, and pneumonia. Some causes of death employ nineteenth-century terminology: "brain fever"—what we would now call meningitis or encephalitis; "dropsy of the chest"— pulmonary edema; "lung fever"—pneumonia; "false membrane on heart"—probably endocarditis or pericarditis; and "bilious fever"—a liver disorder accompanied by elevated temperature.

Some of the terminologies I've noticed in local records are grotesquely blunt: a middle-aged man died of "Insanity and Feeble-mindedness," and a baby with severe birth defects is described as a "stillborn monstrosity." Women sometimes died of "puerperal fever" following childbirth—a post-partum infection of the uterus. The deaths of children were appallingly frequent, often from influenza, rheumatic fever, dysentery, and other water-borne illnesses. Flu periodically killed hundreds of Vermonters each year well before the pandemic of 1918. A diphtheria outbreak in 1863 resulted in nineteen local deaths, mostly among the children, between March and December of that year. Another outbreak, this time during the late summer of 1874, killed eleven local townspeople in little more than two weeks between the final days of August and the middle of September. Hazards specific to rural life also took their toll: "gored by a bull," "scalds," "punctured abdomen by cow's horn," and "killed by fallen tree." Psychological or existential issues caused some deaths as well: "suicide by shooting," "suicide by hanging," and "suicide by slashing throat."

What's clear from the public archives is that despite these many risks, James and Hannah thrived during the 1850s and 1860s. The U.S. Census reports of 1860, 1870, and 1880, however, show that they never had any children—a setback for a rural couple at a time when prosperity relied on offspring to participate in farm labor. Their situation in terms of property is unclear over the years. James and Hannah sold a parcel of their land to someone named B. W. Bartholomew in 1851. Two years later, Robert Bohannon appears to have acquired some of the Whitcomb brothers' acreage but also leased out some of that acquisition to Moses Ring Jr. Just a year later, Moses Jr. sold land to (or back to) Levi Jr. and James. Further uncertainties ensued during the 1860s: transfers take place from Reuben and Louisa Clough to Darius Whitcomb (one of James and Levi Jr.'s brothers) and then from Darius to J. B. Bacon. All of these transfers might suggest that James and Hannah had somehow disengaged from farming the hillside. Yet the 1870 Agricultural Census tells a different story: James now owned 59 acres of "improved" land at that time, while Levi Jr. owned 30 of "improved" and 45 acres of "unimproved" land.

Meanwhile, Robert Bohonon owned land more substantial than the Whitcomb brothers' farm: 80 "improved" and 30 "unimproved" acres. This couple's productivity, like the two Whitcomb couples' productivity, was remarkable. The family harvested wheat, oats, corn, potatoes, hay, and other crops in great abundance. Betsey and her children produced cheese, butter, wool, and garden crops in impressive quantities. How much of this output went toward sustaining such a large family? Surely a lot. But since the era of subsistence-only agriculture had started to ease, the Bohonons, like the Whitcombs, now participated in the cash economy to a greater and greater degree.

Robert and Betsey's marriage lasted until 1869, when Betsey died of "consumption" (tuberculosis). Just two years later, Robert married a local widow named Mary N. Reed. This marriage lasted only until Mary's sudden death a few years later. Then in 1878, Robert, age 64, married a third wife, this time twenty-one-year-old Sophia Sylvester. Robert and Sophia's marriage lasted for thirteen years, until 1892, when Robert died at age 79.

And the elder Moses Ring? I've found no sign of him in the 1870 Vermont Agricultural Census. Given his age in 1850—seventy-nine—it seems likely that by 1870 he would have been long deceased. What of the younger Moses? He fathered five children, among them a son, Barney (born 1840) who in 1869 married Mary Ann Bohonon (born 1841), eldest daughter of Robert and Betsey; and some data exists regarding these and other members of the Ring families. Moses Jr. was alive in 1870 but possibly infirm, and he died in late 1871, age 72, having long survived his wife, Lucinda, who had died in 1854.

❧   ❧   ❧

At this point I have to ask: what do these facts *mean*? Reviewing what I learned during several years of intense research, I can't help but view the data with simultaneous delight and exasperation. Delight, because it's a fact-based portrait of these families. Exasperation, because the facts don't give me what I most want: a glimpse, at least, of faces on photographic glass or paper; a hint, at least, of these families' hopes, fears, impressions, and delights as expressed with ink on paper; a more visceral sense of who these people might have been. The names and dates in ledgers and on tombstones, the numbers and categories in archives, provide both a feast and a famine. I've accumulated an abundance of facts, yet they offer only hints of our predecessors' lives rather than a vivid portrait. The federal census documents and the Vermont state agricultural census records provide a cast of characters and a notion of what their constant toil produced—all those bushels of corn and oats, all those pounds of cheese and wool—but no personal nuance. Despite my strenuous efforts, I've located no letters to or from the Whitcombs, Bohonons, or Rings. Despite my outreach to local descendants of these families, I've gained no access (with just one exception) to photos. The facts I've identified are useful and suggestive but insufficient. I feel as if I'm playing a connect-the-dots game with too few dots and almost no numbers. I can draw lines from dot to dot—so far, so good. The resulting image, however, is angular, simplistic, devoid of human detail.

What are my alternatives?

One option is simply to give up.

Another is to accept limited data and draw limited conclusions.

Or I can resort to other approaches.

This last gambit is what I've chosen to take. By "other approaches" I mean taking what little data I've obtained and putting them to further use. If facts are the kernels of truth available in the storehouses I've visited—archives, libraries, and websites—then I'll plant these kernels and see what sprouts. I'll tend this field and harvest whatever comes up. Drawing from the information gleaned in historical accounts of nineteenth-century Vermonters, I'll grow (for lack of a better word) a sense of the families who once lived here.

In some respects this approach shouldn't be difficult. Edith and I live in the same house that the Whitcombs once inhabited. We walk on the same land that the Whitcombs, Bohonons, and Rings once cultivated. We garden in the same soil, draw water from the same well, cut wood from the same forest. We gaze out onto the same eastern ridge and watch the same moon rise. Five, ten, fifteen decades may separate us from our predecessors, but when I ponder them, the years fall away and reveal a landscape hidden earlier.

September, 1850: Hannah and the Harvest

Hannah and Betsey follow Robert, young Joseph Bohonon, and the three Whitcomb brothers as the men scythe oats. Robert, the tallest of the men, takes the lead, cutting a wide swath with his blade, while Levi, James, Nathaniel, and Joseph each cut a row about five feet to the right and ten or fifteen feet behind the man ahead of him. Hannah, Betsey, and the Welch sisters gather the fallen stalks of grain into sheaves. Betsey's younger boys, Harris and Alva, help tie up the sheaves. Eleven-year-old Mary Ann Bohonon works some yards away to keep her little sisters Fanny and Octavia out of trouble. The toddlers giggle and shriek, surely convinced that the activity in progress is all a big game.

It's a perfect day for the harvest, just cool enough to avoid overheating, overcast but without any threat of rain. The menfolk advance like soldiers in a squadron. The sweep of their scythes is at once beautiful and deadly. The oats fall like the Kushites when King Asa of Judah and his army put them to the sword, or when Joshua stormed the city of Jericho. Then Hannah notices young Joseph lagging behind his father and the Whitcomb brothers. Just at the cusp of manhood, he's trying hard to keep up but is clearly growing tired. Yet the sound of his blade makes the same sound as the grown men's blades, a hush and a rush that is both many sounds and one, five blades cutting through all those stalks, much as a stand of trees catching the wind makes many sounds that are all just one.

The women stop to rest. Betsey turns, smiles, and wipes her brow with the back of her hand. Hannah smiles back, then nods toward her sisters. Sally and Amanda are watching the men. Joseph, especially, draws their attention. Even at thirteen he's a tall boy, and it's clear that in a few years he'll be as big as his father. His arms are long, his hands already huge, no doubt foretelling stature and strength in the same way that a puppy's big paws promise a large dog. His voice has dropped over the past year, yet it spikes at times to girlish notes, prompting the Welch sisters' laughter. Hannah hears the young women whispering and giggling at the sight of this shy, handsome boy-man. Mockery? Or perhaps a lament for the boy's youthfulness? — he's ten years younger than they—as if it's a shame that this kind, still-harmless male will be forever out of their reach.

Hannah watches Betsey too. Though she's Hannah's own age, thirty-four, Betsey looks so much more confident than Hannah feels, and no wonder. All six of her brood, themselves a bounty, have joined her in this harvest. Hannah knows that even as Betsey works, another babe lies dreaming inside her womb. No wonder she can proceed with such confidence. In just a few years she and Robert will work their farm fully on their own, will harvest everything they grow, will have no need of neighborly assistance. Three boys and three girls! Who knows how many more children will arrive in the coming years. Hannah and James, meanwhile? No sons, no daughters. Levi and Louisa? None neither. When Nathaniel marries—probably to sister Sally, it seems—will he and his wife, too, find themselves without offspring? Whose fault is it that these brothers and their wives beget no children? What are the odds that two unrelated women might be the cause of empty wombs and empty cradles? Slim—just like the brothers. Is something wrong, then, with these Whitcombs? What is it about these men that their seed brings forth no harvest? Or has the *seed perhaps fallen on barren ground, Hannah wonders, and for this reason brings forth no yield?*

Envy. First Corinthians, she recalls, warns against this sin: Love is patient and kind; love does not envy . . . How much worse, then, for Hannah to envy her closest friend? Worst of all that she might envy the friend who so generously shares her bounty of sons and daughters; who has even loaned her first-born son to Levi and Louisa; who allows the older girls to walk up the hillside and assist Hannah herself in the household tasks she otherwise would perform alone. No, it is surely wrong to envy such a friend. Beyond wrong—thankless. No one else offers so much help, companionship, and solace. Hannah and Betsey assist each other with their cows, their gardens, their sheep. They share the tasks of cheese making, spinning, sewing, and candle making. They look after each other when sick. Best of all, they sit together talking, they calm and assure each other, they devise how to go on, they plant, grow, and harvest a bounty of words when the men, as so often seems true, are too exhausted, too distracted, too **elsewhere** *to speak.*

9

A Stand of Wheat

The land *is*. Must it also *do*?

From 1790 to 1960, this property was a family farm. The Whitcombs cleared the forest; they planted crops and raised animals; their descendants continued the process for almost a hundred years; and subsequent owners used the hillside as pasture for dairy cows. Since the 1960's, however, the land has lain fallow. The forest has reclaimed most of Whitcomb Hill. The meadow, which for six or eight decades produced sweet hay, now grows milkweed, goldenrod, paintbrush, cornflowers, black-eye susans, and more varieties of wild plants and brambles than I can identify. If Edith and I don't mow this field once a year, it too will soon revert to woods.

Is this situation a problem? Nature doesn't really care what Edith and I do here. Even if we left and no one took our place, Whitcomb Hill would thrive and change in our absence. The land endures. Edith and I are almost irrelevant.

But we're here. We love the place. The question for us, then, becomes: What do we do with it? One answer is: garden. Edith maintains the extensive flowerbeds. I look after the two vegetable gardens. Even by splitting these tasks, we have our hands full with outdoor work throughout the warm months.

During my Colorado boyhood and adolescence, I assisted my father in maintaining a large garden plot on our property in Denver; he taught me extensive skills for growing many kinds of crops; and, decades later, on moving to Vermont, I transferred what I'd learned in the West to Whitcomb Hill's far different ecosystem. Edith and I have grown twenty or more different kinds of vegetables each year since 2010—many varieties of greens, peas, beans, root vegetables, corn, tomatoes, potatoes, artichokes, and whatever else has caught our fancy.

In 2017, fascinated by what we've learned about our predecessors on this hillside, we decide to branch out further. Our meadow is beautiful year 'round, full of robust grasses and flowering plants. Is it possible, however, that we might put some of this open land to more productive use? Could we till the soil, plant crops, and actually grow more than just wildflowers?

Edith is skeptical. "Why do all that work? Don't you have enough going on already?"

"Maybe, maybe not."

"What would you plant, anyway?"

"Wheat."

I have never grown wheat in my life. The only grain I've raised is corn, which presents no challenges for small-scale gardening. I have a lifelong obsession with bread, however; and while living in Colorado, and, later, during each of several long stays in the Peruvian Andes, I often delighted in the sight of wheat rolling surf-like in the wind. Why not reap the benefits—literally—of raising our own grain? Why not enjoy the sight, too, of a breeze cavorting in the field? As I soon learn on the *Mother Earth News* website, my notion isn't implausible. "Wheat is easy to grow almost anywhere in the United States, even as a wide-row crop in your garden," the site explains. "One gardener in Vermont attests to having planted 30 pounds of winter wheat on one-eighth of an acre and harvesting 250 pounds of grain in July. On a somewhat smaller scale, even if you have a front yard that's 20 feet by 50 feet, you could plant six pounds of wheat and harvest nearly 50 pounds of grain."[1] Even these few comments fan the flames of my obsession.

I soon confirm what I recall vaguely from my Colorado youth: there are fundamentally two kinds of wheat. Farmers plant winter wheat during early autumn, let it "overwinter," and harvest the grain between mid-May and late July. Spring wheat is planted in the spring and harvested in the fall. Both spring and winter wheat are further divided into soft wheat (low-gluten) and hard wheat (high-gluten) varieties. Soft wheat is generally used for pastry, hard wheat for bread. (There's also durum wheat, used most often for pasta.) It's clear from further reading that, ideally, I should plant winter wheat; the timing that year, however, prompts me to choose spring wheat instead, since otherwise our planting will be delayed until autumn and the harvest itself until the following summer.

The plan: rototill a fifty-by-twenty-foot plot in the lower meadow, sow seed, and see what happens. As usual, the effort is trickier than it looks. The main problem is that the meadow hasn't been cultivated since at least the 1960's. The mid-twentieth-century farmers who owned this property used it only as pasture for dairy cows. Though surely producing sweet grasses during that era, the meadow is now full of tough, tenacious, deeply rooted plants. Even tilling the small plot with a gasoline-powered rototiller demands strenuous effort. Once I break up the surface, I have to remove hundreds of fibrous plants, shake the dirt off their roots, throw them away, remove dozens of rocks I've uncovered, and till the plot a second time. Adding manure, peat moss, and compost enriches the long-depleted soil. Soon enough, however, I've prepared an expanse of dark-brown dirt suitable for planting.

I order five pounds of wheat from Johnny's Seeds, my favorite provider of seeds and plants, located in Maine. The variety I choose: Glenn hard red spring wheat. Time is tight, so I plant in late May, right after receiving the seeds. An experienced farmer who lives nearby advises me on how to plant such a small plot: "Divide the seed into two piles. Sow one pile in one direction, maybe east to west. Sow the other pile north to south. That's it." I follow these instructions, then use a 1930's-vintage hand tiller to cover the seeds with an inch or more of dirt. Done.

❧   ❧   ❧

What happens next soon exceeds all my expectations. Green sprouts arise from the earth; the sprouts grow into blades. Just two weeks after germination, the plot looks like a lush lawn. I stare at what's growing there and marvel at the obvious: this is *grass*. Then the plants send up stalks, the stalks develop heads, and the kernels on each head start to form. I'm stunned by how quickly the process evolves. The plants reach twelve inches in height, then eighteen or more. Pale green at first, the stalks and the grain gradually turn gray-green. The kernels grow enough by mid-June to make the heads top-heavy, a structure that partly explains why wheat sways so sensually in a breeze. I sometimes walk down into the meadow just to watch the interplay of wind and grass. It's a stirring sight, not only beautiful in its own right but also a hint, a simulacrum, of what made human civilization possible. Wheat has a mixed reputation now, at least in the urban West, blamed for all kinds of ills, including celiac disease, and advocates of gluten-free diets view it almost as a poison. Never mind. I love wheat and look forward to eating whatever I can grow. I also love the voluptuous churning of these plants when the wind rolls through them. I delight in the whisper and hush of air against the grain. If they could see me now, fifteen or sixteen decades after their heyday, the Whitcombs, the Bohonons, and the Rings would surely laugh at my delight—such a little stand of wheat!—but I don't care.

Then, as often happens, reality intrudes on my plans. I walk down to the stand of wheat one morning in late June and notice a disturbing change. A small number of heads have turned dark. I pull one free from its stalk and examine it more closely. The florets have deteriorated, and the entire structure is coated in dark brown powder. Even a city boy like me knows instinctively that there's a problem. A disease, even. Mold, perhaps? An inspection of the stand reveals many more affected heads. *The wheat is infected.*

Unsure what to do, I ask around among local farmers and gardeners. No one can clarify the problem; the mystery remains. Someone at the local Agway is more helpful: "Contact the Agricultural Extension," she tells me. "They'll give you some information." The Extension turns out to be a division of the University of Vermont's College of Agriculture and Life Sciences. I send an email describing the blighted wheat to the Extension's help line. Just a few days later, I receive a response from Ann Hazelrigg, Ph.D., a plant physiologist who runs the UVM Plant Diagnostic Clinic: [2]

> Cool! It is either loose smut (seedborne) or covered smut, not seedborne. We would need to see samples to tell you for sure. It is easy by looking at the spores under the scope. We are currently doing a research project on loose smut and would LOVE to have as many infected seed heads as possible if you need a home for them!

I respond with an offer to provide some of the contaminated plants, and, a few days later, I drop off the samples at Dr. Hazelrigg's office in Burlington.

By e-mail she offers this diagnosis:

> We found both loose smut and covered smut spores in your heads. The loose smut is seed borne as we discussed, and from what I have heard all the hard Glenn is contaminated. The covered smut is more of a "contaminant" in seed but I suspect it is a problem this year due to wet weather.

Loose smut! This sounds like pornography lost in the postal system. More to the point, our wheat has a serious infection. On the same day that I receive Dr. Hazelrigg's message, however, I notice a new change down there in the meadow: few heads show signs of the telltale brown powder. Most of the grain remains unaffected. These signs of diminished infection coincide with the onset of hot, dry weather. Is it possible that

the dry heat has killed the mold? The stand of wheat now looks
... *healthy*.

Perhaps most importantly, Dr. Hazelrigg eases my concerns about any dangers to Edith and me, or to our friends and family, if we choose to eat this grain. I write to ask her about this issue: "My lingering question is this: are these kinds of smut hazardous to humans? If this wheat grows to maturity, is it okay for us to eat the grain?" That same day she responds: "Yes, you should be fine to eat it. You can just let it grow and see what you get."

The summer unfolds. The wheat stalks grow taller; the leaves turn deep green. By mid-July the heads are fat and abundant. Kernels form in a herringbone pattern, each now dusted with pollen and tufted with bristles (which, I learn, are called the beard). When I snip off a head and pry out some kernels, I'm surprised by how green they look, how soft they feel, how sweet they taste. They resemble berries more than grain. What pleases me most of all is what I've hoped for and have expected: the interplay of wheat and air. Even a light breeze prompts the stalks to sway. Gusty wind makes the wheat roll and churn, with different areas within the small stand moving in different directions, the rhythms complex and syncopated. It's a stirring sight. There's a rich sound, too, a complex fugue of hissing, hushing, rushing voices. I walk down the meadow every day just to watch and listen.

This is a city boy's self-indulgence, of course, and I know it. Edith and I aren't dependent on this crop in any way. It's a discretionary project. Sizing up the stand, I can't calculate what our yield may be at harvest time, but I'm guessing perhaps a gallon or two of grain. James and Hannah Whitcomb grew forty bushels of wheat on this property in 1860; that same year, Robert and Betsey Bohonon grew thirty-eight bushels on their adjacent slope of Whitcomb Hill. They would be right to snicker at my delight in raising such a tiny fraction of those yields. Mid-nineteenth-century families who emigrated to the richer soils of the Midwest raised even more grain than the Vermonters did. I'm aware, too, that even the total failure of my experiment would have no consequences for Edith and me. By contrast, low grain harvests in 1867 and in other years caused high prices and resultant hardships throughout American history. More severe shortfalls, such as in Ukraine during the 1930's—the cascading consequences of Soviet agricultural policies, drought, and plant diseases—caused the deaths of between 2.4 and 7.5 million people.[3] What a ridiculous luxury for me to raise wheat and delight mostly because of how it rolls in the wind.

A month passes. The summer remains cool. Except for one hot spell, the temperatures remain below average. The weather turns dry, however, sparing central Vermont from the heavy rains that made life difficult for farmers and gardeners during May and June. The wheat in our meadow turns yellowish, then brassy. The heads grow plump; the beards' whiskers no longer point upward but splay outward. When the wind comes through, the wheat's motions are slower now, languid, producing a hiss and a hush like gentle surf sliding onto a beach.

Soon it's time for the harvest. Early September presents a new decision. Ideally, I'd like to mow the wheat with our grass scythe: easy time travel to the agrarian past. As the *Mother Earth News* site explains, this approach is altogether feasible: "You might use a scythe and cradle. The cradle is a series of long wooden fingers mounted above the scythe blade. The scythe cuts the wheat, and then the cradle carries the cut wheat to the end of each swing and deposits it in a neat pile, stacked with all the heads grouped together." This approach appeals to me in some respects but sounds too complicated. "You could cut with the scythe alone," as *Mother Earth News* warns readers, "but you would spend a lot of time picking up the cut wheat and arranging it for easier handling." Instead, I use a different tool, one that's even more ancient than the scythe. As the same site explains, "Another possible tool for cutting small amounts of grain is the sickle. Hold a handful of wheat in your left hand and swing the sickle with your right to cut the plants at nearly ground level. . . . As you cut handfuls, lay them in small piles with all the heads pointed in the same direction."[4] Purchasing a sickle from Scythe Supply, a Maine-based provider of traditional farm tools, I make quick work of the process: cutting sheaves and propping them upright in bushel baskets. Then it's easy for me to transport our sheaves into the garage—they fill only six small bushel baskets—since that space is empty almost all summer. Resting there, the grain dries within a couple of weeks.

Two tasks remain: threshing and winnowing. Even before starting, I realize that these efforts fall into the category of Things I Should Have Known.

Threshing is the process of separating the straw and chaff from the grain. Even a single kernel of grain consists of many parts, some of which I've never even heard of before. The *palea*, the *lemma*, the glumes, and the *rachis* . . . All of these components must be removed from the kernels. Modern processing plants do the work with high-speed machinery. The Whitcombs, Bonhonons, Rings, and all other pre-modern farmers threshed grain by laborious means. As *Mother Earth News* comments, "One method is flailing. A flail consists of one piece of wood about three feet long—the handle—attached with a leather thong to a shorter piece about two feet long. The shorter piece is flung at the heads of grain repeatedly, shattering a few heads each time." I'm surprised—or maybe not—that it's easy to obtain a hand-flail through the Web. Acquiring the tool isn't what concrerns me. *Mother Earth News* helpfully goes on to note that "If you are using this method, you can expect to produce about three pounds of wheat in 20 to 25 minutes. That's slow work. Also, there's a trick to learning to swing the flail without rapping yourself on the head."[5] (Small wonder that the word "flailing" has negative connotations.)

My alternative: I improvise a gadget to expedite the process. The components are a five-gallon plastic bucket, a power drill, a two-foot-long metal paint mixer, and some short lengths of chain. I attach two three-inch pieces of chain to the paint mixer's head. Placing several quarts of wheat heads into the bucket, I insert the mixer and turn on the drill. The mixer and the lengths of chain whirl through the fluffy jumble of heads and stalks. What settles to the bottom of the pail is grain and light chaff.

The next task, winnowing, is messy but less strenuous: removing the particles of chaff now separated from the grain. "The usual method for winnowing is pouring the grain from one container to another," the *Mother Earth News* site explains, "letting either the wind or the breeze from an electric fan push the lighter chaff out of the grain. Repeat the process a few times to get the grain as chaff-free as possible." This process doesn't sound difficult, but I feel leery about relying on the wind to winnow that big pail of grain. Instead, I use a box fan turned on "high" to blow away the chaff. The process is the easiest of the whole sequence so far. The grain falls straight down into a container; the chaff, sparkling like glitter, floats away. When I tackle the task, Edith watches from a distance, avoiding the particles of chaff as they blow away, her expression revealing the amusement she often shows when I wade into much deeper water than what I've expected.

I prevail. Winnowing the grain proves simple and quick. The yield: just shy of a quart. When I look at the Tupperware box filled with reddish-golden wheat, I'm eager to start baking.

One other issue comes up, however. An online article alerts me to the issue of deoxynivalenol, or DON, also called vomitoxin. This is a toxic agent produced by two kinds of plant pathogens, *Fusarium graminearum (Gibberella zeae)* and *F. culmorum*.[6] These blights can affect wheat during moist weather, which is exactly what Vermont has experienced earlier this year. It's possible that the wheat I've grown is infected. How will I know? There's a test that the Vermont Agricultural Extension can perform to identify contaminated grain. The catch: the test requires a one-quart sample. I can't even provide enough to run the test.

What to do, then? I contact Dr. Hazelrigg at the University of Vermont. "I'm aware that I should get the wheat I've raised this summer tested for DON," I write in an e-mail, "and I know that this process requires submitting a sample to the grain lab. However, the yield from my small stand of wheat is so limited that I don't even have enough to meet the criteria." I offer an alternative scenario: "Is it possible that I could just heavily rinse/wash this small quantity of wheat, then dry it out in the oven at a low temperature (100-150F)? Would that eliminate any concern about DON?"

She writes back a day later:

> Good question. The interesting thing about mycotoxins is that the *Fusarium* fungus can be on the grain and not produce the toxin. Washing would not get rid of it. Whether or not the fungus produces the mycotoxin depends on how the grain is dried and stored. If your grain does not appear moldy (pinkish fungus) and it has been dried, I suspect you would be fine. Especially, since the grain will not be eaten just by itself and will be diluted with other ingredients. However, without testing, it is impossible to know.[7]

I do further research on the issue. The various articles I read confirm Dr. Hazelrigg's statement that eating a small quantity of affected wheat shouldn't be a problem. One blog post states that "Large amounts of grain with vomitoxin would have to be consumed to pose a health risk to humans." Another, written by a Midwestern farmer-author with decades of experience in raising wheat, notes that "I've been eating home-baked bread from wheat flour slightly infected with vomitoxin. I have not vomited, nor have I suffered any ill effects as far as I know." Conclusive? Not really, but I'm not inclined to worry. When I thank Dr. Hazelrigg for her earlier comments and note that "Obviously this is a low-stakes issue," she writes back with a final remark: "I would go for it, live life on the edge and make a pancake!!"

Or, better yet, bake some bread. I contact a friend, Reed, and ask if I can use his grain mill to grind our wheat into flour. He graciously agrees. The output: almost exactly one dry pint. A summer's labor, vigilance, and anxiety for a pint of flour! But that's what we have, so that's what we'll use.

It's quick work for me to mix a batch of dough, and, six hours later, to bake our first loaf. What emerges steaming from the oven is fragrant and delicious, with the nutty flavor I've always loved about whole wheat, as well as a soft, muffin-like texture. It's not the best bread I've ever eaten, but it's the best bread I've ever grown.

10

Sugar(ing)

Vermont = maple syrup.

Maple syrup = Vermont.

So it seems, anyway, in the popular iconography of the American states.

One of our neighbors, Lenny, owns a large sugarhouse right up the road. Lenny is a local merchant whose sugaring operation produces syrup for Vermont wholesalers. Edith and I have chatted with Lenny many times about his sugarhouse, but we never saw it in operation until this past spring, when he showed us around. The sugarhouse is simply a wooden shed, forty by twenty feet in size, with a huge, wood-fired steel boiling trough in the middle and a cupola in the ceiling to vent smoke and steam. Lenny, his son Scott, and their helpers process the maple sap from a thousand trees to produce syrup. Fully stoked, the sugarhouse sends up a huge column of steam and pervades the hillside with a sweet aroma.

Traditional sugarhouses are still common in Vermont, but they used to be a fixture on almost every family farm. During the colonial and early American eras, maple syrup and maple sugar provided the standard sweeteners for most forms of cooking and baking. Later, these products became an important part of the small-farm economy. "Sugar was a cash crop [that farmers] could make at a time when it was otherwise slow on the farm," Stephen Long writes in *Thirty-Eight: The Hurricane that Transformed New England,* and he quotes a farmer named Harry Brainerd on the importance of sugaring in Vermont life:

"'Everybody looked forward to sugaring in my day because it gave you a little bit of extra money to buy things, . . . some extra money to do things with."[1] James and Hannah Whitcomb's efforts generated 450 pounds of maple sugar in 1850, 280 in 1860, and 250 in 1880. Lacking information about the price for this product during the ninteenth century, I can't calculate what their payoff might have been. But farmers generated $600 or more in sugar-related income during the 1930's—the equivalent of $10,400-$13,800 today. This would have been a huge infusion of cash for most families. In any case, maple syrup isn't a staple food in our era; instead, it's now marketed as an artisanal product.

When I comment about Lenny's sugaring operation to Inge, a friend who works at the nearby Agway, she says, "Well, you could make your own."

"Right," I reply sardonically. I'm aware that the ratio of raw sap to finished syrup is forty to one. "I could boil gallons and gallons of sap, work for hours, and end up with maybe a pint."

"A pint is better than nothing."

I nod politely.

"Try it," she says. "Tap a few trees. Boil the sap. You can't go wrong."

Despite my skepticism, her comments embolden me. Why not? Maples are abundant on our property; the sap is running; the process is easy and cheap.

So, following Inge's recommendations, I purchase some supplies: a one-gallon plastic bucket, a steel lid, and a spile. Inge explains how to tap the trees. I retreat to Whitcomb Hill and install these components to launch our minimalist sugaring operation. The spile is a small metal device that combines a spike with a spout. After drilling a narrow hole into one of our old-growth maples, I tap the spile into the trunk, I hang the bucket on the spile, and I secure a lid onto the bucket. Sap emerges from the spile almost at once. The flow resembles a water faucet's slow leak. Shouldn't there be more? I watch for a while, concerned. Leaving to do other chores, however, I return an hour later to find almost a cup of liquid in the bucket. This amount increases to a gallon overnight. We're in business.

The next morning I find the bucket filled almost to overflowing. The fluid is clear except for a few specks of cellulose from inside the tree. I taste the sap: as blank as water. Pleased, I empty the bucket into a copper-bottomed kettle, carry the pot indoors, and prepare to boil. Straining the fluid removes a scattering of particles. I set the kettle on the stove, put the burner on "high," and bring the sap to a boil within eight or ten minutes. Then, turning down the heat, I prepare for the long haul. This quantity is small, however, so the process doesn't take long: even a slow simmer thickens the sap within a few hours. I taste the broth now and then. There's no detectable difference for a long time. Then, little by little, I sense a hint of maple. The flavor emerges almost imperceptibly, much as a house grows visible as one walks toward it in dense fog.

The process goes on—and on. Nothing about the sap's appearance changes until the heat boils away more than half of what remains in the kettle. Gradually, a yellow tinge emerges. The hue deepens over the next hour. At this point I taste the sap again: it's sweet. The color soon turns golden. A short while later, as I sit in the kitchen, I hear the kettle start to hiss; I peer inside and see not liquid but foam. The time has come. I drain the glass bottle I've sterilized, pour in the contents of the pot, and marvel at the outcome. Syrup. Not much, maybe a few ounces, but syrup all the same.

The taste? To mimic oenophiles' wine speak: "This syrup is elegant and full-bodied, offering an intense maple aroma. On the palate it reveals a silky maple personality and finishes long and harmoniously with notes of maple, maple, and maple. It pairs well with waffles or pancakes."

11

A Shed of His Own

"[A] woman must have money and a room of her own if she is to write fiction."

—Virginia Woolf, *A Room of One's Own* [1]

Fair enough. But what about men? What must *guys* have to write fiction?

My answer: a shed. Money wouldn't hurt, but definitely a shed.

The American novelist John Gardner states in *The Art of Fiction* that when writing a novel, a fiction writer's primary goal is to create "a vivid and continuous dream." [2] For me, at least, dreaming the dream requires almost complete isolation. An off-season shack on a beach near Tulum would do nicely. A cabin deep in the Colorado Rockies would be almost ideal. The 1840's-era farmhouse that Edith and I own in Vermont is a good start. But even in this calm rural setting, distractions of any sort threaten the process. The ordinary activities of my family or out-of-town visitors jolt me out of the dream. I lose track of the plot. My characters stop talking to one another. The spontaneous, intense, sometimes torrential flow of words from the mind to the page—what I call "white-water thinking"—slows to a trickle. To dream the dream and, especially, to put the dream down on paper, requires solitude.

Here's how I address this dilemma: I'll purchase a cheap, ready-made wooden shell and have it transported to our property; then I'll upgrade it into a four-season writing space.

Step one of this process is hiring two local carpenters, Alfred and Eugene, to construct the shell where they live in a nearby town. They start work in late June and finish a week later. On the Fourth of July, Alfred and Eugene tow the shell here on a flatbed trailer, drive across our lawn, and back carefully into the meadow. My request for placement causes some concern. I want the shed to sit on slanted ground at an angle that will allow a view down the slope. "We can do that," Alfred tells me, but his tone of voice suggests skepticism. Winching the shed off the flatbed trailer proves touch-and-go for several minutes—there's a risk of it toppling over—but the process takes shape without mishap. Alfred and Eugene use long iron pry bars to shove the shed into the position I've requested. Then they level it with cement blocks.

The result: an austere little shack with lots of potential. Properly shimmed, it's now stable where it stands in the meadow. It isn't ready for writerly activities, not by a long shot, but this shell provides the raw materials for what I intend to create. It certainly possesses the virtue that realtors so often tout: location, location, location. The shack rests about a hundred feet from the house, close enough to allow easy access but far enough to offer privacy and silence. I can't imagine wanting a more serene spot.

> "It [Twain's house in Hartford, Connecticut] has a heart, and a soul, and eyes to see us with; and approvals, and solicitudes, and deep sympathies; it was of us, and we are in its confidence, and lived in its grace and in the peace of its benediction."
>
> —Mark Twain[3]

Over the years I've visited many writers' houses. Among my favorites have been Melville's Arrowhead, located near Pittsfield, Massachusetts; Emily Dickinson's Homestead in

Amherst; Wordsworth's Dove Cottage near Grasmere in the English Lake District; Emerson's mansion in Concord; and Thoreau's shack at Walden Pond (or, more accurately, the original shack's replica). All of these visits revealed aspects of their owners' creative lives, including vivid impressions of the authors' domestic and artistic settings and perhaps a glimpse of how they worked. Especially vivid was a tour of Arrowhead, Melville's residence from 1850-1862 and the locus for his writing *Moby-Dick*. Typical of many large nineteenth-century houses, Arrowhead feels spacious and gracious, and its somewhat musty odor helps to induce an almost immediate illusion of time travel. Most evocative is Melville's study. This sparely furnished room features the broad table that Melville used as a desk, currently laid out with the some of the author's books, a candlestick, an inkwell and two quill pens, and replica pages from long-past works-in-progress. As many visitors have noted, this study's most powerful feature is the large window front-and-center before the desk, a window that looks out on Mount Greylock and the cetacean contour that apparently inspired Melville's vision of the White Whale.

    Why do writers visit other writers' homes? The most obvious reason is curiosity about our literary betters. Passing two hours at Dove Cottage, I could more fully imagine Wordsworth's life and his love of the Lake District. Touring Emily Dickinson's Homestead, I gained a better sense of both the poet's reclusiveness and her activities within a lively New England family. Exploring the state park surrounding Walden Pond and walking to the site where Thoreau's shack once stood, I better understood this place and how its "beauty without grandeur," as Thoreau described it, inspired and infused Walden. Beyond these specific insights, however, something else drives me, something that drives other writers as well, to visit famous authors' homes. It's the hope that some lingering quantum of energy from the brilliant owners' minds will somehow illuminate my work.

The American scholar Ann Trubek notes the folly of this approach: "For me, writers' houses are by definition melancholy," she writes in *A Skeptic's Guide to Writers' Houses*. "[T]hey aim to do the impossible: to make physical—to make real—acts of literary imagination. Going to a writer's house is a fool's errand." Worse, "Writers' houses expose the heartbreaking gap between writers and readers. Part of the pull of a writer's house is the desire to get as close as possible to the precise, generative, 'Aha!' But we can never get there."[4]

At once the question arises: Why bother? If writers' houses are merely secular shrines, as Trubek calls them ("places where one believes a miracle occurred—the penning of a masterpiece, the birth of a genius"), then why bother visiting at all? Maybe it's a waste of time, money, and effort. But Trubek goes on to write that "People trek to pilgrimage sites because they believe it will strengthen their faith to pay homage in person."[5] Faith in what? In the worth of literature? In the possibility that even a far less talented writer than Melville, Dickinson, or Wordsworth may still have something to offer?

"I have enough money now to finish my house."

—William Faulkner[6]

With the pre-fab shell now in place, my own work starts in earnest. The goal is to create what Hemingway called "a clean, well-lighted place." What Alfred and Eugene have constructed, however, is just a dusty, dark, eight-by-ten wooden box. The crude pine floor, the exposed studs and rafters, and the rough-sawn walls won't provide a comfortable workspace even in the summer; during the winter months, it will offer no protection from the cold, the wind, or the snow. Worse of all, there is no light. Making it habitable and congenial will require extensive upgrades.

First and foremost, this means installing lots of windows. I insert two into the south wall and three in the west wall to provide views of the nearby woods. Installing another three windows into the east wall offers a panorama of the larger forest and of the ridge across the valley. Properly inserted and trimmed, these windows will let in the sunshine but keep out the rain, wind, and cold.

Then, to make the shed comfortable year-round, I install a four-inch-thick layer of rigid-foam insulation between the studs and the rafters. A series of intricate tasks follows: wiring two electrical outlets, paneling the interior walls with tongue-and-groove wainscoting boards, installing window trim and sills, sheet-rocking the ceiling, putting down a finished pine floor, and painting the interior. Some of these tasks exceed my skill set. My solutions: 1) if possible, acquire the skills; and 2) if necessary, lower my standards. This shed is a low-risk venture. If I do mediocre work, will there be any negative consequences? None that I can foresee. Somehow I pull off the tasks. The payoff is a cozy space conducive to turning inward. I lay down a rug, move in a table and two chairs, and bring in a small electric heater to complete my labors just in time for November's first snowfall.

"What do you think?" I ask Edith when I show her my finished handiwork.

"It's really beautiful."

"The place is for you too."

She smiles but says nothing.

"Truly," I tell her. "It's for both of us."

"It's *your* place," she assures me.

"No—both of ours."

We set aside the issue. But I'm intent on convincing her eventually to take turns with me.

Like a Pentagon battleship, the project has run late and over budget. Still, the deed is done. The little shed now sits out in the meadow. By mid-November, I start spending several hours there each week, and I feel cozy inside even when the temperature plummets.

Now comes the hard part: writing books.

❦ ❦ ❦

> "If you're lucky, you might have an extra room to set aside for meditation. . . . Whichever room it is, it should be quiet, airy, and free of smoke."
>
> —Bruce Newman[7]

Although Edith and I call this shed "the writer's shack," I've never intended it solely for writing. Meditation has always been part of my agenda. Soon after completing the upgrades, I can tell that the shed will meet my expectations. The isolation, the interior beauty, the sense of calm, the light, and the view down the meadow: all of these attributes make it consistently, deeply conducive to stilling the mind. The shed seems perfect. Soon, however, I begin to wonder if perfection is really what I need. Buddhist teachers often state that meditation should be possible even under less-than-ideal circumstances—indeed, even under difficult, unpleasant circumstances. That's part of the goal: equanimity regardless of external conditions. Would it be better, perhaps, to meditate in an unappealing place? In a setting that offers fewer aesthetic delights and presents more sensory challenges? The American Buddhist teacher Jack Kornfield, for instance, has described how he mastered certain meditative techniques while living in a cacophonous Burmese city.[8] Is it possible that my shed is too pleasant, too calm, too lovely a place for meditation?

To clarify these issues, I consult *Visuddhimagga* (generally translated into English as *The Path of Purification*), a Fifth-century C.E. Buddhist treatise on monastic life. One chapter, "The Five Factors of the Resting Place," outlines the attributes that practitioners in the Theravada tradition consider auspicious

for a meditation site. As translated from the original Pali, here's my phrasing of the Five Factors: [9]
The meditation place should

1. Be neither too far from nor too near the alms resort

2. Be rarely frequented by day nor disrupted [by voices] at night

3. Have little contact with gadflies, flies, wind, burning sun, or creeping things

4. Allow meditators easy access to robes, alms food, lodging, and medicine

5. Have access to elder *bhikkhus* [monks] who are learned, versed in the scriptures, observers of the Dharma, and amenable to questions such as "How is this, venerable sir?" and "What is the meaning of this?"

My shed strikes out on Factor 1 (no "alms resort" in sight), does fine on Factor 2 (minimal disruption), checks out on Factor 3 (no flies, wind, sun, or creepy-crawlies), and scores a bull's-eye on Factor 4 (easy access to food, clothing, lodging, and medicine). Factor 5 is open to interpretation. Do I have access to elder monks? Edith is younger than I am, and she is certainly no monk—or nun—but I regard her as one of the wisest people I know. Is she an "observer of the Dharma?" She doesn't talk the talk, but she walks the walk, so I feel confident that she fits the bill. In short, my shed scores 80% as an ideal locus for meditation.

However, the *Visuddhimagga* goes on to list "The Eighteen Faults of a Monastery." My shed appears to avoid nine of these faults. Is it Large? No. Dilapidated? Nope. Famous? Not a chance. Near a City? Not at all. Near Incompatible Persons? Not in my view. Near a Port of Entry, Border Countries, or the Frontier of a Kingdom? *Nein, non, nyet.* Lacking in Good Friends? No way. Yet further consideration reveals that the shed manifests no fewer than eight of the Eighteen Faults: it is New, Near a Road, Near a Pond, Near Edible Leaves, Near Flowers, Near Fruits, Near Trees, and Near Arable Fields. (The *Visuddhimagga* regards each of these faults as problematic because they draw persons who may distract or disrupt resident monks.) Fault #17—being Unsuitable—is difficult to interpret. What does it mean for a meditation place to be Unsuitable? I can only guess. In any case, *The Path of Purification* states that a meditation place "with any of these faults is not favorable." My shed's score: 50%. In theory, it barely passes muster. In practice, it's what I have, so it's what I'll use.

I start meditating there every day.

"I don't know where it [Faulkner's own literary gift] came from. I don't know why God or gods or whoever it was selected me to be the vessel."

—William Faulkner [10]

Are meditating and writing fiction compatible? Meditation strives to disengage from mental chatter and to dispel the illusions that the mind creates, all of which obstruct a wider, deeper perception of reality. By contrast, writing fiction thrives on precisely that chatter and those illusions—on the flow, even the torrent, of thoughts, emotions, images, and fantasies welling up from within the mind. Properly tapped and channeled, this flow lets writers of fiction create the vivid and continuous dream within a novel. Is *simultaneous* encouragement and discouragement of the mental flow possible? Almost certainly not. These two states require altogether opposite habits of mind. Is it possible, however, that a writer-meditator might somehow make the flow or non-flow *volitional,* much as actors control the process of being "in character" or not? This approach seems a likelier option.

As a writer, I've struggled with these issues for many decades. Almost everything I've written has originated in insights, images, snippets of imagined dialogue, flights of fancy, and dreams that have come to me unbidden. In short, the sources of what I write have welled up from the unconscious. Acquiring these unconscious materials is, of course, just the start of the process. Writing novels, stories, or essays requires taking *la ligne donnée, l'idea donnée, l'image donné*, or whatever else has arisen, then linking, expanding, shaping, and polishing the initial insights into a fully crafted work. I have no doubt that craftsmanship is ninety-nine percent of the artistic task. However, the rational process of crafting the work starts with and relies upon the irrational process of letting insights, images, dreams, snippets of imagined dialogue, and flights of fancy bubble up unobstructed and unfiltered into the light of day. Without access to unconscious material, the conscious mind can't do its work. The intensity, the unpredictability, and even the craziness of the mind: these are the wellspring. For me, as for most artists, everything I've accomplished as a writer has begun with my mind's involuntary ebb and flow.

One evening in 1981, when I was finishing up my workday as the office manager of a clinical psychology program at the University of Denver, I started chatting with a therapist-in-training named Rick. We were discussing the relationship between the arts and psychology. Rick started asking me questions about the experience of being a novelist. He was particularly curious about the process of creating characters and shaping their interactions. "How do you make them do what you want?" he asked.

"Generally speaking," I told him, "I don't. I get them started, then let them do what *they* want."

Rick seemed puzzled. "What do you mean, what *they* want?"

"I try to let them come alive in my mind. Alive to the point that they have autonomy. If I can coax that into happening, the characters make their own choices, take their own actions, and speak their own minds."

"That's really bizarre."

"If I do my job right, they act out the drama and essentially write the book for me."

"You're not . . . *directing* them?"

"Not if I can help it. In fact, they're directing *me*. Or at least they're showing me what should happen. My role as the writer is to leave them alone to the greatest degree possible, then watch them interacting and listen to them talking to one another."

Rick's expression now showed deepening concern. "Don't take this the wrong way," he said, "but what you're saying sounds almost schizophrenic."

"Maybe it is," I admitted. "But if I understand what I hear you guys discussing here at the clinic, the schizophrenic person hears voices and has delusions that he or she mistakes for reality. I hear voices and have delusions that I know *aren't* reality. I observe and listen to what I imagine seeing and hearing. Then I put down what I've witnessed and overheard on paper. I never believe that my experiences are real, and I never attempt to live out the situation myself." What I didn't tell Rick is that the process of observing and listening to characters can grow more and more complex, can proceed for months or even years, can become as compelling as normal reality despite my awareness that the manifestations of this process are illusory. This situation evokes the old wisecrack I heard during my boyhood: "The neurotic builds castles in the air, the psychotic moves into them, and the psychiatrist collects the rent." As a novelist, I have acquired all three roles.

Even at the time of my conversation with this young clinical psychologist, I wasn't concerned that my mind was sliding toward schizophrenia. I had been observing and listening to imaginary human beings since at least the age of five or six. (And not just to human beings: to animals as well. Mythical beasts. Alien creatures. Even inanimate objects.) All young children conjure imaginary worlds and the denizens who live there. The difference for me, and probably for many writers, is that these phenomena didn't fully diminish when I reached late childhood, adolescence, or adulthood. By the age of thirty-one, when I happened to converse with Rick in the offices of the Psy.D. program, I had been having these experiences more or less constantly for over twenty-five years. Were they alarming? Not at all. Disruptive, perhaps? At times. When the voices I overheard and the interactions I witnessed grew intense—and they were often most intense when I was immersed in writing a novel, a story, or a poem—imaginary personages sometimes demanded attention in ways I found annoying. I routinely passed nights during my teens, twenties, and thirties when visions of scenes or snippets of dialogue, arising while I was asleep or half-asleep, felt so compelling that I would get out of bed, turn on the light, scribble some notes in a notebook, and then attempt (often unsuccessfully) to fall asleep again. Gambits such as keeping a notepad beside my bed or using pens with built-in lights intensified rather than dampened the process. Overall, however, I felt that ignoring middle-of-the-night ideas was a bad idea. When the Muse crawls into bed with me at 3 a.m., I don't rebuff her affections.

"All my books were great until I wrote them."

—Virginia Woolf [11]

On September 14, 1982, I sweated through and reveled in my richest and most intense experience of literary inspiration. This experience lasted for several hours but unfolded seamlessly and without any temporal awareness. I was living in Denver at the time but preparing to move East, settle into New York City, and start a new life with Edith. While packing up my rented carriage house (a refurbished garage, actually) near the University of Denver, I was alone late one evening while plotting the logistics of my imminent move. At some point an idea arose spontaneously in my mind. What if during the mid-1530's, when Francisco Pizarro and his band of *conquistadores* arrived in Peru, some of the indigenous population fled deep into the Andean *cordilleras* . . . and then stayed there? What if the Spanish conquest of the Inca empire had been incomplete? What if a remnant of the Incas had not only survived in isolation over the ensuing centuries but had evolved into a distinct culture? In reality, something similar actually took place in the Amazonian rainforest. Isolated, un-Westernized indigenous communities survive to this day in Brazil and perhaps in parts of Venezuela and Ecuador. Anthropologists conjecture that even to the present time, a scattering of "uncontacted" cultures may still exist in South America. It isn't possible that any similar refugees had survived in the Andes all the way to the 1980's . . . but was it plausible that some people might have avoided detection as late as the early twentieth century? Maybe, maybe not. On that September evening, I started mulling over the possibility and began taking notes on the ideas that sprang forth, one after another, without letup. I wrote as fast as I could. One thing led to another. Each concept brought forth two, five, eight, or thirteen more. Images, bits of dialogue, concepts, plot points, questions, conjectures: all of these came to me as fragments, none as coherent thoughts, all of them flighty as hummingbirds, but all related to the conceit of a high-altitude indigenous culture in which mountains were the refuge, the organizing principle, and the object of veneration. My scribbling went on and on. Eventually, dazed and exhausted, I returned to normal consciousness. When I looked at the time, I realized that more than four hours had passed. I had written down forty-seven discrete, often detailed entries in my notes.

Was this event a state of inspiration? Yes, and it lasted longer and was more continuous than any I had experienced before or have experienced since then. Were the resulting notes a work of art? Not at all. My scribblings were only a packet of seeds to plant, water, tend, and cultivate. Bringing them to fruition took ten years of strenuous work. The result: *The Mountain Trilogy.* Spanning 1,200 pages, these three books are the longest and most complex work I've ever written. The first volume, *The Mountain Made of Light,* was published in 1992. The other two volumes, *Fire and Ice* and *The Summit,* followed two years later.

I would have hobbled this process if I'd told myself: *This is just "monkey mind." These are pointless, random delusions. Ignore them, center yourself, and go to bed.* How would I have benefited if I had ignoring the voices and images, the metaphors and notions, and then sat down to meditate, perchance to stop the flow of white-water thinking?

An even more disturbing question: why did I bother? What did I accomplish? *The Mountain Trilogy* remains my most ambitious work of fiction, but so what? Even these complex, carefully thought-through novels fall far short of the vision I received (if that's the right word) in September of 1982. The plot is messy, the characters less fully developed than I'd hoped, the Andean culture inadequately limned, and the philosophical-spiritual implications less ample than what I'd hoped to explore. As a commercial venture, the books had a depressing trajectory. The critical response was positive for each individual volume—at times glowingly so—yet strong reviews didn't generate long-term sales. The first volume, *The Mountain Made of Light,* sold almost a hundred thousand copies—not bad for a first novel back in the early 1990's. The second book, *Fire and Ice,* sold two or three thousand. The third, *The Summit,* sold just a few hundred. All three are now out of print.

I can't help but ask myself two mutually exclusive questions:

Was it good that I shot the rapids and gained the benefit of white-water thinking?

Or would I have benefited far more instead by meditating more often and more deeply over the ten years I devoted to writing the trilogy?

≪ଈ ≪ଈ ≪ଈ

"This is it: the place, the house, the workroom, the time."

—Dylan Thomas [12]

Eight months after Alfred and Eugene transported the wooden shell to Whitcomb Hill, the carpenters stop by unannounced. I chat with them about their work, the weather, and other topics typical of Vermont conversation. I decide on impulse to show them the now-upgraded writer's shack. My hope: they'll say wonderful things about my craftsmanship and will marvel at how I transformed the shell into a fully insulated, handsomely decorated, cozy work space. We walk across the lawn into the meadow. I pull open the bank-vault-like door to reveal the beautiful interior. Alfred and Eugene look the place over. Neither of them comments for a long time. Then Alfred says, "Looks good." Eugene's only comment: "Nice view down the meadow." That's it. No praise, no expressions of surprise, no questions. I'm baffled. Several carpenters within our circle of friends and acquaintances, as well as other friends, have often commented on how beautiful they find the place. From Alfred and Eugene, the craftsmen who made the shed possible by building the shell, I hear next to nothing. Are they so unimpressed that they hold off to spare my feelings from their low opinions of the work? Are they baffled that the shed came out so well? Are they simply not interested?

"This is where you write?" Eugene asks.

"Every day."

"What do you write?"

"Novels, mostly."

Alfred nods.

That's that. Literary work probably makes no sense to these carpenters: my sitting alone for hours in this little place, my attempts to eavesdrop on people who don't exist, my struggle to take notes on imaginary events. I can hardly blame these practical, handy craftsmen for their dim view. They build tangible objects—utility sheds, picnic tables, doghouses. Wisps of ink on paper must seem insubstantial and frivolous. And are.

 I write anyway. I walk down to the writer's shack each morning and hide there for two or three hours. I think and wonder and scribble. During the spring after I've upgraded the shell, I write the second half of a novel that had defied completion for forty-one years. Late that autumn and winter, I finish a second novel, one for which the initial drafting had dragged on since the mid-2000's. I rewrite and publish a novella during January of the new year. I resume work on my long-delayed nonfiction book about Vermont. I'm still not sure what I'm doing, but the river is full, the current strong, the water cold and bracing.

> "We write for the total immersion of experience, the narrowing and intensification of focus to the right here, right now, the deep joy of bringing the entire soul to bear upon a single act of concentration."
>
> —Alan Shapiro [13]

Now that I've waded neck-deep into my sixties, I often have doubts that white-water thinking—the rush of ideas, of imagined scenes, of imaginary dialogue—is truly what I need and want. Coping with the cataract of thoughts, emotions, and fantasies now feels more daunting than in the past. At times it feels worse than daunting: disruptive. Does this chaotic mental process still serve my purposes? If it's the wellspring for writing fiction, am I willing to shoot the rapids despite its potential threat to the equanimity and the insights that meditation confers? To switch metaphors: is building castles-in-air such difficult work—often mind-twisting, mind-warping work—that I should hesitate to undertake these construction projects? Monitoring the gush of unconscious chatter increasingly seems the opposite of the *samatha* (calm abiding) that is the bedrock of

Buddhist meditation. This is never truer than when the castles in question are complex and when the construction projects require strenuous, recurrent, even compulsive effort. I can no longer imagine struggling for ten years to write a 1,200-page trilogy of novels. A failure of imagination? Maybe so. Of will? Perhaps. If I experience a sudden flow of ideas hinting at the possibility of an ambitious novel, I'll consort with the Muse, will give her my attention, will listen to what she whispers in my ear, will take notes on her suggestions. But I'll proceed skeptically. The Muse is a sexy flirt but not a reliable partner. I'll start work only after assessing whatever is necessary to assemble the initial inspirations into something substantial.

I'm uncertain about all these issues, but my uncertainty doesn't stop me from spending time in the writer's shack. I go out there almost every day to write, meditate, or do both. The place is comfortable, quiet, serene. During spring, it's a perfect place for watching the onset of green: first a hint, then a haze, then a luminosity of leaves. In the summer, I revel in the luxury of feeling warm wind blow in through the windows, bringing me the scents of the forest; of watching butterflies, dragonflies, and other insects go about their business in the fields; of hearing Edith's flute melodies—Bach, Handel, Mozart, Fauré—wafting out of the house and down the meadow. In the autumn, yellow sunlight streams through foliage on the nearby trees, and I can smell the leaves and hear their complex rustle and clatter as they fall. In the winter, spending time in the writer's shack is like living inside a snow globe: flakes swarm all around me while I sit in a bubble of warmth. All these modes of sensory richness intensify my experience of spending time there. Both writing and meditating feel deeper and more substantial in that place.

Is it possible that writing and meditation can overlap, or at least coexist? Is it possible that these two radically different disciplines serve a similar purpose? Pondering these questions, I consider the poet Alan Shapiro's observation: "[Writing] is self-forgetful even if you are writing about the self, because you yourself have disappeared into the pleasure of making: your identity ... has been obliterated in the rapture of complete attentiveness. In that extended moment, opposites cohere: the mind feels and the heart thinks, and receptivity's a form of fierce activity. Quotidian distinctions between mind and body, self and other, space and time, dissolve."[14] If Shapiro had been describing meditation rather than writing, his words couldn't have been much more accurate.

❧   ❧   ❧

"One does not find solitude, one creates it. Solitude creates itself. Alone."

—Marguerite Duras[15]

Even before finishing my upgrades to the writer's shack, I've told Edith that I don't consider this place to be mine alone. I want to spend time there, of course, but not to the point of excluding her. In fact, I want her to regard the shed as equally her own. Despite these reassurances (entreaties, even) she never takes me up on this offer. Edith spends time in what we call the upper shed—a larger outbuilding at the high end of our property that I recently emptied of machinery and tools, cleaned up, electrified, and paneled with pine lumber—but she doesn't venture down to what she calls "your shack."

I tell her, "Please take your share of time."

"It's your space," she responds, "so I don't want to intrude."

"You're not intruding. It's an equal-opportunity shed."

"No, it's *yours.*"

I can't persuade her. She sometimes visits me when I'm there, but she won't utilize the writer's shack for her own work. We go back and forth on this issue for months. She never takes up my offer. She won't even use my shack during the winter months, when the uninsulated upper shed is too cold to use.

Following further discussion, however, Edith and I reach a decision: we'll renovate the upper shed into a year-'round cottage. We arrange to have local craftsmen dense-pack the walls with cellulose insulation. We hire them to remove the shabby old metal roof, put down layers of rigid foam insulation and plywood, and re-roof the shed with new sheet metal. Then I add four inches of rigid foam insulation between the rafters and install a ceiling with nineteenth-century-style center-bead boards. After insulating the doors and weather-stripping the jambs, we have a contractor put in a small propane heater and two external propane tanks to heat the place during the cold seasons. Edith and I then furnish the cottage with a bed, a desk, a bookcase, two lamps, and framed art on the walls. The result looks like a small but well-appointed Swiss chalet or a Russian *dacha*.

Finished, both of us are thrilled with the result. It'll be a cozy haven during Vermont's harsh winters. It's beautiful, calm, private. What will Edith do there? That's hers to decide. It's Edith's place now—truly a Shed of Her Own.

12

Scorecard

Livestock, Produce, Crops, Etc.	Whitcomb Family 1860	Bohonon Family 1860	Ring Family 1860	Myers-Poor Family 2018
Horses	1	1	2	0
Milch Cows	8	5	3	0
Oxen	4	2	0	0
Misc. Cattle	8	10	2	0
Sheep	10	17	1	0
Swine	1	1	1	0
Wheat, bu.	40	38	0	.1
Corn, bu.	0	5	30	1
Oats, bu.	70	60	100	0
Peas, bu.	0	0	0	0
Beans, bu.	0	0	0	0
Potatoes, bu.	90	100	200	1
Wool, lbs.	0	60	8	0
Apples, $$	166 [2018$]	0	111 [2018$]	0
Vegs., $$	1,109 [2018$]	0	0	100 [2018$]
Butter, lbs.	200	240	175	0
Cheese, lbs.	0	200	0	0
Sugar, lbs.	280	200	330	0
Hay, tons	40	30	20	0
Meat, $$	5,265 [2018$]	1,386 [2018$]	16,129 [2018$]	0

Novels completed	0	0	0	2
Nonfiction books completed	0	0	0	1
Books published	0	0	0	2
House concerts presented	0	0	0	2

Part Four

Shadows and Light

13

House History—
Changes and Calamities

I. September, 1863: Accounting

The ledger lies on the tabletop; a candle sits near the ledger. Although her eyes struggle to stay open, Betsey forces herself, and Robert with her, to review the numbers. They may as well proceed even at this late hour—otherwise she'll lie awake all night anyway, wondering and fretting.

"Very well," she begins. "Potatoes."
"A hundred and ten bushels," Robert tells her.
She writes the number in the ledger. "Wheat."
"Forty bushels."
"Forty? That's all?"
"It's what we harvested," he says. "Near to forty-five when we finished, but five went bad when the barn roof leaked."
She remains silent for a moment. "Oats, then."
"Sixty-five bushels."
"Is that enough?"
Sitting across the table from her, Robert seems to smile, but Betsey can't tell if the smile shows sadness, fatigue, offense, or something else. "It'll have to be."
She nods. "Barley."
"Ten bushels."
"Indian corn."
"Eight bushels."
"Hay."
"Near to forty tons."

"Forty!" *she mutters, unable to contain her dismay.*

Robert doesn't raise his voice—he never raises his voice—but Betsey can hear what's cloaked inside his calm. "Forty is what we have. Forty is what we harvested. Such a dry summer— Would you expect me to raise more under bad conditions?"

"Of course not."

"Forty is what the Lord has provided."

She sees no point in arguing. It's true: they have what they have. The harvest is the harvest, the numbers are the numbers. They continue to account. Bushels of peas and beans. Bushels of beets, turnips, carrots. Blocks of cheese they've made, slabs of meat they've smoked. Soon, too, jars of tomatoes and pickles that she and the girls will put up. Will this bounty be truly bountiful? Will it be sufficient to feed them all—Robert, Betsey, and so many sons and daughters? God only knows. Each of the older boys, especially—now twenty-three, nineteen, and seventeen—will eat as much as any three of the six younger children combined. How will the family get by? There's a war on, too—far away, thank the Lord. But what if the fighting doesn't stay distant? What if the rebels come north? What if they plunder barns and steal livestock?

Betsey pushes all these thoughts away. Somehow her family will manage. For now, they have no recourse but to account.

"Wool," *she says.*

"Sixty pounds," *Robert tells her.*

II. 1864: Brothers and Comrades

Betsey and Robert Bohanon must have felt a deep sense of foreboding in late December of 1863. Although the Civil War had been raging for more than two years, its catastrophes had befallen other families rather than their own; but now the conflict became far more personal. The couple's older sons—Joseph, Harris, and Alva—had registered with the U.S. government in June of that same year for possible conscription.[1] None of the Bohonons could have been oblivious to the implications. The war had already touched their clan: Robert and Betsey's nephew Albah, who lived in the nearby town of Corinth, had been serving in the Union Army for almost fourteen months, so far without injury. Then, during the last few days of the year, Joseph and Harris both enlisted in the Vermont Ninth Infantry, Company I. Joseph was 25; Harris, 20. Their younger brother, Alva, age 19, enlisted four days into January. Five days later, all three young men went off to war.[2]

In this way began the Bohonons' most calamitous year. Whatever sense of dread Betsey and Robert felt about their sons' collective enlistment, however, must have been swept aside by two tragedies right in their own home. Armina, age five, took ill and died of "brain fever"—meningitis or encephalitis—on January 21st. Less than six weeks later, on March 2nd, Lucy Ann, five months old, died after a brief bout of "lung fever"— probably pneumonia. The deaths of young children were a common aspect of nineteenth century life; even so, it's easy to underestimate how hard these losses hit the parents; and it seems certain that the deaths of the two youngest Bohonon daughters crashed down on their mother and father with devastating force. It's also possible that Betsey and Robert couldn't focus long, or at least not solely, on grieving for their daughters, given what happened next.

The Ninth Vermont Infantry consisted primarily of experienced soldiers. "Most of the men had been with the regiment since it had been mustered in on July 9, 1862," according to Paul G. Zeller, author of *The Ninth Vermont Infantry: A History and Roster*.[3] However, new recruits joined the regiment as the war dragged on. In late 1863 and early 1864, these recruits included Joseph, Harris, and Alva Bohonon, along with several of their cousins. These young soldiers may or may not have possessed any prior knowledge of firearms. "They may have fired shotguns or old style flintlock muskets," Zeller writes, "but they had never touched the new rifled musket. I have copies of many letters from my first book on the 2nd Vermont that indicate they could not hit the broad side of a barn."[4] The Bohonon brothers received only minimal training upon enlistment. Company I, in which the Bohonon brothers served, went into battle little more than a month after their enlistment. This means that the Bohonons probably had benefited from "the rudiments of squad drill" but little more in terms of preparation. Given the emotions that many of their contemporaries expressed about joining the Union Army, the brothers probably felt at once excited and terrified. Perhaps Joseph, Harris, and Alva found solace in having one another as comrades-at-arms.

Who were these young men? No individual photos of them survive, so there's no visual record of each brother's appearance. However, Union Army records suggest that they were robust and large. Joseph, the oldest, was six feet tall. (The *average* height for soldiers in the Union Army was only five feet, eight inches.) Harris was the same height as his older brother. Alva, age 19, stood five feet, ten and a half inches tall. Records note that all three brothers had "dark" hair and "dark" eyes. Joseph and Alva were "dark" in complexion, while Harris was "light." More significant from a military standpoint was that the brothers—farmers all—had spent their youth doing hard manual labor, thus were most likely strong and fit; they were almost certainly handy with tools; and they may have had some familiarity with rifles. In any case, they went into battle less than a month after their enlistment.[5]

On February 2, 1864, more than 2,000 Confederate troops attacked the Union forces holding Newport Barracks, across the river from Newport, North Carolina. The Union troops consisted of the 23rd New York Cavalry and the Vermont Ninth Infantry, backed by Company D of the Second Massachusetts Heavy Artillery. Heavily outnumbered, the Union soldiers fought hard but eventually retreated. "The Ninth Vermont fought quite well, only stubbornly giving up ground as it fought back the main earthwork defenses at Newport Barracks. . . ." according to Eric Linblade, author of *Fight as*

Long as Possible: The Battle of Newport Barracks, North Carolina, February 2, 1864. Lieutenant Colonel Valentine Barney, commanding officer of the Union forces present, realized that "his force could no longer defend the barracks, so he ordered his troops to retreat across the Old Country Road and the railroad trestle. The Union troops barely made it across, thanks in large part to a courageous rear-guard action by elements of the Ninth Vermont." Once over the bridge, Barney ordered his men to burn it, placing the river between his command and the Confederate troops. The Union soldiers then marched twenty-three miles through the night to the town of Beaufort.[6] However, as Paul Zeller writes in *The Ninth Vermont Infantry*, "A number of stragglers, mainly the new recruits who did not know the territory, lost their way and were captured. Others reached the river too late to cross the bridges [which had already burned], so they plunged into the river and swam across."[7] Casualties to the Ninth Vermont resulting from the battle were three soldiers killed and 13 wounded. Two men died later of their injuries. Thirty-eight others, lost or delayed during their flight, fell into the hands of Confederate pursuers.[8]

One of the men taken prisoner was Joseph Bohonon.

Confederate POW camps were notoriously harsh. In an era preceding the Geneva Convention, treatment of prisoners was unregulated and often brutal. The most appalling among the Confederate prisons, was Camp Sumter, later known as Andersonville Prison. Located in Macon County, Georgia, Andersonville became an iconic symbol of Civil War-era brutality. Joseph Bohonon and many other captives arrived there during the spring of 1864 following imprisonment elsewhere. In April of that year, Andersonville had a population of 7,160 prisoners; the census of inmates nearly tripled in number by mid-June; and the camp swelled to a population of 31,693 inmates by late August. Andersonville "was overcrowded to four times its capacity, with inadequate water supply, inadequate food rations, and unsanitary conditions. Of the approximately 45,000 Union prisoners held at Camp Sumter during the war, nearly 13,000 died. The chief causes of death were scurvy, diarrhea, and dysentery."[9] Robert H. Kellogg, a sergeant major in the 16th Regiment of Connecticut Volunteers, described his arrival as a prisoner at Andersonville on May 2, 1864:

> As we entered the place, a spectacle met our eyes that almost froze our blood with horror, and made our hearts fail within us. Before us were forms that had once been active and erect; —stalwart men, now nothing but mere walking skeletons, covered with filth and vermin. Many of our men, in the heat and intensity of their feeling, exclaimed with earnestness: "Can this be hell?" "God protect us!" and all thought that He alone could bring them out alive from so terrible a place. In the center of the whole was a swamp, occupying about three or four acres of the narrowed limits, and a part of this marshy place had been used by the prisoners as a sink, and excrement covered the ground, the scent arising from which was suffocating. The ground allotted to our ninety was near the edge of this plague-spot, and how we were to live through the warm summer weather in the midst of such fearful surroundings, was more than we cared to think of just then.[10]

Over the next months, Joseph Bohonon and the other Union Army prisoners confined to Andersonville endured an experience so wretched as to presage Bergen-Belsen and Auschwitz. The Confederate guards didn't resort to crematoria, but many other features of Andersonville resembled those of the Nazi concentration camps eight decades later. Crowding was severe, shelter rudimentary. Prisoners had little protection from cold, heat, or rainfall. "You must understand that the Confederate government made no attempt to house its Andersonville prisoners," wrote Clark N. Thorp, a Union Army sergeant confined to Andersonville Prison for eleven months. "Here we were, by the thousands, taking the weather night and day as it came, without any covering except the clothes worn throughout the twenty four hours. . . . During a heavy storm none of us could keep from getting soaked and those poor fellows who were without any shelter were much worse off than those who had only a blanket for a roof. . . . Many of them would be dead in the morning and would be carried out to the deadhouse by their comrades."[11] Food consisted of little more than "rice soup" and coarse, low-quality cornmeal bread or mush. Water was foul with fecal pollution. Guards treated prisoners brutally and subjected many to beatings and some to sudden, inexplicable executions. John Ransom, a sergeant in the Ninth Michigan Volunteer Cavalry who managed to chronicle his imprisonment, describes many such incidents in his *Andersonville Diary*: "In crossing the creek on a small board crossway men are often shot. It runs very near the dead line [the start of a forbidden zone near the camp's stockade], and guards take the occasion to shoot parties who put their hands on the dead line in going across. Some also reach up under the dead line to get purer water, and are shot."[12]

In addition to suffering from these inhumane conditions, prisoners endured abuse from the so-called Andersonville Raiders—other Union Army inmates who preyed on their fellows to steal food, clothing, money, blankets, and anything else of value. Men who resisted the Raiders were often beaten or even clubbed to death. "There being no law within the stockade, evil men among us took to robbing from their comrades," Clark Thorp wrote of these predators. "There was an organization of robbers so bold and daring that they would go in squads through the prison and whatever they saw, in the way of clothing or blankets, they captured. For instance, four men would be lying under a fairly good blanket, a raider would come along and lay hold of the blanket and if the men under it attempted to reclaim it each man would quickly receive a blow on the head from a short club in the hands of the raiders [sic] companions. [The] raiders committed several cruel and vicious murders."[13] In response to these predations, a group called the Regulators arose, fought back, captured most of the Raiders, and subjected them to a trial. The jury, selected from the newly arrived Union prisoners, found the Raiders guilty, punished most of them severely with beatings or confinement, and hanged six of the ringleaders. Even with the Raiders eliminated, however, most of the hellish conditions at Andersonville continued or worsened.

An appalling aspect of the situation was that the man in charge of the prison not only tolerated but actively fostered deprivation and abuse of the Union Army inmates. Henry Wirz, born Heinrich Hartmann Wirz, was a Swiss-born Confederate officer. Having served initially in the Fourth Battalion of the Louisiana Volunteers, Wirz took over command of Camp Sumter in April 1864. Many first-person accounts document the harshness of his actions at Andersonville. One such account, John Ransom's *Andersonville Diary*, relates a Union Army sergeant's experience during months of imprisonment. "Capt. Wirtz [is] very domineering and abusive," Ransom wrote during May of 1864. "Certainly the worst man I ever saw." Two months later Ransom noted, "Wirtz punishes very hard now; so much worse than a few months ago. Has numerous instruments of torture just outside the gate."[14] Captain Wirz's reign over the Camp Sumter inmates was so brutal that in May 1865, as the Confederacy collapsed, U.S. Cavalry officers arrested Wirz and transported him to Washington, D. C. A military tribunal (August 23-October 18, 1865) found Wirz guilty of war crimes: conspiracy "to impair the lives of Union prisoners of war"and eleven counts of murder. The U.S. Government hanged Wirz from a scaffold erected near the Capitol on November 10, 1865—one of only two men who were tried, convicted, and executed for war crimes during the Civil War era.

Wirz's eventual fate offered no consolation to the Andersonville prisoners who survived the camp, nor did it provide solace to Robert and Betsey Bohonon or to other relatives of Union soldiers. During 1864, thousands of inmates at Andersonville Prison died of water-borne illnesses and nutritional deficiencies. The Bohonons must have received notice late that year that on October 24, Joseph had died of "scorbutus"—scurvy, a vitamin-C deficiency disease that causes organ failure, edema, and severe diarrhea—while interned at the prison. He is buried in the cemetery there. His nine-month imprisonment and wretched death surely made that final year of his life the most miserable that anyone among Whitcomb Hill's inhabitants had ever experienced. Andersonville Prison must have been the opposite of everything this young man had known back home in central Vermont: not free, but oppressive; not spacious, but wretchedly crowded; not peaceful, but violent; not rich with life, but dense with death. Perhaps the only consolation for his family was that following his death, Joseph's body didn't end up in a mass grave—standard practice at Andersonville.[15]

Unlike Joseph, Harris at least made it back to Whitcomb Hill, but not under the circumstances that he or his parents would have envisioned or wanted. His fate is clear; what led up to its final episode, less so. The records show that Harris continued to serve in the Ninth Vermont Infantry, Company I, almost to the end of 1864. Throughout that year, the Ninth Vermont fought in a series of battles, notably Swansboro and Jacksonville in North Carolina; then Redoubt Dutton, Chapin's Farm, and Fair Oaks in Virginia. What Harris experienced during these engagements is unknown. What is evident, however, is that he took ill at some point, as many troops did, given fatigue, poor food, and contaminated water. Muster rolls tell the story:[16]

- "Admitted to . . . A.b [?] Base Hospt. Pt. of Rocks, Va. Oct. 3. 64."
- "Sent to Point of Rocks [Hospital], Oct. 2 1864."
- "Sick in Corps Hosp. since Oct. 5, 186[4]."
- "Rec'd furlough to his home in Washington, Vt. where he died Nov. 25, 1864."

- "Died of Typhoid Fever."

Exactly when Harris made it back to Vermont isn't clear, but Betsey and Robert at least had the solace of spending a few days with their son, perhaps a week or more, before his death.

And Alva? Two plausible accounts state that Alva "deserted" from the Union Army on November 22, 1864. [17] The events behind this terminology, however, may be more complex than what that one word would suggest. [18] Once again, the Union Army's muster rolls tell a more complex tale. [19]

- "Newport [Barracks], N.C."
- "Wounded through the hand by the accidental discharge of his gun Apr. 24, 64."
- [May and June, 1864:] "[Payment] to be stopped for loss of Arms and equipment Feb. 2/64."
- "Sept. & Oct/64. Sick in Corps Hospital since Oct. 5, 1864."
- "Nov. & Dec., 1864. Transferred to U.S. Hosp'l Vermont—Nov 2/64." How employed: Patient @ Sloan U.S.A. General Hospital, Montpelier, Vt."
- "Transferred to Genl Hosp. Montpelier Vt. Mar 1, 1865."
- "Jan & Feb. 65; Mar and Aprl, 65; May & June 65; June 65; July & Aug 65; Sept. & Oct 65. Absent sick in hospital at Montpelier, Vt."

This is a lot of information, but the gaps are at least as intriguing as the data itself. The first entry indicates that Alva participated in the Battle of Newport Barracks—the messy retreat during which Confederate troops took Joseph Bohonon and other Union soldiers captive. Eleven weeks later, Alva suffered a wound to his hand from his gun's "accidental discharge." It's plausible that the wound was unintentional.

It's also possible that the wound wasn't accidental. Since time immemorial, a self-inflicted wound to the hand or foot has been a venerable ploy for soldiers attempting to avoid military service. Paul Zeller notes: "I have research that one could be accidentally wounded in the hand by a musket. I have also run across incidents where the captain and NCOs suspected the trooper shot himself on purpose, but could not prove it." Zeller's conclusion: "Unless you run across some letters or diaries telling what happened, you probably will never know."

There's the puzzling notation, too, of Alva having been docked pay for "loss of Arms and equipment." Do these annotations suggest that the young man was less than fully committed to the military effort? Or disgruntled by what he had experienced so far? Or so frightened about returning to battle that he shot himself on purpose? Or demoralized by his oldest brother's fate? No answers to those questions are evident from the available information. All that's clear is that a long hospitalization followed—but was it for illness or for the hand injury? There's no way of knowing. In any case, Alva ended up receiving care at Sloan Hospital in Montpelier, just fifteen miles from his hometown, starting on November 2nd.

Which brings us back to the question of the young man's "desertion." The dates are suggestive. Alva "deserted" on November 22, 1864. [20] Harris, now home on furlough but grievously ill, died of typhoid fever on November 25.[21] Records show that Alva was "present" back at Sloan Hospital in Montpelier during December 1864 and for many months during 1865.

The implications are clear. Alva didn't "desert"; he simply left the hospital, either with or without permission, to travel the short distance to his home and spend a few days with Harris before his brother died.

What happened after that visit? Alva returned to Sloan Hospital at some point soon afterwards. A "Muster-out Roll" dated December 1, 1865, provides this notation: "Sick in Hospt

Montpelier Vt." His hospitalization appears to have continued at least through October of 1865. In any case, Alva survived the war. Despite his "desertion," he received a pension for his Civil War service. He lived in central Vermont for many decades and died in Randolph, Vermont, in 1922, age 77.[22]

For Alva, at least, as for Betsey and Robert, the young man's survival must have echoed words from the Job 1:9—words that he and his family would surely have known:

... they are dead; and I only am escaped alone to tell thee.

III. May, 1865: Soil

The oxen pull the plow, the blade cuts the soil, the furrows part. Robert holds the reins and guides the team, but he can only wonder if he's driving the two dumb beasts or if the beasts are leading him instead. They know more fully where to go than he does. They have more will, more spirit. They have more confidence than he that the task is worth doing. Perhaps Robert is simply along for the ride.

Even two years ago his sons would have been here tilling the field with him. Now Harris lies deep in the ground a few miles down the road, and Joseph, far away in Georgia, is himself turning to soil in a military graveyard. Alva is "on the right side of the sod," as the lad himself has joked, but he remains confined to the hospital in Montpelier, his recovery still uncertain.

And Betsey? She's in the garden now with Lydia and Mary Ann, the three of them planting whatever they've decided to plant while the younger girls do their chores inside the house. Robert catches sight of his wife and oldest daughters when the oxen head uphill toward the house, and at times he's aware of Betsey watching him. What does she see? A man whose hard work instills confidence, or one whose constant toil seems merely a dam he's building to stop the tide of sadness, a tide that could swamp the entire family? As if he doesn't notice her own labor, her own construction project. Robert often hears his wife at prayer—O Lord, hold them dear in your embrace—and he listens to his wife console herself when speaking to friends and neighbors: They've gone to a better place. They abide with Our Savior. She's building her own dam, word by word as if stone by stone, to keep from getting washed away.

He also hears over and over what she once told him to his face: "If you hadn't signed for Harris and Alva, the boys would be with us still." Altogether true. No signature, no enlistment. No enlistment, no muster. No muster, no battle, no capture, no illness, no death. But young men go off to war; it's something they do. When Joseph decided to enlist, there was no stopping him: he was four years into his majority and could do whatever he chose. Neither was there any dissuading the younger brothers. To defend the Union, they said. They didn't say, To have an adventure, though surely that was part of what they wanted. They were intent on serving together as their own little squadron. We'll look after one another, Joseph assured his parents. How could Robert have forbidden his sons their right to forge their own destinies—their right to become men? Yet how could he not fear the consequences of allowing them that freedom? Betsey has no idea how sick he felt, how hard the dread washed through him, when he signed those papers at the enlistment office for each of the two younger boys: "I do freely give my consent to his volunteering as a soldier in the army of the United States for a period of three years." Robert wanted to enlist along with them, alongside them, to look over them, but at age fifty-one he knew that the Army viewed him as six years too old. How could he have left, anyway, with a wife and eight other children to feed?

He can't help but recall the story of King David and his son Absalom, how David received the news of the young man's death in the Forest of Ephraim. But King David lost only one son in battle, not two, and he didn't lose two young daughters, struck dead by illness, the same year. What would Betsey have him do? Cry out in a voice like King David's: "O my sons Joseph and Harris, my sons, my sons! Would that I had died for you, O Harris, O Joseph, my sons!"

As he would be tempted to do now. All the same, he must proceed. It's his duty, his fate. God wills it; Robert will obey. This is what it must be, what it will be.

Hence the oxen lumber onward, the plow rolls forth, the blade cuts, the soil parts. No grown sons help Robert with this work, but he will trudge after the beasts and perform the task. Joseph and Harris won't follow their father's team with the harrow. Alva won't take his turn sowing the wheat. Yet in the fullness of time the soil will be ready, the seed will fall onto the dirt, the plants will spring forth, the wheat will make itself manifest.

14

What Would They Think?

If the Whitcombs, the Bohonons, and the Rings could have somehow peered forward in time to observe Edith and me during the early twenty-first century, how would they have viewed my meditative practice? The Rings and the Bohonons, being Irish Americans, were most likely Catholics. The Whitcombs, descended from English immigrants, were likely to have been Protestants. They lived in an era of increasing secularization, but most nineteenth-century Americans were religious. Many held tightly to sectarian beliefs and regarded other denominations with wariness or contempt. Notions of multiculturalism and ecumenism would have baffled many rural Vermonters of that era—would have struck them as peculiar, unappealing, even heretical.

What might have caught these families' notice more than any other issue during their own time was the Millerite movement. Led by a man named William Miller, this millennialist sect believed that the Second Advent of Christ was nigh. Many thousands of Miller's followers sold their goods, quit their jobs, and even abandoned their families in anticipation of the apocalypse certain to occur at some point between March 21, 1843, and March 21, 1844. Jesus, however, was a no-show. Schisms developed among the Millerites thereafter during what historians term the Great Disappointment. I have no idea what our predecessors on Whitcomb Hill thought about these events or about the beliefs that gave rise to them. The likelihood is that the Bohonons, Whitcombs, and Rings were traditional

Christians who would have regarded unconventional religious notions—including those espoused by freethinking contemporaries such as Henry David Thoreau and Ralph Waldo Emerson—as bizarre.

For these reasons, I imagine that they would have been disdainful of my own beliefs and practices. I can only wonder what would they have thought of me. Of a baptized Catholic who rarely attends Mass and is more likely to end up in a Protestant church, a Jewish *shul,* a Tibetan Buddhist *gompa,* or a Zen *zendo?* Over the course of my life so far I've been an impious, contrary-minded Catholic, an indifferent Protestant, an ambivalent, restless student of several Hindu swamis, and, most recently, a less-than-insightful Buddhist. Religiously speaking, I've been (to paraphrase Thersites in Shakespeare's *Troilus and Cressida*) "in all things illegitimate." There is no spiritual tradition I've followed without skepticism, no set of beliefs I've embraced whole-heartedly, no set of practices I've explored without wondering *What's the point?*

Perhaps their disdain would be appropriate.

I feel certain only that the Whitcombs, the Bohonons, and the Rings would have been unimpressed. Worse yet, derisive. Perhaps even contemptuous. Perhaps their low opinion would be appropriate. Perhaps my guardedness and evasiveness are worthy of their derision. Or perhaps whatever their opinion might have been, I've simply undertaken my own task; I'm just trying to untangle my own skein of spiritual yarn. In any case, I have the strange luxury of pondering the Whitcombs, Bohonons, and Rings without the possibility of their pondering me.

Here's how I'll proceed: by paraphrasing John Milton.

They also serve who only sit and write.

15

Lunar Gravity

The house faces east. From the vantage of our hillside, Edith and I marvel at a full-panorama sunrise most mornings—or, in cloudy weather, we benefit at least from a rich glow on the eastern horizon. Depending on the lunar cycles, we often have a full view of the moonrise, too, whether by day or night.

I realized at some point while settling into this house that over the entire course of my life, in all the places where I've lived for extended periods, and in all the countries I have visited, the moon has been one of just two constants. The other, too harsh for human eyes to tolerate, is a presence I can track more by its effects on everything around me than by direct observation. But the moon . . . The moon allows not just awareness but contemplation.

Almost twenty-four years ago, when our son, Cory, was three, I carried him in my arms as we crossed our front yard in New Jersey one summer evening, and he pointed upward at the full moon. We stopped to consider the sight before us.

"Isn't that beautiful?" I asked him.

He responded with a request: "Dad, can you get me one of those some day?"

I don't recall my reply. I have a vague recollection of saying, "I would if I could." I was probably tempted to say, "I'd like to, but finding a good place to put it will be a problem." No doubt the Township of Maplewood strictly regulated the storage of celestial objects in a residential neighborhood. I do remember simply savoring the moment: the warm child in my arms, the bright light in the still-blue sky, and Cory's delicious misperception.

I've noticed over the years that many babies and toddlers, still unaware of how distance affects their notion of an object's size, reach out to grasp at the moon. It's possible that all of us have been subject to the same childhood misunderstanding. Then, growing older, we continue to reach for the moon, not with our hands but with metaphors and similes.

William Shakespeare: "The moon's an arrant thief, / And her pale fire she snatches from the sun; . . . "

John Milton: ". . . Hesperus, that led / The starry host, rode brightest, till the moon, / Rising in clouded majesty, at length / Apparent queen unveil'd her peerless / Face. . . ."

Edward Young: "Thy shaft flew thrice, and thrice my peace was slain; / and thrice, ere thrice yon moon had filled her horn."

Percy Bysshe Shelley: "That orbed maiden with white fire laden, / Whom mortals call the moon."

Robert Southey: "Nor cloud, nor speck, nor stain, / Breaks the serene of heaven: / In full-orbed glory, yonder moon divine / Rolls through the dark blue depths; . . .

Philip Larkin: "The moon, the anchorless / Moon go swerving / Down at the earth for a catastrophic kiss."

I could go on and on, quoting poets not just in English but in every language. Beyond literature, pop music, too, is rife with lunar imagery ("When the moon hits your eye like a big pizza pie, / That's *amore*.") Ever since human beings first began to speak, members of our species have surely attempted to describe and invoke this strange, close-yet-distant object in our field of vision.

❦   ❦   ❦

Traditional Buddhist poetry is full of lunar images. "The moon looms everywhere in Chinese and Japanese poetry," Charles Egan notes in *Clouds Thick, Whereabouts Unknown, Poems by Zen Monks of China,* his collection of Chan poems.[1]

> The moon and pond each carry both general and Buddhist associations. In general usage, the full moon . . . connotes family unity and returning home, due to its perfectly round shape and its associations with holidays on the lunar calendar. . . . The spring of pure water in landscape poetry carries philosophical overtones, as the source of the stream is metaphorically the source of Dao.

He goes on to write:

> The moon and pond together carry additional associations . . . to extend this metaphor: for the individual, the moon may represent original enlightenment and the pond actualizes enlightenment; on a cosmological level, the moon could be the *dharmakāya* in its absolute aspect, and the pond (which reflects ten thousand things) in its phenomenal aspect. These meanings still resonate in Buddhist usage, but are subtly transformed. The moon and pond form a polarity with the multivalent enlightenment message.

Although I have few illusions about the likelihood of ever reaching enlightenment, I can hear this message all the same. I'm aware, too, of a notion implicit in Buddhist teachings: that most if not all of what we "perceive" is a projection from our own minds onto what lies before us. Our beliefs, memories, preferences, fears, biases, hopes, desires, and all the other intellectual and emotional baggage we carry prompt us to impose our own agendas on anything and everything we encounter. No doubt this inadvertent but habitual tendency to project assumptions holds true when we view the moon, just as it does when we view any other object. All the more so, given its primal place in the landscape since time immemorial.

The moon is, after all, nothing more and nothing less than a gigantic stone. Everything else about it—its appearance, its nature, its significance, its symbolism—we ourselves impose. Think of it as a massive, three-dimensional Rorschach blot.

On July 21, 1969, Neil Armstrong and Edwin "Buzz" Aldrin landed their spacecraft *Eagle* on the moon. I had followed the space race avidly through its many achievements, its periodic mishaps, and its occasional tragedies from the time I was ten or eleven. Now, nineteen years old, I felt astonished and moved by what the American astronauts had achieved. I recall stepping out of my house in Denver after viewing Walter Cronkite's CBS broadcast about the moon landing that summer evening, and, walking one block to Merrill Junior High School, I stood in the middle of the athletic track and gazed upward. The summer sky wasn't dark yet. The moon hung almost overhead, full and pale white. I stared for a long time and tried to determine if it looked different now. Had it been transformed? Augmented? Diminished? Violated, even? I certainly didn't feel what some people claimed about the moon landing—that humankind had "conquered" the moon—any more than I believed that Edmund Hillary and Tenzing Norgay, having attained the summit of Mount Everest in 1953, had "conquered" the world's highest peak. Armstrong and Aldrin had somehow succeeded in reaching the moon alive and had set foot on the Sea of Tranquility. That was a huge accomplishment. Both in July of 1969 and over the years since then, I've admired and delighted in what these men achieved.

I also felt a sense of foreboding and dread about this accomplishment at the time, however, a tangle of emotions typical of my response to so many other events during my late teens: a feeling that Western technological advancement was a double-edged sword and that even extraordinary feats like the moon landing fairly screamed out the Faustian bargain our culture had made. Among other things, my dark mood reflected my hypersensitivity toward the U.S.-Soviet Cold War and, especially, toward the arms race between the two superpowers, of which the space race was a major expression—a quasi-military, albeit nonviolent, battle. For reasons I've never been able to explain, I had developed a precocious awareness of the Cold War from mid-childhood on; even at the age of seven, in 1957, I sensed that the Soviets' launch of the first Sputnik revealed a terrible competition that I knew threatened me, my family, and the entire world. The Cuban Missile Crisis of 1962 five years later convinced me that even though we had all somehow survived that crisis, I would eventually die in World War III. Research into that geopolitical conflict has fully confirmed what so many people knew intuitively at that time: that those weeks in October ended with a hair's-breadth swerve away from nuclear war and were (in the words of one historian) "the most dangerous moment in human history." Later phases of the Cold War presented me with a more personal invitation to annihilation. From my mid-teens onward, as the war in Vietnam intensified, I worried that I would soon be drafted into the army, sent to Southeast Asia, and probably killed there in a pointless firefight. (Little did I know in July, 1969, that just two months later I would draw 15 as my number in the nationwide Selective Service System lottery, or that over the next two years I would receive three separate draft notices. I was never actually inducted—I flunked the Army physical all three times for insufficient weight.) So, staring upward at the moon in 1969, I felt both astonishment at NASA's triumph yet also a deep unease over what two human beings on the lunar surface represented.

 Catching sight of the moon over the many years since then, I have ceased to think very often, much less reflexively, about the Apollo astronauts. They do come to mind, however, in one specific way. An exchange took place between Neil Armstrong and Buzz Aldrin during one of their Apollo 11 moonwalks:[2]

> Aldrin: Beautiful view!
> Armstrong: Isn't that something! Magnificent sight out here.
> Aldrin: Magnificent desolation.

This interaction, though embedded in a long series of flat-affect, Right Stuff comments by the Apollo 11 moonwalkers, provided one of the few in which any of the astronauts offered *les mots justes*. Magnificent indeed. Desolation, truly. The oxymoron works. There is indeed a magnificence to the lunar landscape, yet at its core—to human eyes, at least—it's a chilly, even chillingly desolate, panorama. My first sight of the moon through a telescope brought this realization home to me years earlier, though at the time I couldn't even start to describe the impact of what I saw. As an eight-year-old Cub Scout, I participated in a field trip to an observatory one winter evening. There, gazing through the first big telescope I had ever used, I examined the brilliantly illuminated lunar panorama. The sight made me catch my breath. But even more than the sheer expanse of terrain, what astonished and shocked me was realizing that only three components made up everything I saw: rock, light, and shadow. Worse yet, shifting my attention from the central *Mare Tranquillitatis* to the right, where the *Mare Crisium* curved away and tapered off, I saw—*nothing*.

In a way, the insight I reached as an eight year old gazing through that telescope, and the insight that has hit me time after time in the years since then while contemplating the moon, is what has mattered most to me. The moon is a *memento mori*, or perhaps more accurately a *memento nihili*. Yet at the same time, when gazed at from the earth, at least, the moon is also a *memento vitae*, a constant reminder of the vibrant life all around us. "If we only paid attention," Edward Abbey wrote, "we would see that Earth is the only heaven we will ever need."

On a late-May evening well before dusk, I spotted the moon almost overhead. The sky held nothing but its own diffuse blue and that one bright object. I'm not sure why, but darkness reduces the moon to a luminous disk, while daylight lets it appear more fully three-dimensional. Now the moon was waxing gibbous, the left-hand quarter lacking the impact of enough solar rays to make it visible, and the missing fourth of its surface left the rest looking all the rounder. As songbirds in the woods started calling out to one another, I stood in the meadow and marveled to see the moon so clearly a sphere, the earth's atmosphere and the space beyond so transparent that nothing at all seemed present to stop me from reaching a quarter of a million miles to touch the lunar surface.

A former girlfriend once admonished me during our mid-1970's cohabitation about the risks of staring too long at the moon: "You might burn your eyes."
"*Burn?*"
"Moonburn. From staring too long."
I assumed she was joking. "And I suppose I also shouldn't lie out too long on moonlit nights?"
"Right. Your skin could get moonburned."
"What you're saying doesn't make sense. Moonlight isn't intense enough to burn. It's only reflected sunlight, right? I don't think it even has the UV rays that make sunlight so damaging."
Bright and well educated, she nonetheless persisted in this tenacious belief: "That's my point exactly. It's reflected sunlight. So if you're out there in the moonlight, and especially if you're staring at the moon, you really could get moonburned."
Our argument reached a slow boil and simmered for many months. This same issue cropped up time and again. Nothing I said could dissuade her. Nothing she said could persuade me. More and more annoyed as I persisted in my folly, she often

warned me when I continued to gaze at the moon.

In the decades since my then-girlfriend and I parted company, I've contemplated the moon often enough and for long enough that if her theory had any merit, I would probably have gone blind many years ago, or else I would have suffered some bizarre form of skin cancer. Who knows. I feel confident only that this smart, ambitious woman had missed a major business opportunity: in the New Age-y 1970's, she could have produced and marketed a line of lunar protection products—Diana's Shield MoonBlock™—each with its own MPF number.

One February night, I stepped out to give Sammy, our Shetland sheepdog, her last bathroom break before sleep. The temperature was eighteen or twenty degrees below zero. Clear sky. No wind. While Sam went about her business, I gazed out toward the east, where at once I found the moon. The air felt like glass shards shoved up my nostrils. The sight of the moon—icy, hard, empty—felt like the spiritual equivalent of glass shards shoved up my nostrils.

According to Buddhist legend, Prince Siddhartha, following the forty-nine days of meditation that culminated his years-long search for wisdom, looked up from where he sat under a huge tree and, catching sight of the morning star in the pre-dawn hours, attained enlightenment. Perhaps that pinpoint of light triggered the Buddha's moment of clarity. Perhaps having spotted the morning star was coincidental to the culmination of his protracted struggle—simply what happened to appear in his field of vision at that moment. *Buddha* means The Awakened One. In any case, he saw that celestial glint as he reached full wakefulness.

Seeing the moon that night in February woke me, but only as a splash of cold water would have wakened me. I felt only a jolt and a shudder.

Can I go back to sleep now, please?

❧   ❧   ❧

I audited a writing workshop some years ago in which the professor was a well-regarded American poet. My initial interactions with her developed cordially enough, but after a few more class sessions she grew testy, irritable in response to my classroom comments and at times mildly insulting toward me in front of the other students. I have no idea why. I shared her interest in formal poetry; I respected her work; I contributed to discussions in what I regarded as occasional, appropriate, and fairly unobtrusive ways; and I submitted poems that I considered more than adequate in comparison to other students' contributions. Perhaps she resented my presence as a contemporary among her much younger, more compliant students. In any case, she became more and more dismissive toward me as the semester took shape. At one point, when I submitted a poem whose subject matter included the moon, she exclaimed, "The moon, of all things!" As if I shouldn't write about the moon. As if a classic object of contemplation were somehow inappropriate. As if originality of subject matter were a necessity—or even a possibility. As if I shouldn't face (and write about) what is so often right in front of me.

I've been fascinated for many decades by the obsession with originality of subject, theme, and so forth within the contemporary literary establishment. "Make it new," Pound insisted, or commanded, and his motto expresses and represents genuine virtues. Literature advances as old assumptions, styles, topics, and modes of thought fall way, yielding to innovations. In some non-Western traditions, however, some things may be more important than originality—at least for the individual writer. Think of all the Chinese and Japanese poets who have written about the moon. Imagine if their Chan and Zen masters had admonished them: "The moon, of all things!" They didn't write to plow new ground in the literary field. They wrote simply as part of a spiritual practice. (The most extreme instance of this approach may be the Zen practitioners of *jisei*, deathbed poems; these aspirants wrote haiku and other traditional forms during their final moments of life as a final reach for enlightenment.[3]) No matter how many people had written about the moon in the past, they would proceed to contemplate and to write. So would I.

Lunar Gravity

Steeped both in light and shadow—
what a sham you are, feigning
radiance to hoodwink lovers,
farmers, sailors, and all the rest
of us into a belief
that you'll illuminate our lives.
Bone-white, you leach even the stars
out of the night sky till what's left
is just a brilliant emptiness.

And yet what troubles me
isn't just your lie, but the promise
within it, not just your stark
offer, but my urge to accept.

Now, while camping, I awaken,
leave the tent, and walk in darkness
to the river. I do not know why.
Ignorant of what I seek,
I know what I find: the moon
twisting in swift water. Even
the icy woods turn opulent
by comparison. Yet the sight
does not frighten, it only stirs me—
perfection not of this world.

One can hear the siren song of oblivion and admit that it's a catchy tune but still decide not to join the chorus. Better to stay lashed to the mast. Better to sail on. No matter how messy, ambiguous, fraught, strenuous, and often painful life may be, there's no good reason to get too tidy about the situation. There will inevitably be a time to participate in what the American poet Edgar Bowers called "the perfect order trusted to the dead."[4]

Beautiful view!
Isn't that something! Magnificent sight out here.
Magnificent desolation.

"Dad, can you get me one of those some day?"
"I would if I could."

The moon, of all things!

Part Five

What Lasts and What Doesn't

16

House History—
Remnants and Ruins

When Edith and I descend into our woods, we sometimes spot abandoned farm equipment. There's a dark green machine down among the trees, complete with metal wheels, a metal seat, a long-handled brake, and a transverse boom armed with a row of five-inch-long blades. Dating from the late nineteenth or early twentieth century, it's a horse-drawn mower. There's a caisson-like cart, too, still deeper in the forest. Some kind of wagon? The purpose it served isn't clear to city folk like us. Most alarming in appearance is a rack of spikes that looks like hardware left over from the Spanish Inquisition. Despite the resemblance to an "iron maiden," however, it's just a harrow, essentially a mega-rake used to loosen plowed soil before sowing seeds. What's evident when we encounter these machines is that our predecessors abandoned them on what was once open farmland. As farmers stopped cultivating the fields on Whitcomb Hill, saplings sprang up, they grew and spread, and the fields reverted to forest. The machines are now engulfed in woods. Some of these devices have trees literally growing out of them.

Lost down there, too, are old stone walls. Most are about two feet tall. Some are still in good shape; others are dilapidated. All are encased in moss and lichens. Did the early farmers here build walls to mark off property lines? No: walls would have been a too-strenuous way of doing what could be accomplished by simpler means. Rather, these walls are remnants of the early-nineteenth-century sheep craze. In 1811, a retired diplomat named William Jarvis imported 400 Merino sheep from Spain to Vermont; the Merinos and their offspring thrived in the state's hilly ecosystem; and sheep became the pastoral mainstay for over three decades. (In 1840, Vermont had a population of only 280,000 people but 1,681,000 sheep.[1]) Now the sheep are gone, the shepherds are gone, and the walls remain.

Is it possible that other relics of our predecessors are still present? When I contacted Doris and Paul to raise this issue, Doris responded in the affirmative. "A historian and Carl [a former neighbor, now deceased] went looking for Reuben's grave on the property."(Reuben Whitcomb, you may recall, was the late-18th-century paterfamilias of his clan.) "He [Reuben] lived in a house on the farther south side," Doris told us. "The granite foundation is still out there. Paul [Doris's husband] saw it." A further e-mail from Doris includes this clarification: "Paul tells me the house foundation is deep in the woods between you and Jeff." This news intrigues Edith and me. Reuben's grave? An old foundation? The notion of finding these remnants is irresistible. So, like Hiram Bingham searching for the Lost City of the Incas, we set off into the forest.

Edith and I often walk in our own five-acre section and in our neighbors' adjacent and much larger woods. The whole area is new-growth forest on what was cultivated farmland up until the 1960s. Although "young," the woods are remarkably dense. Usually we follow the paths. There's the VAST trail, a track maintained by a Vermont snowmobilers' club. A few old roads, too, cut through the forest. Starting with the paths we know, Edith and I explore sections nearest to our own property. We see no signs of ruins. Then, over a period of several weeks, we venture off the trails. We walk south into Jeff's woods, then southeast into Brooke and Donna's. Still no luck. One rainy afternoon, I head off alone, first following old stone walls to see where they take me, then using an improvised grid system to work through the terrain more systematically. None of these various approaches yields any results. It dawns on me that we've undertaken this effort in the worst possible season: early summer. The trees and plants are the most florid they'll be all year. I'm lost in a green labyrinth. Saplings, ferns, ground cover, and full-grown pines, birch, ash, and maples surround me in every direction. I could be standing twenty feet from an old foundation and never see it.

"Are there maps of local properties?" I ask Carol, the town clerk.

More than anyone else, Carol keeps this community running. She knows everything about its present and more than anyone alive about its past. Carol has stayed patient with my many visits to her office and with my endless questions over the past five or six years. "We have maps on file," she tells me.

"For everyone?"

"For every owner who did a survey."

"Am I allowed access to them?"

"Of course. They're public information."

I remove five or six maps from the rack she shows me. Most are three feet long and at least two feet wide. When I start examining them, I see that each shows a property as surveyed in recent decades. The oldest map that interests me dates from the 1960's; the most recent, from around 2010. All show land either adjacent to or fairly near the property that Edith and I own near the top of Whitcomb Hill. Why do I bother checking? Because a map might show the old foundation that Doris mentioned. Surveyors sometimes note long-lasting objects as reference points on a property: a dilapidated stone wall, an abandoned well, a collapsed shed. Why not a ruined foundation? For this reason, I scrutinize the maps. Jeff's. Brooke and Donna's. Lenny's. Other owners'. Even our own.

Nothing I see on paper shows any evidence of what I'm looking for.

❧   ❧   ❧

For many weeks throughout several summers, Edith and I venture back into the forest. Sometimes we search together; sometimes I look alone. We search at least two or three times per week for the old graves and for the lost foundation. The weather is unusually hot. Wandering through the damp, buggy woods isn't always appealing, and the warm weather has stimulated the florid growth of ferns, weeds, and other ground plants that complicate our efforts to spot what may already be plant-shrouded blocks of granite. We persist anyway. We search systematically on some days, randomly on others.

During these walks we spot few marks of humanity on the land. Other than the stone walls, most signs are recent: the VAST Trail, some other paths, a scattering of POSTED signs, Jeff's hunting shack. Now and then we notice tantalizing remnants of nineteenth-century inhabitants. Most are slabs or chunks of granite but not foundations as such. Rather, they are fragments of boulders that the Whitcombs or Bohonons must have split to acquire foundation stones. The standard practice in that era was to locate a boulder, drill a line of three-inch-deep, evenly spaced holes into its surface, and then tap a set of small wedges into the rock until its crystalline structure gave way, producing a clean fracture line. Edith and I see several of these split boulders lying on the forest floor. The drill marks are obvious. The rectilinear shape of the slabs makes it clear that someone was harvesting granite blocks for a construction project. People wouldn't have exerted so much effort if they weren't building a foundation; and in an era when moving heavy slabs of rock required teams of oxen, special sledges, block-and-tackle, and lots of strong men, settlers split boulders as close as possible to the construction site.

Where would that site be? We still don't know.

I contact several of our neighbors by e-mail or through the postal service to ask for suggestions. No one replies. When I phone Jeff, however, we have a useful discussion.

"You know anything about an old foundation in the woods?"

"Yeah, there's one in there someplace."

"Any idea where?"

"I saw it a long time ago, but I can't recall exactly where. It's hard to spot. It's so overgrown you'd hardly see it."

We discuss the possibilities. "Over by Brooke and Donna's place?" I ask.

"Probably not."

"Maybe closer to the California sisters' property?"

"No, not that way."

"Farther to the south?"

"To the west. Or the southwest."

This is useful information. Edith and I set off again, even more intent now than before.

What explains my obsession with ruins? Am I just channeling my inner Wordsworth, all the better to ruminate on the passage of time and the evanescence of our brief lives on earth? Maybe so—but not only that. Among other things, I'm connecting with longstanding interests of more tangible sorts. Though raised in Denver, I lived in Peru for a year at age ten and then for another year at age fifteen. My parents, my brothers, and I traveled throughout the country during each of those stays and visited a dozen or more archaeological sites. Not just Cuzco and Machu Picchu but Nazca, Paracas, Pachacamac, and Chavín de Huántar were among the ruins we visited. Many of the ruins were still largely unexcavated back then. Scrambling around on the remnants of ancient civilizations was a heady experience for a kid from Colorado, where "old" meant miners' shacks built in 1880. Even our daily life in Lima included bumping into (sometimes literally) the ancient past. An upscale supermarket called Todos, for instance, had a thousand-year-old pre-Inca *huaca* (burial mound) right next to its parking lot. Later, during the 1970's, I returned to Peru on my own and explored the country more extensively and with the freedom, and sometimes in the risky ways, feasible for a male in his twenties. I hiked into the backwoods of the

Andes and, among other things, camped in Inca and pre-Inca sites dating from the 1480's. The result: I have an unshakable obsession with old ruins.

The Lost City of the Whitcombs is small change compared to an unexcavated pre-Columbian *huaca*. Even so, it's hard to shake the bug once you catch it. I find it almost impossible to see ruins of any era or in any place without starting to wonder who lived there, what the inhabitants' lives were like, and what became of them.

Edith and I can't seem to locate the foundation, but we find many other things in the forest. We find more stone walls crisscrossing the woods. Once two or three feet high and fairly even, these walls are now as crenelated as castle parapets. The individual stones are green with moss. We find more pieces of abandoned machinery, too: rusted, broken-up cars, trucks, and wagons. One chassis sports a pair of 1967 license plates, though another looks old enough to be a Model T. We find split boulders, too. In addition to these durable, inanimate objects, however, we find the woods teeming with animals. Toads and harmless snakes scoot or slither across the forest floor. A few squirrels scurry overhead among the branches. Now and then a chipmunk spots us, freezes, then vanishes so abruptly that it may as well have teleported itself to another dimension. Once or twice we spot a deer. Pushing through a thicket of underbrush, we startle a bevy of grouse that explode out of the underbrush. We hear even more birds than we can see: wild turkeys, blue jays, phoebes, nuthatches, wood thrushes. One evening, walking in the forest later than we should have, we hear the bizarre conversation of two barred owls. One asks, "Who cooks for *you*?" and the other inquires, "Who cooks for you *well*?"—before erupting into their notorious caterwauling, as maniacal as a grade-B movie villain's laughter. We can't find the past, but we find the present around us everywhere.

Edith is a strong walker and can out-walk me on a long haul.

With my thin frame and decades of experience hiking and climbing, I'm more agile and quicker on slopes and uneven terrain. I also have an almost unerring sense of direction. These attributes, combined with my tenacious curiosity about the lost foundations, prompt me to venture alone into the woods. During a recent summer I take walks day after day. I explore in every direction. I push into areas I didn't even know existed. I work systematically from a grid system. I experiment by using concentric circles and spirals. When all else fails, I just wander aimlessly, following my hunches. Having once imagined the forest adjacent to ours as consisting of fifty, sixty, seventy acres, I now find myself exploring woods that spread out over a square half-mile. The place is huge. I always find my way out, but day after day I fail locate what I'm seeking.

Probing the dense woods near Jeff's hunting shack one afternoon, I wade waist deep among the ferns. It's a muggy mid-July day. Trees, saplings, and forest floor are as green and lush as they'll be all year. This area is so dense with ground plants that I have to push hard to get through. Brambles interwoven among the ferns grab at me and scratch me through my clothes. Logs hidden underfoot keep tripping me. I feel as if I'm awash in dense surf. An irrational thought arises: what if I drown? A ridiculous notion. This "water" is dense, dry, green, prickly. Yet only by shoving hard through the plants am I able to emerge. A less preposterous, more metaphorical idea comes to mind: I'm searching for an old shipwreck, a lost boat submerged not in water but in ferns. I could be standing next to the foundation and never spot it. I could be standing *on* it and never know.

Then, two surprises.

One takes place as a result of my trolling the Web. While doing research on various members of the Whitcomb, Bohonon, and Ring families, I start using a genealogy-related site called Find-a-Grave.com. This site lets members post and access information about cemeteries and the graves located there. At some point I notice that someone whose "handle" is *eriboh* has posted information about the Bohonon family. I've grown tired of sending out inquiries to contacts and then receiving no responses, so I almost hold back from writing. On impulse, however, I send a message to *eriboh*. I receive an answer just five or ten minutes later. The result? My first breakthrough in communicating with latter-day Bohonons. The woman who contacts me—I'll call her Erica—isn't a direct descendant of Robert and Betsey. She's a distant cousin, however; and, more importantly, she is knowledgeable about genealogy in general and about her own family tree in particular. The resulting correspondence yields less information than I crave but more than I've acquired so far—a couple of photos, some contacts within her clan, and access to the massive family tree that Erica has assembled.

After a few weeks of e-mailing back and forth, Erica and I make a plan for meeting up in Vermont. She and her boyfriend, Bob, drive north from western Massachusetts and arrive on a mid-August Sunday afternoon. The goal: sharing information. I'll take Erica and Bob on a tour of local cemeteries to show them the Bohonon gravesites I've located; in exchange, Erica will describe what she knows about her ancestors. Over a period of five hours, we drive around the area and visit five small graveyards and a large municipal cemetery. Erica snaps photos of her ancestors' and relatives' markers. Bob checks names off a list and takes notes. Our various stops and the drives between them allow time for me to ask my questions. Erica states that she has no breakthroughs to offer about Betsey and Robert, but she offers some useful context for why I've had so much difficulty while doing my research.

At one point, when the three of us are eating lunch while seated in a small, serene cemetery, I ask her, "Why are the modern-day Vermonters so reluctant to talk with me? I've made it clear that I'm writing about their ancestors with respect and admiration, but nobody will even answer my inquiries. Why are folks so buttoned-down?"

"Because we're Yankees!" Erica exclaims with a laugh. "We're New Englanders! We don't like sharing information with outsiders!"

"Even outsiders who are respectful and admiring?"

"Of course! We're afraid you'll find the skeletons in our closets!"

"Well—*you* aren't afraid. At least you don't seem to be."

"True. I'm talkative and nosy," Erica tells me. "But you know what? Even my own relatives don't want to answer my questions. Some of 'em, anyway."

"So, what do you recommend?"

"Just don't take it personally."

I don't. Despite Erica's generous sharing of her family tree and other archives, however, I still wish I could obtain more.

The second surprise happens about a month later. One September day when Edith is out of town on business, I hear what sounds like a shout coming from outside the house. I go to the front window and see a car in our parking area. Going downstairs and out onto the porch, I find a woman standing on the lawn.

"Hello?" she asks.

"Sorry— Can I help you?"

"I'm Jolie. My family used to own this house back in the 70's."

I recognize her name at once. She is one of the "California sisters," as they're called by local folk—three women, now in their mid-forties through early fifties, who own the land adjacent to Edith's and mine. For some years now I've considered contacting them but have never gotten around to it. Now, unannounced and unexpected, here is Jolie.

What ensues is a full day of conversation about Whitcomb Hill and many other topics. Jolie, age 46, is a forester and environmental educator based in the Bay Area. Her sisters, Monique and Nicole, live in southern California, as does their mother, Susan. The sisters grew up in Port Washington, Long Island (by coincidence, Edith's teen-years hometown). Their parents had purchased the Whitcomb Hill property in 1971, used it as a summer place, and then sold the house and ten acres of land in 1978. They retained almost fifty acres of the hillside, however. This property is held in trust for the sisters.

Jolie is in Vermont now for a brief stay, a chance to explore the area and visit her land. She has been camping in the woods for a couple of days; now she's here in hopes of seeing the old house. "I visited in 1988," she tells me, "after I'd heard a rumor that the place had burned down. I had to see if that was true. I was relieved when I saw that it was still standing. I talked with Doris and Paul at that time—they were really welcoming. So, I was glad to see the place intact and being cared for."

Then, after reminiscing for a while, Jolie mentions another reason for making this trip: she wants to walk the property line and get a better sense of the land that she and her sisters own. I ask if she'd like some company. I'm a little concerned about Jolie's wandering into the woods alone at the start of deer-hunting season, and I'm curious to hear any other stories she might want to tell me. She says yes. So, after putting on our boots, we head off together into the forest.

The hours we spend hiking are uneventful. I find it interesting, however, to learn about her work as an environmental educator in California and to hear a little more about her childhood visits to Whitcomb Hill. "Remember, I was just two years old when my parents bought the place," she tells me, "and just ten when they sold it. My sisters and I came up here only in the summer—maybe one or two times each year. So, what I remember is bits and pieces. I remember cows on the open land. I remember horses that lived on the other side of the road. Carl took care of them. In fact, Carl was the caretaker of our place when we were away." (Carl, our neighbor Lenny's brother, was the man who had alerted Doris and Paul to the existence of a lost foundation.)

What does Jolie recall about the house?

"Not much. The house wasn't that significant to me."

What was, then?

"The land. The place. I remember the meadow, the view, the flowers, the horses—riding the horses!—and a huge tree. It was down the meadow. It was this huge, welcoming, beautiful tree. When I think about coming back here, I think of that tree."

Jolie and I descend into the woods, we follow the survey map that she brought along for the visit, and we explore the property. As a trained forester, she tells me a lot about the ecosystem. These trees are thriving; those others are looking stressed. We discuss climate change and the dangers it presents to New England. We note various kinds of trash in the woods—beer cans, cigarette packs, and other refuse—and we speculate about who's been trespassing and littering. At some point, while using Jolie's map to gain our bearings, we note a symbol that indicates an old foundation. "There used to be other houses on this hillside," I tell her, "and maybe this foundation is what's left of one." This is the first confirmation I've seen that my quest may have an actual destination. Where, though? The map isn't precise. No coordinates are indicated on the printout. We decide, however, to try locating what's noted on the map.

For at least an hour we shove our way through the ground cover and work our away among the trees. The task seems as difficult as what Edith and I have undertaken over the past several months. Even now, in mid-September, the foliage remains lush and dark. The trees haven't even started turning yet. Jolie and I often can't see clearly where we're going, much less spot clear evidence of foundation stones among the ferns, brambles, saplings, and bushes. Soon we decide that my obsession with the old foundations shouldn't distract Jolie from her own agenda: getting an overview of her property.

Moreover, I don't want to commandeer the visit and put it to my purposes. I ask her if she feels comfortable proceeding on her own. She says yes, which I take to mean that she'd like some time alone anyway. So, leaving Jolie with her map, I retreat, work my way northeast, and return to the house.

The weeks after Jolie's brief visit prompt Edith and me to do what we've already been doing, only with even more focus and intensity. We look and look. I feel more obsessed even than before—so much so that Edith grows irritable about my returning to the woods day after day.

"Is it possible that you're going a bit overboard?" she asks me one evening. "A little carried away?"

"Probably," I admit.

"How long will this continue?"

"Hard to say. For a while but not forever."

"That's a relief."

"I'm not hurting anything, am I? It's not as if I'm a compulsive gambler throwing money at the roulette wheel. Tell me if I'm wrong, but I'm doing all the tasks I need to be doing for us—my own work, the house chores, and interactions with you and Robin and Cory."

She nods.

"I just want to poke around in the woods long enough to satisfy my curiosity," I tell her. "We know something's in there—Jeff confirms that. Something is marked on Jolie's map, too. So, I want to see it. That's all."

I know I'm pushing my luck here; somehow I've annoyed Edith or jeopardized her trust in my priorities. For this reason, I avoid going into the woods when she's around, and I don't insist that she come along unless she's already interested in what we call a "woodsy walk." (Edith walks several miles a day, but mostly on the local roads.) When she's away, however—when she's out of town on business, visiting with local friends, or running errands—I sometimes venture back into the forest on my own. I explore areas that seem auspicious, given the data on Jolie's map. I use the grid system, the spiral system, the random-wandering system. I search at midday when the sunlight pours straight down through the increasingly leafless trees. I search at dusk with a powerful flashlight that might throw foundation stones into relief. I search by looking closely. I search by paying no intention to what's visible and by just following my hunches, intuitions, and impulses. I follow paths that angle this way and that through the forest but show me no ruins. I follow old walls but discover that they lead nowhere. I wait for all the leaves to fall and reveal more of the landscape, but even then I locate no Lost City of the Whitcombs, no Lost City of the Bohonons. I look, I see, I do not find.

Until I do.

One afternoon early in October, while attempting to work my way out of a brambly, unfamiliar part of the sisters' property, I realize that I'm standing inside a rough rectangle of stones. The stones are so fully covered with moss that they resemble old tree stumps. So many stones surround me, and in such clear alignment, that I feel no doubt that I'm standing on a human-made structure. Trees grow out of the rectangle. One tree must be ten inches across at the base; others are three to four inches in diameter. The stones around the trees almost certainly predate their growth. These moss-covered chunks and slabs of rock have been here for a long, long time. For what purpose? The rectangle is only about eight by twelve feet in size. This can't possibly have been the foundation for a house—least of all a house big enough for raising twelve children. What was it, then? A shack? A shepherd's hut, perhaps, dating from the sheep craze two hundred years ago? That seems more likely. In any case, it's a real foundation, and it probably dates from the Whitcombs' and Bohonons' era.

The other issue on my mind after finding this foundation: its location. This rectangle of stones isn't in the place shown on Jolie's map. It's too far west and too far north. Where, then, are the ruins on the map? Weeks of pacing back and forth in the likeliest area haven't paid off. Does the lack of success tell me that I've not been searching for the place on the map? Or is it possible that the map itself is mistaken? Perhaps Jolie's survey map is approximate, not precise. If so, perhaps the foundation isn't located exactly where it's marked.

I start searching farther to the south and the west, both being areas I've tended to ignore until now.

I find a second foundation almost immediately. It's much bigger than the first, twenty feet long at and least twelve feet wide. Like the smaller one, this foundation is a jumble of stones. Some are huge—a yard long, two feet wide, and a foot or eighteen inches thick—while others are smaller, a foot or two square and five or six inches thick. Still others are just random chunks in random sizes and shapes. All are heavily coated with moss and lichens. All are dilapidated in ways that challenge my ability to discern a clear shape to the foundation itself. I can see a clear depression in the ground, however, and I can see how the stones border this depression. Some trees grow out of the hollow that the foundation stones create, and some fallen logs and branches fill the hollow in the middle. It's clear that a house once stood here. When I look more closely, too, I see more than just stones: I also notice discarded items among the stones, branches, and leaves. I step carefully into the hollow and start examining what I find there. Glass jars and bottles. Rusted buckets, pots, and pans. A metal grill of some sort. Corroded cans. When I examine these items, it occurs to me that their presence may contradict my assumption about a foundation. Maybe this place is just a dump. But that makes no sense; the people who lived on Whitcomb Hill wouldn't have undertaken the arduous work of shaping, moving, and setting massive granite blocks just to create a garbage dump. They would've done what people have done for millennia before the advent of landfills—they would've simply strewn their trash in the nearest and most convenient place. No, the huge stones served as the base of something more significant: a house.

Finding what I've found, I feel vindicated. At least partly. Is this the Lost City of the Whitcombs? Probably not. As nearly as I can tell, the Whitcombs always lived farther to the north, chiefly where the current house stands now. The Lost City of the Bohonons, perhaps? That's more likely. But I'm not convinced. As large as this second foundation may be, however, it doesn't seem substantial enough to suggest a house where Robert and Betsey could have raised twelve children. Yes, nineteenth-century American families packed their kids into tight sleeping quarters; the notion of each child having his or her own bedroom—or even doubling up with just one brother or sister—was eighty or a hundred years distant. But this second foundation just doesn't seem big enough.

What is it, then?

The answer comes to mind quickly: it's a starter house. Robert and Betsey acquired land on Whitcomb Hill in 1853. They had to begin somewhere, and this place was where they began.

17

Heat

"There is no place more delightful than one's own fireplace."

—Marcus Tullius Cicero

1

Warmth is a god in Vermont, and the wood stove is the sacrificial altar where we make burnt offerings to ensure our wellbeing each day throughout the autumn, winter, and spring.

2

Keeping warm isn't just a task here; it's a culture. Vermonters endlessly discuss which heat sources are best, where to obtain the various kinds of fuel, how to maintain stoves and boilers, and how to keep warm for the least money and the least effort. At the same time, Vermonters wax lyrical regarding how hard they work to stoke all their heat sources. Heating with firewood, especially, is an obsession: where to buy the cheapest cordage, when to stockpile a supply, how to split the wood most efficiently, how to calculate the ideal amount for a given winter. People express great pride in the primal aspects of heating with firewood: *It's what Real Vermonters do.*

3

This state endures some of the coldest winters in the United States. Only Alaska, Maine, Minnesota, North Dakota, South

Dakota, and Wisconsin are colder. The mean temperature in Vermont during January, for example, is 16.41 degrees Fahrenheit.[1] But this statistic doesn't even begin to reveal what we experience from day to day. Each winter in Vermont brings months of sub-freezing weather and weeks of sub-zero temperatures. The lowest temp that my wife and I have experienced while living here is minus-30. The wind chill on that particular night was 40 or 50 degrees below zero. Lows of minus 15-20 are routine. Small wonder that the residents of this state are obsessed with keeping warm.

4

The question is how—and at what cost. Vermont's total energy consumption is the lowest of any state in the nation, but the percentage of energy used to generate heat is high. Since Vermont has no coal reserves and receives natural gas only through a small-capacity pipeline from Canada, the favored fuels for generating residential and commercial heat are oil, propane, firewood, and wood pellets. Three-fourths of the state's surface is forested, which provides abundant supplies of renewable products.[2] As a result, nearly one fourth of all energy consumed in Vermont comes from renewable sources, and almost one-third of school children attend facilities heated by wood products, such as wood chips or pellets. Use of wood products to heat residences clocks in at 14%, but this figure is higher than anywhere else in the country.[3]

5

Even as Edith and I prepared to buy the property we now own, we realized that an 1840's-vintage house would require complex, expensive upgrades to make it comfortable and safe during cold weather. The home inspector's report prompted us to make multiple changes once we took possession. The insulation contractor we hired added fourteen inches of cellulose "loft" into the attic. He dense-packed the walls with the same material. A carpenter replaced the leaky first-floor windows. We installed a pellet stove insert into the existing fireplace to heat the first floor more efficiently than would have been possible with an open hearth. We acquired two high-performance Danish woodstoves—one for the living room and the dining room, the other for the second floor. These changes transformed the house from a drafty icebox into a cozy lair.

6

When I drive from our place down to the nearby village, the view I see on winter days often includes a pall of smoke hanging over the valley. Most people in the area heat their homes with the cheapest fuel: firewood. Many have indoor wood stoves, and some use outdoor wood boilers—freestanding units notorious for low efficiency and high output of pollutants. As a result, even a small town like ours can have winter air quality as bad as that of a large city. Edith and I are fortunate that up on our hillside, where we're surrounded by woods and farms, we have only a few neighbors, hence minimal air pollution.[4] But the upshot is clear: use of renewable fuels doesn't necessarily avoid all environmental problems.

7

Nathaniel Hawthorne, writing in "Fire Worship" (1843), laments the advent of cast-iron wood stoves as a replacement for open hearths. "It is a great revolution in social and domestic life," he states, "this almost universal exchange of the open fireplace for the cheerless and ungenial stove. . . . " Missing "that brilliant guest, that quick and subtle spirit" of the open flame, Hawthorne proclaims that "we have thrust him into an iron prison . . . I never shall be reconciled to this enormity. Truly may it be said that the world looks darker for it." Human interactions, he believed, would suffer from the absence of a fireplace as the gravitational center within a home. Open hearths open hearts. Wood stoves—dark and shut tight—would lead to dark, tight communication. "Conversation will contract the air of debate," writes Hawthorne, "and all mortal Intercourse be chilled with a fatal frost."[5]

I can relate to Hawthorne's lament. Other than a campfire in the wilderness, no heat source provides more solace than an open hearth. But at what cost?

8

Here's a sad truth: the traditional brick fireplace is fundamentally an appliance for pumping heat out of a house. Some heat radiates from an open fireplace into the room, of course; but, as Benjamin Franklin observed, "the strongest heat from the fire, which is upwards, goes directly up the chimney and is lost."[6] Worse yet, the upward draft creates negative air pressure inside the house, a partial vacuum that sucks ambient air up the chimney as well. The result: the open fireplace is one of the most inefficient heating devices available—so inefficient, in fact, that it may even *cool* the living space it's intended to warm.

This inefficiency is a vexing environmental problem. The amount of firewood burned in households throughout New England's history defies belief, the quantities are so vast. In his biography of Henry David Thoreau, Robert Richardson notes that during Thoreau's years at Harvard College (1833-1837), each student received an allotment of six cords of wood annually to heat his dorm room.[7] Nineteenth-century families in Vermont and elsewhere in New England often expended twenty cords of firewood each year heating their relatively small houses.[8] (A cord is the amount of wood that, when "ranked and well stowed"—that is, arranged so that the pieces are aligned, parallel, touching each other, and compact—occupies a volume of 128 cubic feet.[9] This amount corresponds to a well-stacked woodpile four feet high, eight feet long, and four feet deep.) Has the situation changed in the supposedly efficient, energy-conscious modern era? The answer isn't encouraging. As many as 12% of Vermont homeowners heat their houses with wood, but not necessarily in efficient ways. [10] One of our neighbors, a highly skilled farmer who lives in a medium-sized house, burns, like nineteenth-century Vermont families, twenty cords of firewood each winter.

9

Would I be willing to burn twenty cords of firewood to heat our little house? Never. Would I accept not only the intense labor involved in using that quantity but also the huge output of greenhouse gases in exchange for the psychological benefit of an open hearth? No—that's out of the question.

But if open hearths are such an inefficient way to burn firewood, and if wood stoves are (to use Hawthorne's word) "ungenial," what's a good alternative? Fortunately, heat sources have evolved dramatically over the past three centuries. The oil shocks following the 1973 OPEC embargo prompted the Danish government, for instance, to mandate increased use of renewable fuels, including firewood; Danish companies responded with innovations in heating technologies. Other European industries took similar actions. In more recent decades, Germany and other countries have promulgated plans to foster energy efficiency. One example: the Energiewende, the German government's "Energy Transition," launched in 2010 "in hopes of . . . slashing the country's overall carbon emissions to 40 percent below 1990 levels by 2020." [11] (The United States, by contrast, has focused primarily on finding and exploiting new sources of fossil fuels.) Among other innovations, the Morsø company in Denmark has created a line of stoves that burn wood in almost hermetically sealed fire boxes, that recycle hot gases within the chamber and increase the fuel efficiency. The result: less wood burned, more heat generated, less CO_2 emitted. [12]

There's also a delightful aesthetic payoff of the Danish approach. Each of our two Morsø wood stoves has a heat-resistant window in front. The glass maintains the hermetic seal of the firebox but allows Edith and me to watch what's burning inside. The result: what we call Flame TV. We have the pleasure of viewing what Hawthorne called "that brilliant guest, that quick and subtle spirit" but without the drawback of ripping through vast quantities of firewood. Even during our years of heating the house almost exclusively with wood, we've burned little more than a single cord each winter.

10

A log in the woodstove has flamed itself into embers. It's now orange-pink and intense, bright as a radioactive salmon. Having placed this wood in the firebox, I've watched for thirty minutes as it transforms into a radiant replica of its formerly substantial self. It looks exactly like a log, complete with growth rings on the end, striations on the surface of what had once been bark, and little stumps jutting out from the trunk, but the whole thing is now made of embers—dark areas of carbon delineated by orange light. I continue watching as the intensity diminishes. Orange fades to red. Red fades to an ashen surface that emanates a strange glow from beneath the surface, much as molten lava appears as it oozes down a volcano's slope. The glow dims. Then what remains of the log collapses little by little into ash.

11

Few sights are as calming and beguiling as flames in a fireplace. One of the wildest phenomena in nature, now domesticated, resides there in a safe place. The warmth provides a tangible sense of wellbeing; the orange-yellow light offers solace. But the delight I feel while watching flames twist inside the Morsø woodstoves is inherently problematic. Each time I place a new log in the firebox, I commit a crime against the earth. Burning one pound of firewood combines with oxygen to create and release 1.76 pounds of carbon dioxide into the atmosphere.[13] There is no easy way around this fact and the dilemma it presents.

12

How many trees do Edith and I burn during the cold months each year? That's a difficult question to answer, since trees vary greatly in overall height and girth, in the number and size of branches, and in other variables. However, a University of New Hampshire website allows an educated guess. I'll assume that the quarter-split pieces of firewood we purchase locally come from logs about twelve inches in diameter. The site's calculator suggests that three and a half trees with twelve-inch trunks will yield a cord of firewood. Since Edith and I currently burn about a cord of firewood each winter, we burn 3.5 trees during the winter months.[14]

13

In addition to firewood, we burn kindling cut up from scrap lumber, broken furniture, and various discarded wooden items. Here's what we sent up the chimney over the past several winters:

- Scrap lumber from many projects
- Boards from a flimsy, worn-out bookcase
- A busted-up rocking chair
- A severely weathered picket fence from Maplewood, New Jersey
- Three warped hiking staves
- A collapsed barrel dating from the 1910's
- A broken safety gate of the type used to protect toddlers
- Five broken fence posts
- Cut-up rails and rungs from a wooden stepladder
- Three deteriorated bushel baskets

- A ten-foot length of a warped bannister
- Six or eight sawed-up shipping pallets of many sizes
- The wooden bases from two rat traps and half a dozen mouse traps
- Two ugly coat racks
- Three chopped-up birdhouses.

14

An old New England saying: "Heating with firewood warms you thrice—once when you split it, once when you stack it, and once when you burn it."

15

Perhaps heating a house with wood is the thermal equivalent of killing the animals you eat. Purchasing shrink-wrapped meat at the supermarket distances you from the violence of slaughter and butchery, yet pigs, steers, and chickens still die in the process of becoming food. Likewise, nudging the thermostat in a suburban home distances you from the process of extracting oil or natural gas from the earth, but the environment still suffers each time you raise the temperature. Heating with wood is carbon-neutral, thus less harmful than burning oil or gas, but doing so still releases carbon into the atmosphere, as well as large amounts of particulates. This situation prompts me to ask: Is there any moral advantage to heating with wood? Perhaps. Doing so avoids using a fossil fuel. In addition, firewood often comes from local sources, thus requiring a smaller carbon footprint for transport. Heating with wood also puts you face to face with your own actions. It forces you to connect physically and sensually to the reality of burning fuel.

These issues prompt Edith and me to consider some alternatives. If firewood isn't a truly clean fuel, what might be better?

16

While simply walking inside the house one winter evening some years ago, I felt a searing pain inside my left knee. I knew immediately that I'd ripped a ligament. The damage, as an MRI showed two days later, was a classic "bucket-handle" tear of the medial meniscus. An orthopedist performed arthroscopic surgery on my knee late that week and ordered me to limit my normal activities for more than a month. Among other things, that meant no more hand-splitting logs or hauling bushel baskets loaded with firewood.

The upshot: for over a month, Edith and I couldn't heat adequately our house using firewood. I managed to hand-pick small pieces of wood from the stockpile in our garage. Soon, however, we ran out. Splitting more logs was beyond what I could manage in my state of temporary disability. We had no choice but to fire up the old oil boiler in our basement. Doing so felt like a defeat. Worse than a defeat: this reliance on using a dirty, expensive fossil fuel felt like committing a crime.

What disturbed us most intensely was realizing that this incident gave us a glimpse of the future. A minor injury had literally kneecapped my ability to stoke our fires. I was sixty-four at the time. Even if I remain hale and hearty into my seventies and eighties, I can't assume that I'll maintain sufficient strength and agility to split and carry firewood. Edith and I can burn oil, of course, but doing so feels unacceptable. The problem goes beyond environmental objections: oil is expensive. What, then, were the alternatives?

17

In response to this situation, Edith and I purchased an Austrian pellet-fired boiler. Andy Boutin, the green-energy engineer at a local company called Pellergy, sold us the hardware. Steve Gilbert, our friend and neighbor who runs an excellent plumbing-and-heating company, installed the boiler in our basement. Tied into the existing system of baseboard heaters, this boiler now heats the entire house by burning about forty pounds of pellets—compressed sawdust—per day. The Windhager boiler resembles a medium-sized refrigerator and is fully automated. Within just a day or two of using this appliance, Edith and I realized that we will now be safer and more comfortable even during the coldest months of the year; we'll have far less work to do each winter; and if we want to stay in Vermont into our eighties, the effort to stay warm won't be the reason not to.[15]

18

Meanwhile, the news about global climate disruption has grown worse and worse. January 2016 was the hottest January ever. May 2016 was the hottest May ever. July 2016 was the hottest July ever. Overall, 2016 was the hottest year worldwide since observers started compiling records in the 1880's, and it followed two other years that had broken all previous records.[16] 2017 was the third-hottest year on record. Specific consequences of the warming trend continue to be alarming. Glaciers world-wide are retreating. The Greenland ice sheet is melting so fast as to exceed climate scientists' worse-case predictions. The Arctic ice cap now melts almost completely each summer. Huge regions of the Antarctic ice sheets are melting. A region of the Antarctic ice sheet has melted so fully as to disengage altogether from the continent. During the summer of 2015, wildfires ravaged not only large areas in California but also in Washington State—including parts of the Olympic peninsula's rainforest. Wildfires in 2017 and 2018 destroyed thousands of homes in California and elsewhere. A recent study published by James Hansen (the former director of NASA's Goddard Institute for Space Studies) and other climate scientists now predicts a rise in the sea level of at least ten feet by 2050.[17] A separate study recently published in the journal Science indicates that global sea levels could reach twenty feet by that same year, and it warns that a rise of 75 feet isn't out of the question. Meanwhile, much of the world's population continues to heat with fossil fuels, to generate electricity with fossil fuels, and to travel in fossil-fuel-powered vehicles—in short, to keep spewing carbon into the atmosphere with an abandon that suggests there's no tomorrow.

What difference does it make, then, if I'm heating with wood or with pellets? Will a relatively clean conscience make any difference (or offer any consolation) if our species stokes the grill of climate change and barbecues the whole planet to a fare-thee-well?

19

Amount of carbon dioxide emitted into the atmosphere each year: 38.2 billion tons.[18]

Amount of CO_2 emitted into the atmosphere by generating domestic heat: approximately 8% of the total, or 3,056,000,000 tons.[19]

20

Being cold some of the time may confer spiritual benefits. How can I grasp the seasons of my life if no seasons unfold around me? How can I catch a proper existential chill if I never feel a chill in my flesh? When I talk with people who live in perennially temperate climates—southern California comes to mind—I often get the feeling that their warm surroundings inspire delusions of immortality. (An apocryphal story: a Scotsman recounts his perplexity while visiting the United States. "Back in Scotland," he says, "we believe that death is imminent. Then I visited Minnesota, where I learned that death is inevitable. Then I visited Los Angeles, where I learned that death is optional.") Better, I think, to see winter coming at me in October, to see the snow fly in November, to watch the drifts accumulate in December, and to feel the slap of sub-zero air in January and February. Those transitions show something about the arc of a lifetime. A gloomy vision? Not at all. This is just reality. Grasping the presence of cold can inspire a great delight in what's warm—both in the literal and figurative senses of the word. Grasping the presence of cold also helps me perceive and relish the changes in March and April: how the light brightens and deepens, how the air grows sweet, how the birdsong rises once again from the meadow.

21

Based on measurements of cosmic microwave background radiation, the average temperature of the universe is apparently about 2.73 kelvins.[20] This temperature is the equivalent of minus-454.49 degrees Fahrenheit or minus-270 degrees Celsius. Here's what I find terrifying about these numbers: although they take into account the vast emptiness of space, they also factor in all of the stars, the exploding supernovae, the vast clouds of super-heated gas, and all of the other incendiary matter in the universe.

Here, however, is what I find reassuring: even when the outdoor thermometer reads minus 20 degrees Fahrenheit on a winter morning, the hillside where Edith and I live is 434.49 degrees Fahrenheit *warmer* than the average temp for the universe. Even Vermont in the dead of winter is a cozy place.

22

Edith and I sit watching Flame TV. The warmth emanating from the Morsø is gentle and even. Since we can precisely control the flow of air into the firebox, what we see there aren't flames in the usual sense; rather, the sight resembles a slow-motion tornado made of iridescent orange-yellow plasma. The thin logs below this firestorm appear to be made not of matter but of red radiance. This sight is intense but beguiling.

Then my vision shifts—or else my imagination shifts—and I see the fire in a different light. I gaze at this sight and see far more than radiant wood and boiling light. I see a city in flames, its houses consumed, its skyscrapers alight, its skyline hemorrhaging fire. I see a forest ignited—the trees like torches, the hillsides churning with fire, the air whirling with smoke. I see a conflagration spread, the flames smiting all nations like a host of avenging angels.

Then it's over. My vision reboots. I see nothing but a log in the firebox, the wood emanating brilliant gases, the light lovely and consoling.

18

Past Present, Present Past

"The past is never dead. It's not even past."

—William Faulkner

"The past is gone."

—Gautama Buddha

December 6, 1884: James and the Snowfall

Staring out the window, James watches the flakes descend without wavering or billowing. He ought to feel agitated, he tells himself, but he doesn't. He ought to be afraid but isn't. No matter how stark, the snow tells him that all is well. It's possible that he has never seen a more beautiful sight. He lies propped up in the bed and simply watches. A bounty of snow. After all the years of growing corn, oats, wheat, and barley, now this bumper crop of snow. How many snowflakes in a bushel?

From the far end of the house he hears the women. The tones are hushed—not Mary's and the nieces' usual vivacity—but their high voices carry. What are they saying? He can't tell. What are they cooking? He doesn't care, for he has no appetite. He wants them to eat. He worries that they're exhausted, fussing over him these past several weeks, not sleeping well, not nurturing themselves. It's not good, depleting themselves as they take turns sitting up all night. He has what he needs: this bed, this window, the snowfall beyond the pane, their voices in the background.

The bed. What a bed it's been over all these years. Where he and Hannah lay together so many times. Where they hoped that she would bear the sons and daughters who never deigned to grace their lives. Where Hannah herself, depleted and swollen and unable to catch her breath, died eleven years ago. Did she feel the embrace of this bed, as he does now?

The women enter the room and disrupt his thoughts. Even his nieces are women now. Lucy and Ella Jane, both in their twenties. Edna, sixteen. His wife Mary, just shy of fifty, still looks youthful.

The nieces sit nearby, his wife closer.

"James, we made you a tasty soup."

He says: Thank you, Hannah, but I'm just not hungry. Then he realizes that he didn't speak the words, only thought them. He grasps too that the wife leaning toward him is Mary, not Hannah.

"Please try some."

He shakes his head once, twice, until he realizes that he hasn't actually moved.

"Just a spoonful?"

She doesn't understand that there's no need. He feels no hunger. His body is already nourished, his appetites all sated. These women have fed him well.

Amazing, all the years they've harvested. How many years in a bushel?

How does their past change our present? Does it matter to Edith and me that James and Hannah worked so hard? That Robert and Betsey raised so many children? That Hannah, Betsey, and Lucinda Ring all predeceased their husbands? That the Bohonons lost two daughters and two grown sons in a single year? In some ways, no. If I had never heard of these families—if I had never pulled the threads that led me into the fabric of their lives—my own cloth would be outwardly the same. Yet it's hard not to think about them, to wonder about their joys, frustrations, delights, and sorrows. It's hard not to feel changed by what I've learned.

I've heard people who own old houses comment that they feel the presence of those who once lived there. Living now on Whitcomb Hill, I don't sense our predecessors' presence, but I feel their absence. The more I learn about the Whitcombs, the Bohonons, and the Rings, the more I think about who they were and what they did; and the more I think about them, the more they seem missing. I can't help but wonder about the lives they lived, the children they raised, the work they performed from dawn to dusk. I can't help but contemplate the losses they suffered and speculate about the joys they experienced. I can't help but admire the strength and stamina they must have possessed to work their teams of oxen, to grow and harvest 75 bushels of corn, 400 of potatoes, and 100 of oats; to produce 800 pounds of butter and 200 of cheese; to shear 24 pounds of wool and spin it into yarn; to raise a bumper crop of five, six, eight children all the way to adulthood. I can't even begin to grasp the grief they must have felt to suffer the loss of so many sons and daughters.

Now they are gone. James and Hannah Whitcomb are gone. Levi Jr. and Louisa: gone. Betsey and Robert Bohonon, too, are gone. Moses and Lucinda Ring: gone as well. Nathaniel Whitcomb? Gone. Later residents on Whitcomb Hill—John S. Hall, J. D. Eastman, Albert and Ida Whitcomb, Leonard and Laura Flint, the Moran brothers—all are gone. The 1960's-era owners, Joe and Pat Rafferty, may still be alive but don't live here now, so they, too, are gone. Doris and Paul continue to thrive, but not on Whitcomb Hill. All of these people are gone.

Is this the big takeaway from Whitcomb Hill? That everything passes? If so, it's the most brilliant insight I've reached since age of four, when I informed my parents that the sun always rises in the east. All the same, what strikes me hardest when I review the data I've amassed about the Whitcombs, the Bohonons, and the Rings is the contrast between the complexity and richness of the lives they lived in their day compared to the simplicity of their absence now.

❧ ❧ ❧

Among the few people who have described their time on Whitcomb Hill to us are Paul and Doris, our immediate predecessors, who owned this property from 1983 until late in 2010. "The house was up for foreclosure," Doris told us recently, "and it had been vandalized." Despite the deteriorated state of the house, Doris and Paul saw its potential right off and purchased it; however, they immediately faced the huge task of cleaning up the mess and correcting all the problems that had festered in recent years. Doris described the squalid state of the place: "The garage was full of garbage bags filled with baby diapers. The shed by the road was a total takedown. The well pump's motor had burned out. The furnace was also burned out. The fireplace chimney needed to be replaced. There were huge holes in the plaster throughout, feces in the tub, and electrical wires exposed. The [light] fixtures had been taken and the stove also. The septic system needed a new cover. There had also been water leaks from the heating system." Paul and Doris responded by hiring people from the nearby town to start correcting the property's shortcomings. "We hired a local person to clean out the garbage and debris in the house and garage," Doris told us. "Since the heating system wasn't operating, we hired a friend to put in a new boiler. We also hired a local carpenter to rebuild the shed, repair the fireplace, take down the bar in the living room, remove a wall in the dining room, replace broken windows, replaster some of the walls, fix the water system, the septic system, and so forth. He worked for months to do all the repairs."

Later, Paul and Doris hired the carpenter and a plumber to install an upstairs bathroom. They also fixed up the kitchen, wallpapered several rooms, and painted the house both inside and out. By the time they finished making improvements in the mid-1980's, the house on Whitcomb Hill was a modern dwelling for the first time ever. Paul and Doris lived here each year from May through September. Accomplished gardeners and landscapers, they planted both a huge plot of vegetables and several flowers beds, and they groomed the rolling meadow to create the lovely property that Edith and I had admired even during our six years of summering in a rented cottage down the road. We've felt moved to hear Doris and Paul's stories about how they rescued the house and then delighted for all of thirty years in what Doris calls "our slice of heaven."

What would James and Hannah Whitcomb think of the house if they could see it now? From the outside, it would look familiar—visually brighter, perhaps, given its fresh coat of cream-colored paint, but otherwise recognizable. Inside, too, the house wouldn't seem altogether alien. Our style of décor would look spare to nineteenth- or early-twentieth-century homeowners, but the rooms themselves wouldn't strike time-traveling visitors as altogether bizarre. Other features of our life would be difficult or impossible for them to grasp. The electric well pump ... The solar-powered water heater ... The digitally controlled pellet boiler and the central heat it makes possible ... The high-speed Internet connection and the access it provides to the entire world ... The propane-powered backup generator that keeps the house electrified during outages ... These and other aspects of the house would bewilder them.

What would James and Hannah think of how the land has changed during the almost one hundred eighty years since they built their house on Whitcomb Hill? What would they think of their twentieth-century successors having let the fields revert to forest—fields that Reuben, Levi Sr., and the Whitcomb brothers labored so hard to clear? What would they think of our not *needing* the fields? Edith and I obtain most of our food by driving a few miles to the local supermarket and selecting from over 300,000 items on the shelves. That cornucopia would be incomprehensible.

What would they think of our children's lives? Of Robin's and Cory's easy, work-free childhoods? Of their almost perfect good health from birth through their late twenties and early thirties? Of their years in school, during which our fellow twenty-first-century parents' anxieties focused on test scores, their kids' "academic resumés," and the risk that other moms and dads might bring in cupcakes or cookies for the children rather than a healthy snack?

What would James and Hannah think of us? Would they find it baffling that I earn my income by tapping little alphabetic squares on a metal slab? Would they feel perplexed that I breed words and sentences rather than cows, pigs, and chickens? That I harvest metaphors, tales, images, and insights rather than oats, hay, and potatoes? Would they consider my life foolish, even pointless? Or would they regard it as just enviably less stressful than their own, much as a shopkeeper's life was easier than a farmer's in their own day?

What in turn would I think of them? When I conjure images of James and Hannah or of Robert and Betsey, I find it easy to believe that they were my superiors. For what must have been their great physical strength. For their obvious stamina. For the abundant, varied skills they possessed as they worked the land so productively. For their ability to withstand hardship and loss. I feel astonished, even humbled, when I consider their ability to manage all of the tasks they undertook, to raise their families despite having such limited resources available, to cope with a harsh climate without modern heat sources.

At the same time, I'm aware that these couples were members of the generations who started the process of damaging the American environment. Reuben and Levi Sr. took part in clearing of the Vermont landscape—a standard, crucial phase of early settlers' efforts to dominate nature. Then James, Levi Jr., Nathaniel and their wives; Robert and Betsey; Moses Jr. and Lucinda—all of them continued the process. What they regarded as "improved" land was land denuded of woods that had flourished for thousands of years. The result was the destruction of wildlife populations, damage to natural watersheds, increase in flooding, and early-phase harm to the global climate. James and Hannah, Robert and Betsey, Moses and Lucinda, and their offspring, too, continued the process. Could they have grasped what they were doing? Almost certainly not. They had simply inherited their cultures' values, expectations, and goals, which included killing or evicting the Native American population, "taming the wilderness," and subjecting nature to human dominion in accordance with nineteen-century assumptions about God's will. It's worth noting, however, that early environmentalists of their own era—not just Henry David Thoreau but also Zadock Thompson and George Perkins Marsh, the latter two being Vermonters of Betsey and James's own generation—were already sounding the alarm about environmental destruction. Mid-nineteenth-century observers weren't oblivious to the worrisome changes spreading around them. In any case, I temper my admiration for these people with concern for the environmental damage they set in motion.

Yet I admire them. I delight in what must have been the satisfactions in raising enough food to feed their families. I resonate with the dread and sadness they surely felt when witnessing so many of their children fall sick and die. I conjure them at times, usually when I meditate, and wonder what they thought of this hillside, a place that gave to them and took from them in equal measure.

Did our predecessors love this place back then as Edith and I do now, and perhaps for the same reasons? Did they delight in the sweet air during the warm seasons, in the clear light each autumn, in the welter of stars on winter nights? Did they revel in the wood thrushes' songs at dusk? Did they stir at the sight of the moon rising over the eastern ridge? Or did they resent this land, perhaps even hate it, for the hardships that living here forced on them? For the brutal winters. For the unceasing labor. For the loneliness endured while living in an isolated little house. For the untreatable illnesses and sudden deaths. I'll never know.

My hope is that our predecessors somehow felt enough joy and pleasure to counterbalance the weight of their hardships and their grief. I can't help wondering how many nights Betsey Bohonon lay awake thinking about the calamities that 1864 visited upon her family, and how many nights Robert lay awake beside his wife wondering how to console her, and himself. I can't help wondering about James and Hannah—what they gained during their time here, and what they lost. I can only hope that for them, and for the families that followed them through the nineteenth and twentieth centuries, that living here wasn't just a vale of tears, that the cargo this house carried was more than just loneliness, that spending their brief time on Whitcomb Hill was (in E. B. White's words, quoting the meadow larks) a "sweet, sweet interlude."

Afterthoughts

Lovely, Dark and Deep

Midway in the journey of our life
I came to myself in a dark wood . . .

—Dante Alighieri, *Inferno* I 1-2[1]

Of our ten acres on Whitcomb Hill, five are open land, five are forest. The open land covers most of the plot's high end, an acre of lawn surrounding the house and four acres of meadow rolling downward to the woods. A trust owns the large expanse of land to the south. Our wooded terrain declines further to the east and abuts another neighbor's forty- or fifty-acre plot. What's down there delights us in many ways. The previous owners cleared brush and saplings to create hiking paths; there's a little stream along the northern property line; and the woods are dense enough that when we walk there, we quickly lose a sense of scale and imagine our snippet of forest to be large. What we own is actually a small property by local standards. With our neighbors' land unfenced and undeveloped, however, and with coyote, fox, deer, and moose footprints crisscrossing the snow all winter, the woods around us somehow feel expansive and wild.

During our second year of living in Vermont, Edith and I decided to contact Brooke and Donna, the couple who own the property to the south of ours. They had "posted" their land—that is, had put up signs warning against intrusion. State law requires people to contact the owners in writing before setting foot on posted land. Our request for permission received a cordial note in the mail: "We welcome our neighbors to enjoy exploring our little woods on foot year 'round. In the summertime the trail should make for a great hike to town."

Following this go-ahead, we started venturing deeper into the forest to reconnoiter. The month was February, the weather cold but less snowy than during our first winter. The snowpack was a crusty ten inches deep. Edith chose to use snowshoes, while I preferred to wear knee-high insulated boots. Together we headed due south from our property; we slogged until we hit a spur of the VAST Trail, a network of paths maintained by the statewide snowmobilers' club; and we then angled east over a hilltop until we hit the main path. From there the trail wound its way down to the farms bordering the roads below it. We had the woods to ourselves. We saw many animals' tracks in the snow but no sign of the animals themselves.

"You Will Be Fine"

> This is the forest primeval.
>
> —Henry Wadsworth Longfellow,
> *Evangeline*, Canto I[2]

This is not the forest primeval. While inspiring illusions of being ancient, Vermont's woods are relatively new. European settlers in the 17th and 18th centuries clear-cut huge areas of the Northeast to create their farms; then, during the 19th century, as the frontier moved west and emigration started easing population pressures in New England, a process of natural reforestation began. This trend continued during the 20th century and into the 21st. Deep in our own woods, we have found agricultural machinery abandoned in what had been open farmland many decades earlier. Three fourths of Vermont's land is now forested; in its percentage of total surface area, this state is the fourth-most wooded in the nation. Our property is typical of this countryside. But because the process of reforestation is so recent, most of the trees here are small: maples thinner than the lodgepole pines of my Colorado youth. Old-growth maples, oaks, and other big trees are now uncommon.

Even so, the forest can feel ominous. Our neighbors Brooke and Donna warned us outright in their message: "Please be aware that a black bear has her den on our land, and there are numerous transient predators, including red fox, wolves, and coyotes. Exercise a degree of caution, and if you see them, give them their space, and you will be fine." All very reassuring. Even so, crossing paths with any of these animals face to face would be an encounter we choose to avoid. We see their footprints. We hear the coyotes' howls and yips at night. We keep our distance.

Stopping by Woods

> "Friends who were present told me that after reading it, he looked up startled and said, 'Well, now, that does have a good deal of the ultimate about it, doesn't it?' Is it possible that he really had forgotten?
>
> —W. D. Snodgrass regarding Robert Frost's poem "Stopping by Woods on a Snowy Evening"[3]

In late June of 1922, after an entire night of writing at his kitchen table in the South Shaftsbury, Vermont, house where he lived with his family, Robert Frost realized that morning had dawned. "Having finished 'New Hampshire,'" Frost wrote later, "I went outdoors, got out sideways and didn't disturb anybody in the house, and about nine or ten o'clock went back in and wrote the piece about a snowy evening and the little horse as if I'd had an hallucination." This experience of "piggybacking" one poem on another wasn't unusual for Frost. "Sometimes one [poem] would grow out of an idea, leaving me relaxed. At other times the idea would produce a second growth, coercing itself as a Siamese twin on its predecessor. 'Stopping by Woods on a Snowy Evening' was written just about that way . . . But I must admit, it was written in a few minutes without any strain."[4] Frost immediately recognized that he had written something unusual. In a letter to Louis Untermeyer, Frost described this poem as "my best bid for remembrance." "Stopping by Woods" received widespread acclaim following its publication in 1923, and it is arguably the best-known, best-loved of Frost's works.[5] Many generations of schoolchildren have read it in their English classes, countless mourners have heard its last lines quoted at funerals, millions of people have cherished it, and millions of others have mocked it for what they perceive as its picture-postcard sentiments.

> Stopping by Woods on a Snowy Evening[6]
>
> Whose woods these are I think I know.
> His house is in the village though;
> He will not see me stopping here
> To watch his woods fill up with snow.
>
> My little horse must think it queer
> To stop without a farmhouse near
> Between the woods and frozen lake
> The darkest evening of the year.
>
> He gives his harness bells a shake
> To ask if there is some mistake.
> The only other sound's the sweep
> Of easy wind and downy flake.
>
> The woods are lovely, dark and deep.
> But I have promises to keep,
> And miles to go before I sleep,
> And miles to go before I sleep.

What has amused and puzzled me about "Stopping by Woods" ever since I first encountered it as a teenager has been the disparity between the poem's sunny reputation and its more fundamental, darker nature. This reaction may be partly a consequence my habitual tendency to see the skull beneath the skin. It's also possible that during my adolescence, one or another of the writers who visited my parents at our family's house—among them the American Studies scholar Stuart James, the novelist John Williams, and the poet Alan Stephens—pointed out the shadows in Frost's snowy landscape. In any case, I never felt inclined to see this poem as the dollop of maple syrup that many people believe it to be.

Frost himself struggled with its implications. Although he wrote the first draft quickly, the ending caused him considerable difficulty. Jay Parini, one of Frost's biographers, has written: "The whole poem may have come to Frost in a flash, but he had great trouble with the last stanza. It was some time before he thought of solving the problem by simply repeating the last line: 'And miles to go before I sleep.'"[7] Even early on, many readers caught the ambiguous but troubling implications that result from the repetition. Some raised the issue with Frost at public events, though "in countless readings of the poem in public, he would leave it open to the listener to decide what was meant by the poem's suggestive final stanza." Now and then he would be more explicit, even reassuring. "To an audience at Bread Loaf," writes Parini, "he once said that the ominous-sounding last lines don't necessarily mean that 'you're going to do anything bad' when you get home."[8] Frost even took umbrage over suggestions that the final stanza suggests a longing for death. As late as 1962—the year before he died—Frost was still denying that *thanatos* suffuses the poem. The American poet Louise Bogan commented on a November reading that year: "He insisted that 'Stopping by Woods' was NOT concerned with Death . . ."[9]

My own belief is that the poem itself refutes Frost's denials. Another of Frost's biographers, Jeffrey Meyers, has written:

"The theme of 'Stopping by Woods'—despite Frost's disclaimer—is the temptation of death, even suicide, symbolized by the woods that are filling up with snow on the darkest evening of the year. The speaker is powerfully drawn to these woods . . . and wants to lie down and let the snow cover and bury him. The third quatrain, with its drowsy, dream-like line: 'Of easy wind and downy flake,' opposes the horse's instinctive urge for home and the man's subconscious desire for death in the dark, snowy woods. The speaker says, 'The woods are lovely, dark and deep,' but he resists their morbid attraction." [10]

Moreover, I believe that the darker aspect of the poem hinges on a single comma—or, rather, on the absence of one. The first line of the final stanza appears in two different ways in several different editions. *The Poetry of Robert Frost*, edited by Edward Connery Lathem, places a comma after "dark." [11] The mid-1990's Library of America edition deletes this comma. The presence or absence of that tiny punctuation mark subtly but profoundly changes the line's significance. "The woods are lovely, dark, and deep" presents the forest's attributes as loveliness, darkness, and deepness. "The woods are lovely, dark and deep" states both that the woods are lovely and that their loveliness consists of being dark and deep. The distinction isn't a question of pedantry but of existential substance. The critic Richard Poirier describes the situation bluntly: "In fact, the woods are not, as the Lathem edition would have it (with its obtuse emendation of a comma after the second adjective in line 13), merely 'lovely, dark, and deep.' Rather, as Frost intended in all the editions he supervised, they are 'lovely, [i.e.] dark and deep'; the loveliness thereby partakes of the depth and darkness which make the woods so ominous." [12]

Do that comma and its implications matter? In a world where almost two billion people lack sufficient food, where dozens of armed conflicts kill innocent civilians every day, where more than sixty million people are refugees, and where all inhabitants of the planet are threatened by climate disruption and environmental degradation, the obvious answer is No. Yet perhaps the comma (or its absence) may be significant anyway—on a literary level, at least, and perhaps on other levels as well. I would suggest three reasons why.

First, because the comma or its absence reveal Frost for what he is—a writer far more interesting and complex than the benign, grandfatherly New England farmer often celebrated in popular American culture. He is a writer whose portraits, both of the land and of people, reveal as much shadow as light.

Second, they matter because "Stopping by Woods," like others among Frost's finest poems, delivers an existential jolt. As Poirier states it neatly, "the woods are lovely and . . . their loveliness consists of being dark and deep." The shadows have their own magnetic pull. One can resist their pull, one ought to, but it's a mistake to deny the reality of this gravitational tug.

Third, they matter because ultimately this poem shows that the woods—their loveliness, darkness and deepness—aren't external.

Una Selva Oscura

> I am walking alone in a dark forest and I notice that I have lost my way.
>
> —C. G. Jung, *The Red Book* [13]

Entering the Dark Forest or the Enchanted Forest is a threshold symbol of the soul entering the perils of the unknown," writes J.C. Cooper in *An Illustrated Encyclopaedia of Traditional Symbols*. The forest is "the realm of death; the secrets of nature, or the spiritual world. . . . " In many folk tales, legends, and survival stories, the "[r]etreat into the forest is symbolic [of] death before initiatory rebirth."[14] Consistent with this view, the psychologist Bruno Bettelheim believed that wooded environments represent the inner realms of the mind. "Since ancient times the near impenetrable forest . . . has symbolized the dark, hidden, near-impenetrable world of our unconscious. [When] we succeed in finding our way out we . . . emerge with a much more highly developed humanity.[15] Stories about entering dark woods and struggling with strange experiences range from fairy tales ("Little Red Riding Hood," "Hansel and Gretel," "Vasilisa the Beautiful") to children's books (Frank Baum's *The Wonderful Wizard of Oz,* Gary Paulsen's *Hatchet,* and George MacDonald's *Phastastes*) to classical drama (Shakespeare's *A Midsummer Night's Dream*) to musical theater (Stephen Sondheim and James Lapine's *Into the Woods*) to canonic poems as varied as Dante's *Inferno* and Spenser's *The Faerie Queene.*[16]

Why is forest imagery so common, and what accounts for all the dark symbolism? Robert Pogue Harrison, writing in *Forests: The Shadow of Civilization,* an exploration of forests in Western thought and imagination, states that most inhabited lands throughout the West were more or less densely forested in the past. Western culture literally cleared its space in the midst of wooded places. The dark, densely vegetated areas thus defined the limits of civilization—the line between the Known and the Beyond. The forest has tended to represent "an outlying realm of opacity which has allowed . . . civilization to estrange itself, enchant itself, terrify itself . . . in short, to project into the forest shadows its secrets and innermost anxieties." Writing of the brothers Grimm, for instance, Harrison notes that

> Anyone familiar with the Grimms' fairy tales knows how prominently forests figure in the collection as a whole. These forests typically lie beyond the bounds of the familiar world. They are the places where protagonists get lost, meet unusual creatures, undergo spells and transformations, and confront their destinies. Children typically "grow up" during their ventures in the forests. The forests are sometimes places of the illicit—Little Red Riding Hood learns her lesson in the forest, telling herself at the end of

the tale: "Never again will you stray from the path by yourself and go into the forest when your mother has forbidden it"—yet more often than not they are places of weird enchantment.[17]

Christian traditions, especially, have tended to view forests as symbolic of the Other. Harrison goes on to state that "The Christian Church . . . was essentially hostile toward this impassive frontier of unhumanized nature. Bestiality, fallenness, errancy, perdition—these are the associations that accrued around forests in the Christian mythology. In theological terms forests represented the anarchy of matter itself . . . " Culturally, they "represented for the Church the last strongholds of Pagan worship. The darkness of forests—full of dangerous beasts both real and imagined—stood in opposition to the light of divinity cast from above." Harrison adds that "Where divinity has been identified with the sky, or with the eternal geometry of the stars, or with the cosmic infinity, or with 'heaven,' the forests became monstrous."[18]

> As the underside of the ordained world, forests represented for the Church the last strongholds of pagan worship. In the tenebrous Celtic forests reigned the Druid priests; in the forests of Germany stood those sacred groves where unconverted barbarians engaged in heathen rituals; in the nocturnal forests at the edge of town sorcerers, alchemists, and all the tenacious survivors of paganism concocted their mischief.[19]

Beyond all these issues of European history, symbolism, theology, and tale-telling lurks a simple, more visceral aspect of the situation. Woods can be scary places. Straying off a forest path—straying literally, not symbolically—almost always inspires dismay, concern, dread, alarm, and even panic. Spending a night lost in the woods leads to a state of hypervigilance. Every rustle of the leaves inspires uncertainty and fear. Is that creaking noise just the wind in the branches? Or is it a bear's approach? Uncertainty and fatigue leave the nerves jangled. Time slows to a crawl. Dawn seems eons distant. All of life's other problems shrink and vanish. As Walker Percy once noted: If you wish to cure yourself of modern existential angst, just spend a night lost in the bayou. You'll be eager—desperate—to trade the tangible, acute miseries and potentially life-threatening dangers of moment-by-moment survival for the familiar anxieties of contemporary life.

Not, Not, Not

One late-November morning a few years ago, Edith and I visited the Robert Frost Stone House Museum, currently maintained by the Friends of Robert Frost, in South Shaftsbury, Vermont. We had stayed overnight in Bennington with intent to visit the Stone House early the next morning, all the better to avoid the schoolchildren who often tour the place on field trips. The parking lot was almost empty—a good sign for crowd-averse visitors like us. Then we noticed a small slate hung on a fence near the path to the house: CLOSED TODAY. The museum's website hadn't mentioned this disruption of the schedule, so how could we have known? Edith and I stood near the car for a while and discussed our options. We could come back some other time, of course . . . But South Shaftsbury is a two-and-a-half-hour drive from our town, so we weren't thrilled to contemplate making another trip. Maybe we could have a look anyway? We walked up to the house, spoke with some of the contractors whose renovations had prompted the closure, and got their permission to explore the grounds, at least.

The house, built circa 1769, is fairly unremarkable in appearance despite its age. Two stories tall, it has a stone front and gabled ends. Double windows flank the centered front door. There's a pointed dormer in front and a single, very wide dormer with three windows in back. Brick chimneys rise from each end of the roof. The main roof slants down to a long closed-in back porch with sashed windows and plaid curtains. The window trim throughout is maroon. The back door opens out onto a small, stone-bordered plot of grass, then a much larger lawn stretching out toward a big gray barn, a single large white birch, and the woods beyond. Circling the house, Edith and I peered in through the windows but couldn't see much, given the bright reflections on the window panes, and we didn't want to annoy the nearby workmen; then, feeling abashed to behave like a pair of literary peeping Toms, we left the house and walked west across the back lawn toward the line of trees.

It wasn't as if I had necessarily expected Frost's South Shaftsbury woods to be The Woods as described in his iconic poem. I hadn't even assumed that these woods were his inspiration. The forest he described in "Stopping by Woods" was a grove in his mind, not on his land. Even so, I wanted to see the property he had owned during his decade in South Shaftsbury. I wanted to walk among the trees that Frost might have gazed upon through his kitchen window as he wrote early one morning in June of 1922.

Edith and I walked down a grassy path—once a road, surely—that took us away from the Stone House and across its back lawn. Dilapidated stone walls bordered the path, with rough meadow grasses rising alongside the rocks. This path declined for a hundred yard until it reached the forest. The trees were bare of leaves. Maple and birch predominated, though I saw a few stout pines as well. What seemed most striking was the thorny underbrush. Brambles rose both to the left and the right along the path and deep into the forest. Walking off-trail would have been possible but not easy or fun; pushing through the thicket would have left us scratched and bleeding. Edith and I kept to the footpath, which was wide and even. We proceeded for several hundred yards. The trail angled to the right, then started to decline. Many of the trees ahead were damaged, with ragged limbs and fallen branches angled this way and that. We continued on the footpath, letting it take us gradually downward until it opened up rather quickly into . . . a swamp. I was struck at once by the unappealing nature of these woods—not lovely, not dark, not deep.

Treeness

In her memoir *Living with a Wild God,* Barbara Ehrenreich describes a series of experiences, including one occurring at the edge of a forest, that troubled her as a teenager.

> I had wandered off and was leaning on a fence, staring at the woods in the pale late-summer sunlight, feeling nothing but impatience . . .
> And then it happened. Something peeled off the visible world, taking with it all meaning, inference, association, and words. If anyone had asked, I would have said I was looking at a tree, but the word "tree" was gone, along with all the notions of treeness that had accumulated in the dozen or so years since I had acquired language. Was it a place that was suddenly revealed to me? Or was it a substance—the indivisible, elemental material out of which the entire known and agreed-upon world arises as a fantastic elaboration? I don't know, but I was alarmed to discover that when you take away all human attributions—the words, the names of species, the wisps of remembered tree-related poetry, the fables of photosynthesis and capillary action—that when you take all of this away, there is still something left.
> I snapped out of it soon enough. . . .[20]

Driving home after the family excursion that afternoon, Ehrenreich settled in for the evening with her parents and sister. She ate dinner with her parents and sister, then withdrew to her room, where she read poetry until bedtime. "They were just doing their job, these poets, which is really the job of all of us—to keep applying coat upon coat of human passion and grandiosity to the world around us, trying to cover up whatever it is that lies underneath." She mused uneasily over what had taken place earlier that day. "I decided that evening that whatever I had experienced . . . had to be an aberration, like the retinal floaters that sometimes intruded on my vision after I'd been in the car too long on a hot, bright day. . . . Sleep deprivation does odd things to the mind, and this must be one of them, I thought—except it kept happening, and it gained legitimacy through repetition." After a sequence of these experiences in different settings over a period of several years, Ehrenreich struggled to interpret what had been happening. Eventually, she writes, "I came up with my own explanation, patched together from fragments of psychology I had picked up at the Lowell Public Library, which suggested that the most routine perception requires an impressive creative effort." The human sensory apparatus and the brain collaborate, she realized, not so much to perceive reality as to construct it. "There was plenty of input still pouring in as colors and lights and sound, but it wasn't getting sorted and categorized." She goes on to state that "There is a word for the episodes I was experiencing, though it was not available to me at the time: 'dissociation,' described in the psychiatric literature as 'feeling unreal' (either that one is unreal or that the world around one is unreal, if those two conditions can even be distinguished)." Describing this phenomenon as general cognitive breakdown, Ehrenreich then quotes the *Diagnostic and Statistical Manual of Mental Disorder*s regarding "the disruption . . . in the normal integration of consciousness, memory, identity, emotion, [or] perception." And she comments about herself: "in other words, one of these areas is not working correctly."[21]

❧   ❧   ❧

The American novelist Reynolds Price, writing in his memoir *Clear Pictures,* describes his own experience in a forest—a sense of relating *to* a forest. Living with his family at the time on the rural outskirts of Asheboro, North Carolina, Price spent long afternoons roaming through the woods. There, at the age of six, "with no knowledge of Wordsworth, Thoreau or the other pantheist nature poetry of England and America, I came upon a faith of my own, parallel to theirs but newly found."

> I wedged my hunting knife into the soft bark of a pine tree. I pressed my lips to the dull edge of the cool blade. In that moment as I felt the tree's life in the steel, I knew that the world beyond me—every separate thing that was not Reynolds Price—was as alive as I. Through means that, then or now, I couldn't begin to explain, I knew that all matter was alive and aware—listening, seeing, hearing or feeling in its own way. . . . Every thing knew, or knew of, every other thing; and each understood its kinship with all. . . . I perceived an immense created being, dispersed in millions of things. And I worked to press myself toward the being. I wanted it to know me as fully as possible and for me to know it.[22]

Unlike Ehrenreich, who has described herself repeatedly and consistently as an atheist, Price framed his own experience as theistic from the start: "Since I'd heard a lot about God, I assumed God had made this single thing. But I knew God wasn't it—God was not a rock, and he surely wasn't me. He was watching us though, with hope and a set of powerful rules that I needed to learn.[23] At later stages of his life, Price both accepted and pulled back from his boyhood experience, and he refined his sense of what he had experienced.

When I moved out of my trees-and-rocks mysticism into my years of church religion, it took me a while to see that I'd done two sizable things. One was good; one was ultimately bad. . . . The good was a slow discovery that my early sense of the connection, the union, of all things could lead me to a serious error. Tempting as the notion of that union was . . . I ran a grave risk in thinking that all things were not only one thing but that each thing contained its rightful portion of God the maker. I'd almost believed we're made out of God, and that's as risky an error as any.[24]

The Romantic movement, both in England and elsewhere in Europe, included beliefs that would have rejected the notion that being "made out of God" was "as risky an error as any other." Wordsworth, Coleridge, and Shelley in England all subscribed to variants of what Coleridge called "the latency of all in each." Similar pantheistic beliefs held true for Goethe in Germany and, later, for Whitman in America: beliefs that the Universe or Nature as the totality of everything is identical with divinity, as well as beliefs that an immanent God suffuses Nature or the Universe. None of these ideas was new. They are prominent in the early Vedas, in some aspects of ancient Egyptian religion, in some of the Presocratics, in some of the Stoics (starting with Zeno of Citium), in Marcus Aurelius, and in some of the early Gnostic Christian groups. During the Renaissance, Giordano Bruno espoused the concept of an immanent and infinite God—a heresy against Catholic doctrine that contributed to his excommunication and to his being burned at the stake in 1600. The most prominent premodern exponent of pantheism, however, was Baruch Spinoza, whose *Ethics* countered Descartes' emphatic dualism—the belief that the body and spirit are completely separate. By contrast, Spinoza held that body and spirit are the same, and he regarded God as the unity of all substance. (This concept led to Spinoza's own excommunication from the Jewish community in Amsterdam.) Pantheism gained adherents in the eighteenth century and eventually found widespread expression among the Romantics throughout Europe.

Wordsworth, writing in "Lines Written a Few Miles above Tintern Abbey," expresses these beliefs emphatically and eloquently:

> ... And I have felt
> A presence that disturbs me with the joy
> Of elevated thoughts; a sense sublime
> Of something far more deeply interfused,
> Whose dwelling is the light of setting suns,
> And the round ocean, and the living air,
> And the blue sky, and in the mind of man,
> A motion and a spirit, that impels
> All thinking things, all objects of all thought,
> And rolls through all things. Therefore am I still
> A lover of the meadows and the woods . . .[25]

Therefore am I still / A lover of the meadows and the woods ... The "presence" inherent "in all things"—Coleridge's "the latency of all in each"—is the immanent God coexistent and coequal with Nature. As H. W. Piper describes the situation: "One of the most prominent features of English Romantic thought is the belief that the universe was a living unity . . . [,] the belief that this life could be found in each natural object and that, through the imagination, a real communication was possible between man and the forms of nature."[26] Wordsworth doesn't describe a tree as such in "Tintern Abbey." If young William had confronted an individual tree in the same way that Ehrenreich and Price did during their respective youths, I believe that he would have perceived it as a manifestation of the imminent God.

Unmedi(t)ated Experience

> "[M]editation empties mind of words, concepts, and stories, the preoccupations that distance us from the immediate presence of earth's ten thousand things."
>
> —David Hinton, *Hunger Mountain*[27]

Barbara Ehrenreich, writing about her unnerving adolescent experience, states that while staring at the woods, she found that "[s]omething peeled off the visible world, taking with it all meaning, inference, association, and words." She decided later that same day that "whatever I had experienced ... had to be an aberration"; and, later still, she concluded that this experience was the result of dissociation—a pathological state. But what if Ehrenreich's experience—"looking at a tree, but [with] the word "tree" ... gone, along with all the notions of treeness that had accumulated in the dozen or so years since I had acquired language"—what if this experience isn't necessarily dissociation but, instead connection? Perhaps "taking [away] all meaning, inference, association, and words" isn't necessarily a psychiatric aberration but, instead (at least under some conditions), a normal and rich experience. An experience that, far from isolating the person who undergoes it, returns her to the ground of her being. The question I'm raising here invokes the Buddhist concept of "unmediated experience." Is it possible that the human sensorium, collaborating with the human mind, can perceive objects, events, and experiences without the trappings of "meaning, inference, association, and words," as Ehrenreich puts it? That is, can a person experience the world itself rather than a heavily filtered, interpreted, potentially distorted view of the world? Attempting to answer these questions can benefit from considering the Buddhist concept of mindfulness (in Pali: *sati,* also translated as "bare attention").

First, however, an aside—and a caveat. Over the past ten or fifteen years, the concept of mindfulness has been extracted from the realm of Buddhist philosophy and meditation and has been adapted to an almost infinite array of mainstream purposes. Or, to put the situation more bluntly, mindfulness has been kidnapped from the meditation hall and put to work in the marketplace. You can now attend workshops on mindfulness is schools, churches, and storefronts throughout the land. You can buy DVDs, online courses, and iPhone apps to teach you mindfulness. Medical clinics teach mindfulness to help patients manage chronic pain. Psychologists teach mindfulness to help clients ease anxiety and depression. Corporations teach mindfulness to help sales reps, assembly line workers, managers, and executives cope with workplace stress, increase productivity, and achieve organizational goals. Several branches of the U.S. military teach mindfulness to help soldiers reduce stress and focus on their duties. In short, non-Buddhists have adopted and commodified mindfulness in a thousand different ways.

Some benefits may accrue from this phenomenon. However, even a cursory review of this commodification warrants concern. Many Buddhists are concerned that mindfulness has been co-opted, diluted, and cheapened. At the same time, some non-Buddhist observers feel concerned that if mindfulness can be so easily adapted to such varied and sometimes questionable purposes, perhaps it doesn't have any substance after all. These are legitimate concerns. I can understand the sources of the backlash currently developing against the fad of mindfulness. I sympathize with a thoughtful friend who exclaimed, "I'm sick of all this mindfulness!" At the same time, I believe that rejecting the fundamental Buddhist concept and practice of *sati* on account of faddish spinoffs is like bulldozing a lush, vibrant orange grove because you hold Tang in contempt.

Returning to the main point, however: the concept of mindfulness may clarify Ehrenreich's experience and its implications.

Here's how a prominent Buddhist monk and teacher, Bhante Guranatana, describes the nature and value of mindfulness:[28]

> When you first become aware of something, there is a fleeting instant of pure awareness just before you conceptualize the thing, before you identify it. That is a state of awareness. Ordinarily, this state is short-lived. It is that flashing split second just as you focus your eyes on the thing, just as you focus your mind on the thing, just before you objectify it, clamp down on it mentally, and segregate it from the rest of existence. That flowing, soft-focus moment of pure awareness is mindfulness. In that brief flashing mind-moment you experience a thing as an un-thing. You experience a softly flowing moment of pure experience that is interlocked with the rest of reality, not separate from it. . . . [T]his moment of soft, unfocused awareness contains a very deep sort of knowing that is lost as soon as you focus your mind and objectify the object into a thing. In the process of ordinary perception, the mindfulness step is so fleeting as to be unobservable. We have developed a habit of squandering our attention on all remaining steps, focusing on the perception, cognizing the perception, labeling it, and most of all, getting involved in a long string of symbolic thought about it. That original moment of mindfulness is rapidly passed over.

Guranatana further clarifies the nature of mindfulness by describing these attributes [with my italics]:

> *Mindfulness is pre-symbolic.* It is not shackled to logic.

> *Mindfulness is not intellectual awareness.* It is just aware.

Mindfulness is participatory observation. The meditator is both participant and observer at one and the same time.

Mindfulness is mirror-thought. It reflects only what is presently happening and in exactly the way it is happening.

Mindfulness is nonjudgmental observation. It is the ability of the mind to observe without criticism. It does not take sides. It does not get hung up on what is perceived. It just perceives.

Mindfulness is non-conceptual awareness. . . . It is not thinking. It does not get involved with thoughts or concepts. It does not get hung up on ideas or opinions or memories.

Mindfulness registers experiences, but it does not compare them. It does not label or categorize them. It just observes everything. It is . . . the direct and immediate experiencing of whatever is happening, without the medium of thought. It comes before thought in the perceptual process.

Mindfulness is present-time awareness. It takes place in the here and now. It is the observance of what is happening right now, in the present moment.

Mindfulness is non-egotistic alertness. It takes place without reference to self. With mindfulness one sees all phenomena without references to concepts like "me," "my," or "mine."

Mindfulness is awareness of change. It is observing the passing flow of experience. It is watching things as they are changing. Mindfulness is watching things moment by moment, continuously.

Mindfulness is objective, but it is not cold or unfeeling. It is the wakeful experience of life, an alert participation in the ongoing process of living.

Mindfulness adds nothing to perception and it subtracts nothing. It distorts nothing. It is bare attention and just looks at whatever comes up.

To summarize: *sati*—mindfulness or bare attention—is a state of awareness. It's now widely understood even outside of the Buddhist community that mindfulness involves being "in the moment." However, mindfulness isn't *only* a matter of being in the moment. Most central and most important to *sati* is what one does with the moment. The goal is a full waking awareness of whatever is happening. As the American Buddhist writer Joseph Goldstein writes in his description of sati: "Bare attention . . . brings the mind to a state of rest. Bare attention means observing things as they are."[29]

Revisiting Ehrenreich's account of her unsettling adolescent experience, it's worth revisiting her succinct description: "I would have said I was looking at a tree, but the word "tree" was gone, along with all the notions of treeness that had accumulated in the dozen or so years since I had acquired language." Viewed from a Buddhist perspective, it appears that Ehrenreich experienced a state of precocious, unbidden, involuntary mindfulness. Every aspect of what she describes here coincides with Buddhist assumptions about *sati*—bare attention. This experience is vivid, intense, fundamental, and stripped of the assumptions, biases, memories, fantasies, and intellectual frameworks that can be rich in their own right but that also filter and even obstruct our perceptions. How and why did Ehrenreich's state of bare attention arise? That wasn't clear to her at the time, and she remained uncertain about its sources for a long time afterwards; otherwise she wouldn't have spent the next several decades attempting to make sense of what happened. What she describes, however, fits the description of what occurs during moments of intense mindfulness. Ehrenreich found this event disquieting, even alarming. States of unease and alarm aren't inevitable during meditation or under other circumstances conducive to mindfulness, but neither are they uncommon. Mindfulness strips away the habits of perception that prompt us to take the world for granted. Mindfulness removes the familiar context from the objects, events, thoughts, and emotions we perceive. As Ehrenreich succinctly states, "Something peeled off the visible world, taking with it all meaning, inference, association, and words." Mindfulness was the peeler. What remained after the process of peeling was (in Buddhist parlance) unmediated experience. Ehrenreich saw a tree, but she saw the tree with the word "tree" . . . gone, along with all the notions of treeness that had accumulated. The result was profoundly unsettling: "I was alarmed to discover that when you take away all human attributions—the words, the names of species, the wisps of remembered tree-related poetry, the fables of photosynthesis and capillary action—that when you take all of this away, there is still something left."

Or, to paraphrase Gertrude Stein's famous dictum: A tree is a tree is a tree.

This situation immediately drops us into deep waters: the question of what constitutes perception. For many years I've repeatedly mulled over Immanuel Kant's notion of *das Ding an sich*. This phrase is most commonly translated into English as "the thing in itself" or "the thing as such." What would it mean to perceive *das Ding an sich*? Given the nature of the human sensorium, would a perception of any *Ding an sich* even be possible? Stated another way: can I perceive something by a means (any means) that bypasses the senses I'm equipped with? The answer seems an obvious No. Since I'm a human being, the only way by which I can perceive anything is through the ordinary human senses. My senses necessarily keep me at a distance from what I perceive.[30]

Suppose that while walking in the woods, I notice a tree several hundred yards away. The tree suddenly falls over. I observe the trunk strike the ground and, just an instant later, I hear the crash. Which perception—the sight or the sound of the tree falling or the resulting crash—is the actual *event* of the tree's fall? The answer: neither one. Light travels faster than sound, so initially I saw the tree strike the ground; then, once the sound waves reached my ears after a brief lag, I heard the crash. But both sensory impressions were my delayed experience of an event that was already over before I "perceived" it. The same circumstances would hold true even if I perceived a stationary tree over a longer period time—for instance, by staring at or even meditating upon the tree. Try as I might, I would only experience my sensory impressions of the tree; I would never perceive *der Baum an sich*.

Is it possible, however, that under some circumstances I might perceive the tree in a less cluttered way—that is, through a less obtrusive filter of "meaning, inference, associations, and words"? This possibility is where *sati* enters the picture. By means of bare attention, I might attain a state of openness and clarity—what some schools of Buddhism call Big Mind—that would allow me something closer to perceiving the tree itself rather than the tree festooned with the preconceptions, memories, emotions, attitudes, biases, preferences, aversions, and fantasies that I would habitually and unconsciously impose on it otherwise. That perception might lead to (or at least be part of) a more complete apprehension of the world than if I insist on imposing my own grab bag of impressions and preferences. While I might not perceive "the tree in itself," I might come closer to perceiving the tree more clearly, more fully, and in a less distorted way. Or, as the English literary critic John Banville states the situation: "Entire mythologies, entire theogonies, have been invented to shore up our manifold illusions. Human creatures pass their days in gloriously irresponsible denial of the cold reality staring them pitilessly in the face. . . . [T]he only solution must be to turn back to the thing, the *Ding* if not quite the *Ding an sich,* and refuse to be distracted by mere chattering: the thing, that is, and not our notions of it."[31]

More than four decades ago, a friend who practiced a form of meditation similar to my own told me, "What we're trying to do while meditating is to observe the world like babies—to see things as if for the first time. But we're trying to do that consciously." I resisted this notion at the time. As a twenty-four-year-old, I resented the possibility that babies might be more perceptive than I was in the full flower of young manhood. In my late sixties now, after having helped raise a daughter and a son from birth through young adulthood, I can grasp and accept the wisdom of children—including babies. They do indeed see the world for the first time. The downside of their perceptions is lacking the context that years of experience allows. Perhaps, then, the benefit of bare attention is to see the world as if for the first time but in a state of full, volitional, wakeful consciousness.

Whose Woods These Are I Think I Know

One afternoon in late spring I start meditating in the woods. There's no hut there, not even a crude platform, only a folding metal chair that I carried down the first time around and then abandoned among the maples for future use. It's easy to cross the meadow, enter the forest, find the chair, do my sitting, and leave.

Whenever I descend to that meditation place, I'm struck time after time that the woods are indeed lovely, dark, and deep—and also lovely, dark and deep. This place is just a few hundred yards from the house yet seems a separate world. Unlike our meadow, the forest can't be taken in at a glance; it can't be grasped. I walk among the trees but can see only fifty or a hundred feet ahead, often less. Overall, this isn't a dangerous place. I can't become literally lost in this Dark Wood—it's too small. A one-minute walk west and I'm back in the meadow. Our woods lack the sheer scope of the forested landscapes I've faced in the Rockies, the Olympics, and the Andes. While it's true that wild animals live here—the fox, coyote, deer, moose, and bear whose tracks Edith and I have seen—these creatures generally keep their distance. Something jolts in a nearby tree, and I startle . . . but the marauding beast is only a blue jay. No, the creatures aren't a menace. What's alarming in the woods is what's alrming anywhere: the otherness of the Other. Only in this sense am I playing with fire. How great is the risk? Hard to say. Connect with that power and I may as well grab a high-voltage wire. What will I do, then, if the woods truly reveal themselves—if they overturn my comfortable assumptions that the tree trunks, the branches, the twigs, the leaves, the birds, and the scraps of sky visible overhead are only the beautiful surfaces they present to me?

Even so, meditating in the woods quickly becomes a routine that I enjoy and deeply value.

The woods in springtime . . .

The bare branches are budding. Sunlight remains weak but still manages to penetrate the sparse foliage. The breeze plays the tiny leaves: a fugue of rustles. Phoebes call out in intervals of descending minor seconds. Meditation in this setting is so easy that it's difficult: there's a constant risk of falling asleep. I try my best to stay alert. Almost at once, however, I doze off and immediately plunge into REM sleep. My dream: sitting in these same woods and fretting about my recent diagnosis of sleep apnea. I perceive myself recalling the initial consultation with the somnologist, my overnight sleep study at the medical center, and the follow-up visit with the doctor, who informs me: *We have many treatment options.* My eyes snap open. I'm bewildered to find myself not in the doctor's office but in a forest. For a moment, everything I see around me is black-and-white. Last year's leaves lie at my feet, a few fallen branches among them, and stick-like maple saplings rise before me.

The woods in summer . . .
 Full foliage now, deep green drenched in shadow. Not just the canopy but the underbrush as well are fully leafed, blocking my view beyond half a dozen yards. Birdsong is continuous: the sparrows' twitters, the jays' shrieks, the crows' caws, the robins' exclamations, and, late each afternoon, the wood thrushes' liquid notes. Beyond the birds I hear the wind in the trees: cyclical, heavy, surf-like. The air is warm enough to feel like an embrace, so I'm comfortable and feel no distractions from my own body. It's hard to avoid feeling that this place is perfect. Time slows and stops. There is nowhere else on earth.

The woods in autumn . . .
 This fall has been the most colorful that Edith and I have experienced so far. The leaves started turning early, stoked to incendiary reds and oranges, and stayed brilliant much longer than usual. Why? We had an unseasonable cold spell in late September—temps in the low twenties—so perhaps the hard frost jump-started the colors. Beyond that, who knows. The consequences for me are a meditation spot that stays temperate and radiant a week into November. Sitting in the woods is effortless and serene. As the leaves fall, clicking and clattering around me, the sunlight intensifies day by day. Soon I'm basking in warm, yellow light even in the middle of the woods.

My question day after day, week after week, month after month, season after season: to what degree does meditating here reveal the woods at all . . . or does sitting here reveal only more layers of my thoughts and feelings about the woods?

A tree is a tree is a tree. The woods are the woods are the woods.

The Longest Evening of the Year

> His soul swooned slowly as he heard the snow falling faintly through the universe and faintly falling, like the descent of their last end, upon all the living and the dead.
>
> —James Joyce, "The Dead" [32]

On the winter solstice I venture down the hillside to my meditation spot. This part of the forest was open land throughout most of the 19th century; the Whitcombs, having farmed these slopes for decades, surely grazed their sheep here. Whitcomb Hill is now fully wooded. I arrive here at just past four in the afternoon, but the light is already fading. This is the longest evening of the year. We've had such heavy snowfall in recent weeks that I'm startled to realize that today is just the first day of winter. A layer of snow almost two feet thick blankets the ground. I haven't come here in over two weeks, so I locate my meditation chair only after several minutes of probing with a trekking pole. I tug it out, dust it off, and shove the legs back into the snowy substrate. I have to clear a space in front of the chair so that my legs have a place to rest. These preparations make for an awkward start. Yet despite the stark setting and the chilly air—it's eighteen degrees out—I'm intent on meditating here. I've prepared by wearing long johns, a turtleneck shirt, a sweater, a fleece, a parka, insulated boots, and ski mittens. I sit and settle in.

Light snowfall sifts through the trees. When I look straight up, I notice tiny clusters of flakes spiraling toward me. Their impact on my face feels lighter than the touch of gnats in summertime. The sky above is ashen. All around I see countless dark twigs, each one sheathed in ice from last week's storm, the ice in turn coated with snow from a few days ago. The almost total lack of wind leaves the snow intact. There must be some kind of breeze jostling the upper reaches of the trees, however, because I hear not so much a hiss as an intricate rustle like that of a hundred thousand shreds of cellophane being crumpled and uncrumpled.

I sit as I always sit. I watch my breath in the usual way. After the effort of slogging down here and digging out the chair, I need a few minutes before I can settle down and settle in. Our property is almost always peaceful, and this little spot deep in the woods offers peace within the peace. Soon I grow calm.

Then a recurrent worry surfaces: how alone am I here, anyway? Sportsmen sometimes venture onto our land. The various hunting seasons are now long over, so the presence of intruders is unlikely. (Just to be safe, I've worn my day-glo orange pullover cap to avoid the possibility that an off-season "jack hunter" might somehow mistake a meditating Buddhist for a deer.) If not people, what about animals? The local bear is surely hibernating... but maybe not, since climate change has altered many large mammals' winter patterns. What will happen if I see her loom through the snowfall and approach me? How eager will I be to have an unmediated experience of nature? To grasp *die Bär an sich?* Or, more likely, to be grasped *by* her? No thanks. Sitting there, I'm relieved when it's clear that our neighborhood *Ursus americanus* won't bother to visit. I'm relieved, too, when I receive no attention from *der Fuchs an sich, der Wolf an sich,* or *der Elchbulle an sich*—although neighbors have recently mentioned spotting a fox, a wolf, and a moose in the area. I'm here alone. Except for the hiss of snowflakes all around me, nothing moves or makes a sound.

I sit for a long time. Nothing happens. As is typical of my meditation, I reach no insight. Or perhaps the insight is simply that I've reached no insight. I'm here. That's it. That's all.

What, exactly, am I expecting? What am I trying to accomplish? Do I hope that by sitting among the trees I may feel something like what Barbara Ehrenreich felt when she found the word "tree" gone, along with all the notions of treeness that had accumulated over the years, yet still discovered something left over? Or am I hoping to perceive, as Reynolds Price appears to have concluded, that if all things "were not only one thing, [with] each thing [containing] its rightful portion of God the Maker," then there's an unbridgeable gap between God and Creation? Or am I hoping that, like the young Wordsworth, I might perceive "a sense sublime / Of something far more deeply interfused, . . . / . . . [that] rolls through all things"?

What would any of these perceptions tell me? If I could look at the woods and fully experience their loveliness, darkness, and deepness, what would I perceive?

Would I perceive that

$$God = Nature$$
$$and$$
$$Nature = God$$

and that for this reason the forest itself, as part of Nature, harbors a portion of divinity?

Would I perceive that

$$God \neq Nature$$
$$and$$
$$Nature \neq God$$

and in fact that God and Nature lie on opposite sides of a chasm—that God is the Creator and Nature is the altogether separate and subordinate Creation? And that as a tiny mote within Creation, I can perceive the splendor of what lies around me but never perceive the Creator as such?

Or would I perceive that

$$nature = nature = nature$$

and nothing more—that the woods are devoid of any divine substance and equally devoid of a Creator's mark—that is, that the trees are the trees, the forest is the forest, the snow is the snow, end of story?

Perhaps this is why the woods—lovely, dark and deep—inspire both longing and dread. The woods are beautiful indeed. If perceived clearly, however, they are vast, unfathomable, non-human, soulless. They have the potential to absorb without a trace anyone who, entering their realm, doesn't step carefully. Yet the woods' vastness and beauty are precisely what often draw me into them.

Sitting there and starting to shiver, I can't answer my own questions. In fact, I can't even ask the questions any more clearly than I have in the past—less so, perhaps, since I'm now growing more uncomfortable with each passing moment.

I'm disappointed but not surprised. What do I expect, really, coming down here to meditate in eighteen-degree weather? Enough already. Time to quit. Time to cover my chair with the black garbage bag I use to protect it and trudge up the hillside back to the house.

Then, unbidden, a strange interlude. While sitting there with my eyes closed, I watch the blankness of my shut-down field of vision open up and erupt into clouds of light. I say clouds because what I see appears almost meteorological in its scope and intensity, much as I've watched thunderheads billow toward me above timberline while hiking in the Rockies. The light is somehow at once orange-pink and pale blue. It simultaneously unfolds before me and washes over me. My first thought is that sunlight striking my face has triggered this phenomenon. But I'm facing east, the sun has already set at my back, and dusk is deepening into nightfall. When I open my eyes, everything before me is darker than when my eyes are closed. The light resumes fulminating when I close them again. The sight is both dazzling and subtle, voluptuous and insubstantial. It's so lovely that I can't stop watching. I've seen this brilliance before, though not in recent years. It's always a delight, always marvelous. What does it mean? Probably nothing. Is it . . . *significant?* Unlikely. The meditation teachers I've studied with, as well as many Buddhist writers whose books I've read, all state that no matter how impressive and enjoyable such experiences, they aren't important and may even be risky. Why? Because they are distractions and potential stumbling blocks. Like all thoughts, emotions, and experiences that arise during meditation, they are best simply observed and allowed to pass. For this reason I observe what's before me, I steep in this billowing cloud, and I let it diminish and fade away. [33]

By now I'm engulfed in slate-gray dusk. I could stay in the woods and accomplish little beyond getting chilled. If I persist, I'll suffer acute hypothermia. How long will it take before I experience confusion, decreased heart rate, metabolic shutdown, respiratory failure, and cardiac arrest? These are the outcomes that Frost's protagonist would have faced if he had abandoned his sleigh, entered the woods, and allowed the forest to absorb him. What would he have gained by doing so? Perhaps a realization of being a thread in the fabric of nature, fully interwoven as part of the tapestry yet also insignificant and transitory. A worthwhile insight. However, gaining it at the cost of death by exposure isn't what I have in mind. Meditating here is perfect, calm, serene—the only sound's the sweep of easy wind and downy flake—but after another ten minutes I've had enough. I want to go inside. I want to be back in the house with the lights on and a fire in the woodstove. I want to fix dinner for Edith and our son and our daughter, Cory and Robin, who are visiting for the holidays. I want to sit with them, share the meal, and enjoy the warmth of their companionship. *Sati*—bare attention? I want that too. *Bodhi*—full waking consciousness? Maybe I'll attain that some day as well—and, who knows, maybe even while sitting in our little forest. Not tonight, though. Not here.

The woods are lovely . . . dark . . . opaque . . .
But I have promises to make,
And miles to go before I wake.
And miles to go before I wake.

Notes

Chapter 1—House History: Glimmerings

[1] *Land Records*, Vol. 12, unpublished log of deeds and mortgages in the town hall archives for Washington, Vermont.

[2] *Town Records, Vol. 1—1795-1834*. Unpublished records in the town hall archives for Washington, Vermont. Also relevant is the log titled *Births, Deaths, and Marriages—1857-1867*. All otherwise uncited references to past local residents mentioned in this book have their sources in these town archives.

[3] C. G. Jung, *Memories, Dreams, Reflections* (New York: Vintage, 1989), pp. 158-160.

[4] Sigmund Freud, "The Dream; X. Symbolism in the Dream," in *A General Introduction to Psychoanalysis* ([City unknown:] Andesite Press, 2015), p. 254.

[5] Jan Albers, *Hands on the Land: A History of the Vermont Landscape* (Cambridge, Mass.: The MIT Press, 2002), p. 102.

[6] Ibid., p. 106.

[7] "Balloon Framed Houses," HereAndThere.org, http://www.hereandthere.org/oldhouse/balloon-framing.html.

Chapter 3—The Cheerful Reaper

[1] Robert Frost, "Mowing" in *Robert Frost: Collected Poems, Prose, and Plays*. Richard Poirier and Mark Richardson, eds. (New York: Library of America, 1995), p. 207.

[2] Barry Newman, "Who Needs a WeedWacker When You Can Use a Scythe?" *The Wall Street Journal* online, June 29, 2012, http://online.wsj.com/article/SB10001424052702304782404577490583379647566.html.

[3] David Tresemer, *The Scythe Book: Mowing Hay, Cutting Weeds, and Harvesting Small Grains with Hand Tools* (Chambersburg, Penn.: Alan C. Hood & Company, Inc., 1981, 1996), pp. 30, 34.

[4] Jónas Hallgrímsson, "Mowing Song" ("Sláttuvísa"), University of Wisconsin Digital Collections, http://www.library.wisc.edu/etext/jonas/Slattu/Slattu.html

[5] Frost, p. 26.

[6] Richard Poirier, *Robert Frost: The Work of Knowing* (Stanford, Calif.: Stanford University Press, 1977, 1990), p. 287-288.

[7] Leo Tolstoy, *Anna Karenina*, Richard Pevear and Larissa Volokhonsky, trans. (New York: Penguin Classics, 2004), p. 247-249.

Chapter 4—House History: One Hill, Three Families

[1] "Revolutionary [War] Soldiers Buried in Washington, Vermont," unpublished document in the archives of Calef Public Library, Washington, Vermont.

[2] *Town Records, Vol. 1 — 1795-1834*. Unpublished records in the town hall archives for Washington, Vermont.

[3] Lynn A. Bonfield and Mary C. Morrison, *Roxana's Children: The Biography of a Nineteenth-Century Vermont Family* (Amherst, Mass.: University of Massachusetts Pres, 1995), p. 173.

Chapter 5—Sound of Water

[1] Matsuo Basho, tr. Robert Hass, in David Landis Barnhill, "Basho's Hokku," http://www.uwosh.edu/facstaff/barnhill/es-244-basho/bashos-hokku.pdf

[2] Amy Lowell, "The Pond," *The Complete Poetical Works of Amy Lowell* (New York: Houghton Mifflin Company, 1955, 1983), p. 384.

[3] Tim Matson, *Earth Ponds: The Country Pond Maker's Guide to Building, Maintenance, and Restoration,* 3rd ed. (Woodstock, Vermont: Countryman Press, 2012), p. 126-131.

[4] Charles Egan, (trans./ed.), *Clouds Thick, Whereabouts Unknown: Poems by Zen Monks of China* (New York: Columbia University Press, 2010), p. 120.

[5] "Northern Spring Peeper—*Pseudacris crucifer*," The Cleveland Museum of Natural History online, http://www.cmnh.org/site/ResearchandCollections/VertebrateZoology/Research/Treefrogs/NSpringPeeper.aspx

[6] Basho, op cit.

Chapter 6—Night Fliers

[1] Adelaide Crapsey, *The Complete Poems and Collected Letters of Adelaide Crapsey*, Susan Sutton Smith, ed. (Albany, N.Y.: State University of New York Press, 1977), p. 86.

[2] Emily Dickinson, *The Complete Poems of Emily Dickinson*, Thomas H. Johnson, ed. (New York: Little Brown and Company, 1961), p. 841.

[3] Tracy V. Wilson, "What's the Difference between Moths and Butterflies?" HowStuffWorks.com, http://animals.howstuffworks.com/insects/moth-versus-butterfly.htm

[4] Percy Bysshe Shelley, "To—," PoetryFoundation.org, https://www.poetryfoundation.org/poems/45145/to-

[5] James Thurber, "The Moth and the Star," *Fables for Our Time* (New York: Harper Perennial; Harper Colophon, 1939; 1983), p. 17.

[6] Herbert Gold, "Vladimir Nabokov, The Art of Fiction" in *The Paris Review*, Issue 41, Summer-Fall 1967, https://www.theparisreview.org/interviews/4310/vladimir-nabokov-the-art-of-fiction-no-40-vladimir-nabokov

[7] Simon Karlinsky, ed., *The Nabokov-Wilson Letters, 1940-1971* (New York: Harper & Row, 1979), p. 302.

[8] Virginia Woolf, *Death of the Moth and Other Essays* (New York: Harcourt Brace and Jovanovich, 1974), pp. 3-6.

[9] Walter de la Mare, "The Moth," *Collected Poems 1901-1918* ([City unknown:] QontroClassic Books, 2010), p. 231.

[10] David Beadle and Seabrooke Leckie, *Peterson Field Guide to Moths of Northeastern North America* (New York: Houghton Mifflin Harcourt, 2012), p. 2.

[11] "Butterfly as Christian Symbol," Catholic Saints Info, http://www.catholic-saints.info/catholic-symbols/butterfly-christian-symbol.htm

[12] Annie Dillard, *Holy the Firm* (New York: Harper & Row, 1977; Harper Perennial, 1988, 2003), pp. 16-17, 35-36, 46-48, 74-76.

[13] Yosa Buson, *Haiku Master Buson*, Yuki Sawa, tr.; Edith Siefert, ed. (Torrance, California: Heian International, Inc., 1978), p. 37.

[14] Johan Christian Fabricius, "Biographical Sketch" in *The Bulletin of the American Museum of Natural History*, 1901, pp. 61-62.

Chapter 7—The Whiteness of the Weasel

[1] Herman Melville, *Moby-Dick; or, The Whale* (New York: Harper Perennial Classics, 2011), pp. 193-201.

[2] "Radio Rudy vs. Ferret Man," New York Observer online, http://www.observer.com/1999/08/radio-rudy-vs-ferret-man/

[3] Melville, pp. 544-546.

Chapter 8—House History: Working the Land

[1] United States Census for 1850.

[2] *Vermont Agricultural Census for 1850—Orange County:* unpublished logbooks located at the Vermont State Library, Montpelier, Vermont.

[3] Christopher McGrory Klyza and Stephen C. Trombulak, *The Story of Vermont: A Natural and Cultural History* (Hanover, N.H., and London: University Press of New England, 2015), p. 73.

[4] Ibid, p. 80.

[5] Bonfield and Morrison, p. 12.

[6] Ibid., pp. 39-40.

[7] Ibid., p. 29.

[8] Ibid., p. 11.

[9] Ibid., p. 11-12.

[10] Ibid., pp. 8-9.

[11] Richard Steckel, "The Health and Mortality of Women and Children, 1850-1860," in *The Journal of Economic History*, Vol. 48, No. 2, "The Tasks of Economic History" (June 1988), pp. 333-345.

[12] Bonfield and Morrison, pp. 8-9.

[13] Ibid., p. 34.

[14] Ibid., pp. 10-11.

[15] "Life Expectancy by Age, 1850-2011," Information Please, http://www.infoplease.com/ipa/A0005140.html

[16] "The Science of Longevity in the Twentieth Century," Slate.com, http://www.slate.com/articles/health_and_science/science_of_longevi_in_the_20th_century.html

Chapter 9—A Stand of Wheat

[1] Sarah Pitzer, "Growing Wheat of Your Own," in *Mother Earth News*, February/March, 2010, http://www.motherearthnews.com/real-food/growing-wheat-zmaz10fmzraw?pageid=1#PageContent1

[2] Personal correspondence with Ann Hazelrigg, Ph.D. A pertinent document I also found useful was the U.K. Agriculture and Horticulture Development Board publication titled "Wheat Disease Management Guide," https://cereals.ahdb.org.uk

[3] "Soviet Famine of 1932-33" in Wikipedia, https://en.wikipedia.org/wiki/Soviet_famine_of_1932–33

[4] Pitzer, op. cit.

[5] Ibid.

[6] Gleason, Ben and Theresa, "Growing Wheat in Vermont," a privately produced PDF document.

[7] Ann Hazelrigg, Ph.D., personal correspondence with the author.

Chapter 10—Sugar(ing)

[1] Stephen Long, *Thirty-eight: The Hurricane that Transformed New England* (New Haven: Yale University Press, 2017), p. 106.

Chapter 11—A Shed of His Own

[1] Virginia Woolf, *A Room of One's Own* (New York: Harcourt Brace & Co., 1989), p. 1.

[2] John Gardner, *On Becoming a Novelist* (New York: Norton, 1999), p. 45.

[3] Francesca Premoli-Droulers, *Writers' Houses* (New York: The Vendome Press, 1995), p. 168.

[4] Ann Trubek, *A Skeptic's Guide to Writers' Houses* (Philadelphia: University of Pennsylvania Press), p. 5.

[5] Ibid., p. 46.

[6] Premoli-Droulers, pp. 69-70.

[7] Bruce Newman, *A Beginner's Guide to Tibetan Buddhism* (Ithaca, New York: Snow Lion Publications, 2004), p. 63.

[8] Jack Kornfield, "Natural Freedom of the Heart: The Teachings of Ajahn Chah" in *Voices of Insight,* Sharon Salzberg, ed. (Boston and London: Shambhala, 2001), p. 37.

[9] Bhadantácariya Buddhaghosa, Bhikkhu Ñáóamoli, trans. "The Five Factors of the Resting Place," from *The Path of Purification (Visuddhimagga)* (Colombo, Sri Lanka: Buddhist Publication Society, 2010), pp. 113-116.

[10] Premoli-Droulers, p. 71.

[11] Woolf, Virginia: source uncertain.

[12] Premoli-Droulers, p. 154.

[13] Alan Shapiro, "Why Write?" in *Best American Essays*, Robert Atwan, ed. (New York: Mariner, 2006), p. 205.

[14] Ibid., p. 206.

[15] Premoli-Droulers, p. 4.

Chapter 13—House History: Changes and Calamities

[1] Military records accessed on Fold3.com.

Alva Bohonon's name appears in the records spelled both "Alva" and "Alvah" (e.g., the Bohonon brothers' enlistment documents, other U.S. records, and Vermont Civil War online.) Military records from the Civil War era generally list the youngest Bohonon brother as "Alva." The back of a portrait photo dating from around 1900 states the subject's name as "Alvah Bohonon." In this book I spell his name without the terminal *h* to avoid any confusion with his cousin Albah. Typical of that era is the Bohonon family members' many variant spellings of their surname—Bohonon, Bohonan, Bohonnon, and so forth.

Upon enlistment, Joseph, Harris, and Alva each received a "bounty" of $267, worth $4,878 in 2016 dollars, to be paid in installments. It's evident (and poignant) that on December 30, 1863, Robert Bohonon signed documents granting his two younger sons, both of whom were younger than twenty-one, permission to enlist: "I do hereby freely give my consent to his volunteering as a soldier in the army of the United States for the period of three years." Robert's signature is clear and vigorous; Harris's likewise, though the letters are less elegantly formed; and Alva's looks almost boyish.

[2] George Grenville Benedict, *Vermont in the Civil War* (Burlington, Vt.: Free Press Association, 1888), p. 226.

[3] Paul G. Zeller, personal correspondence with the author.

[4] Zeller, personal correspondence with the author.

[5] Military records accessed on Fold3.com. Additional information originates in "Civil War Soldiers," Historynet.com, http://www.historynet.com/civil-war-soldiers.

[6] Eric Lindblade, "The Newport Barracks" (blog), http://newportbarracks.blogspot.com

[7] Zeller, *The Ninth Vermont Infantry: A History and Roster* (Jefferson, North Carolina: McFarland & Company, 2008) p. 139.

[8] Ibid., p. 140.

[9] "Andersonville National Historic Site" in Wikipedia, https://en.wikipedia.org/wiki/Andersonville_National_Historic_Site

[10] Ibid.

[10] "Andersonville Prison Camp," HistoryNet.com, http://www.historynet.com/andersonville-prison-camp

[11] "John Ransom's *Andersonville Diary*," Kansas City Public Library online," http://www.kclibrary.org/blog/kc-unbound/john-ransoms-andersonville-diary

This remarkable document includes the author's day-to-day comments on the mounting death toll. See also John Ransom, *Andersonville Diary* (Auburn, N.Y.: 1881):

> April 9: "About thirty or forty die daily"; "Scurvy and dropsy taking hold of the men."
>
> April 11: "Everybody sick, almost, with scurvy—an awful disease. New cases every day."
>
> May 6: "There are about eight-five or ninety dying now per day, as near as I can find out."
>
> May 19: "Hundreds of cases of dropsy. Men puff out of human shape and are perfectly horrible to look at."
>
> June 8: "More new prisoners. There are now over 23,000 confined here, and the death rate 100 to 130 per day, and I believe more than that."
>
> June 26: "They die now like sheep—fully a 100 each day. New prisoners come inside in squads of hundreds, and in a few weeks are all dead."
>
> July 8: "Over a hundred and fifty dying per day now, and twenty-six thousand in camp."
>
> August 2: "Two hundred and twenty die each day."
>
> August 20: "Some day three hundred now die each day."

[12] Ransom, pp. 50-51.

[13] "Andersonville Prison Camp," HistoryNet.com, http://www.historynet.com/andersonville-prison-camp.

[14] "Captain Henry Wirz," National Park Service online, https://www.nps.gov/ande/learn/historyculture/captain_henry_wirz.htm

[15] "Soldier's Record for Bohonan, Joseph," in Vermont in the Civil War online, http://vermontcivilwar.org/get.php?input=9793

[16] "Soldier's Record for Bohonan, Harris," in Vermont in the Civil War online, http://vermontcivilwar.org/get.php?input=9791

[17] "Soldier's Record for Bohonan, Alvah," in Vermont in the Civil War online, http://vermontcivilwar.org/get.php?input=9779

[18] "Desertion in the Civil War Armies," www.civilwarhome.com/desertion.html

According to this article, the consequences for desertion were more complex than generally assumed:

> To suppress desertion the extreme penalty of death was at times applied, especially after 1863; but this meant no more than the selection of a few men as public examples out of many thousands equally guilty. The commoner method was to make public appeals to deserters, promising pardon in case of voluntary return with dire threats to those who failed to return.

Paul Zeller, responding to my questions in an e-mail, notes other aspects of Alva's situation:

> Finding "deserted" in a soldier's file is not uncommon. I don't know why [this term] was used so quickly. Sometimes I think it is used instead of AWOL. I have many cases where a kid was in the hospital, but was marked deserted in his company. If Alva got a government disability pension after the war the "deserted" in his record was corrected. And since he was not court martialed it was probably just an erroneous entry. Leaves/furloughs were given do freely at Sloan Hospital I don't see why he would have had to desert to go home.

[19] Muster roles and other military records accessed on Fold3.com.

[20] "Soldier's Record for Bohonan, Harris," in Vermont in the Civil War online, http://vermontcivilwar.org/get.php?input=9791

[21] Ibid.

[22] Ibid.

Chapter 15—Lunar Gravity

[1] Egan, p. 120.

[2] "Magnificent Desolation: Walking on the Moon," *Apollo 11 Lunar Surface Journal*, "One Small Step," http://en.wikipedia.org/wiki/Magnificent_Desolation:_Walking_on_the_Moon_3D#cite_note-2

I find it interesting, however, that although the Apollo astronauts were quintessential technicians—trained chiefly to perform the complex and dangerous tasks of flying spacecraft to the moon and, if possible, returning to earth alive—some of them related experiences far outside their roles as test pilots. Edgar Mitchell, for instance, underwent some sort of unitive experience during the return voyage of Apollo 14. "As he approached the planet we know as home," Mitchell has written of himself, "he was filled with an inner conviction as certain as any mathematical equation he'd ever solved. He knew that the beautiful blue world to which he was returning is part of a living system, harmonious and whole—and that we all participate, as he expressed it later, 'in a universe of consciousness.'" This description isn't inconsistent with what practitioners of Buddhist meditation and other spiritual disciplines strive for.

[3] Here are two examples of *jisei* that incorporate lunar imagery:

> Holding back the night
> with increasing brilliance
> the summer moon
>
> —Tsukioka Yoshitoshi (1839-1892)

> I pondered Buddha's teaching
> a full four and eighty years.
> The gates are all now
> locked about me.
> No one was ever here—
> Who then is he about to die,
> and why lament for nothing?
> Farewell!
> The night is clear,
> the moon shines calmly,
> the wind in the pines
> is like a lyre's song.
> With no I and no other
> who hears the sound?
>
> —Zoso Royo (1192-1276)

Source: http://www.quietspaces.com/deathpoems.html

[4] Edgar Bowers, "The Astronomers of Mont Blanc," *Collected Poems* (New York: Alfred A. Knopf), 1997.

Chapter 17—Heat

[1] "Data U.S. Climate, NOAA.gov, http://www.esrl.noaa.gov/psd/datausclimate/tmp.state.19712000.climo

[2] "Analysis by State," U.S. Energy Information Administration, http://www.eia.gov/state/analysis.cfm?sid=VT

[3] "Residential Use by State," eeere.energy.gov, http://apps1.eere.energy.gov/states/residential.cfm/state=VT#sources

> 59% of Vermont residents heat their homes with fuel oil; 12% use natural gas; 10% use propane; 5% use electricity; and 14% rely on "other," mostly firewood and wood products, such as pellets and biomass. Source: U.S. Department of Energy.

[4] "Health," vtwoodsmoke.org, http://www.vtwoodsmoke.org/health.html

[5] Nathaniel Hawthorne, "Fire Worship," *Mosses from an Old Manse* (Newcastle-upon-Tyne, U.K.: Cambridge Scholars Publishing, 2009), p. 93.

[6] Spike Carlsen, "Warming Up Fireplaces," in *The Family Handyman*, September, 1996, Vol. 46, Issue 8, p. 121.

[7] Robert D. Richardson, *Henry Thoreau: A Life of the Mind.* (Berkeley: University of California Press, 1986), p. 9.

[8] Bonfield and Morrison, p. 12.

[9] "Glossary of Forestry Terms in British Columbia," British Columbia Ministry of Forests and Range, https://www.for.gov.bc.ca/hfd/library/documents/glossary/Glossary.pdf

[10] "Vermonters Return to Wood Heat: It's Still the Way to Go," in Vermont Woman.com, http://www.vermontwoman.com/articles/2015/0215/05-woodheat/woodheatarticle.html

[11] Richard Martin, "Germany Runs up against the Limits of Renewables" in MIT Technology Review, May 24, 2016, https://www.technologyreview.com/s/601514/germany-runs-up-against-the-limits-of-renewables/

[12] "Products," Morsoe.com, http://morsoe.com/us/indoor/products

[13] "Calculator," TallahasseeGovernment.com, https://www.talgov.com/eper/eper-about-calc.aspx

A carbon-footprint calculator available from the state of Florida indicates that "the CO^2 emission factor for seasoned Live Oak is around 7,392 lbs. per cord, or 115 $kgCO^2$ per MMBtu." Edith and I burn "mixed hardwoods," primarily sugar maple, with a CO^2 emission factor somewhat different from oak. However, the approximate output is likely to be approximately 7,400 pounds of carbon per cord.

[14] "Estimating Firewood from Standing Trees," The University of New Hampshire Cooperative Extension, http://www.familyforests.org/research/documents/Estimatingstandingfirewood.pdf

[15] Windhager.com, http://www.windhager.com/int_en/

[16] "The Ten Hottest Global Years on Record," Climate Central online, http://www.climatecentral.org/gallery/graphics/the-10-hottest-global-years-on-record

[17] A Dutton et al., "Sea-level Rise Due to Polar Ice-sheet Mass Loss During Past Warm Periods," http://www.sciencemag.org/content/349/6244/aaa4019)

This article notes that global sea levels could rise by at least 20 feet, even if governments manage to keep global temperature increases to within the agreed upon "safe" limit of two degrees Celsius. The study warns that it is quite possible that 75 feet of sea level rise could well already be unstoppable, given current carbon dioxide levels in the atmosphere; and recent studies that show how rapidly Greenland and several Antarctic ice sheets are melting.

[18] "Carbon Dioxide Emissions Rise to 24 Million Pounds per Second," CBS News.com, http://www.cbsnews.com/news/carbon-dioxide-emissions-rise-to-24-million-pounds-per-second/

Last year, all the world's nations combined pumped nearly 38.2 billion tons of carbon dioxide into the air from the burning of fossil fuels such as coal and oil, according to new international calculations on global emissions published Sunday in the journal *Nature Climate Change.*

[19] "Climate Change," Environmental Protection Agency online, http://www.epa.gov/climatechange/ghgemissions/global.html

[20] "What Is the Current Temperature of the Universe?" Reference.com, https://www.reference.com/science/current-temperature-universe-9a4d7f89e72e21c3

Afterthoughts—Lovely, Dark and Deep

[1] Dante Alighieri. *Inferno.* Robert Hollander and Jean Hollander, trans. (New York: Doubleday, 2000), p. 3.

[2] Henry Wadsworth Longfellow, *Evangeline* (Mineola, N.Y.: Dover Publications, 1995), p. 11.

[3] W. D. Snodgrass, quoted in Jeffrey Meyers, *Robert Frost: A Biography* (Boston: Houghton Mifflin, 1996), p. 184.

[4] Louis Mertins, Robert Frost: *Life and Talks-Walking* (Norman, Oklahoma: University of Oklahoma Press, 1965), pp. 81-82.

[5] Nancy Lewis Tuten and John Zubizarreta, *The Robert Frost Encyclopedia* (Santa Barbara, Calif.: Greenwood Publishing, 2001), p. 347.

[6] Robert Frost, "Stopping by Woods on a Snowy Evening" in *Robert Frost: Collected Poems, Prose, and Plays*, Richard Poirier and Mark Richardson, eds. (New York: Library of America, 1995), p. 207.

[7] Jay Parini, *Robert Frost: A Life* (New York: Henry Holt and Company, 1999), p. 208.

[8] Parini, pp. 212-213.

[9] Meyers, p. 327.

[10] Ibid., p. 180.

[11] Frost, *The Poetry of Robert Frost,* Edward Connery Lethem, ed. (New York: Henry Holt and Company, 1969), p. 224.

[12] Richard Poirier, *Robert Frost: The Work of Knowing* (London: Oxford University Press), p. 181.

[13] C. G. Jung, *The Red Book* (New York: W. W. Norton & Co., 2009), p. 261.

[14] J. C. Cooper, *An Illustrated Encyclopaedia of Traditional Symbols* (New York: Thames & Hudson, 1987), p. 287.

[15] Bruno Bettelheim, *The Uses Of Enchantment: The Meaning and Importance of Fairy Tales* (New York: Vintage Books, 2010), p. 112.

[16] A striking but not unique instance of how the Christian imagination can conflate actual woods with a dangerous spiritual landscape appears in Nathaniel Hawthorne's description of forests in *The Scarlet Letter*. Typical is this passage in Chapter 16, "A Forest Walk":

> The road, after the two wayfarers had crossed from the peninsula to the mainland, was no other than a footpath. It straggled onward into the mystery of the primeval forest. This hemmed it in so narrowly, and stood so black and dense on either side, and disclosed such imperfect glimpses of the sky above, that, to Hester's mind, it imaged not amiss the moral wilderness in which she had so long been wandering.

Nathaniel Hawthorne, *The Scarlet Letter* (New York: Penguin Classics, 1962, 2016), p. 170.

[17] William Pogue Harrison, *Forests: The Shadow of Civilization* (Chicago: University of Chicago Press, 1993), p. 169.

[18] Ibid., pp. 171.

[19] Ibid., pp. 61-62.

[20] Barbara Ehrenreich, *Living with a Wild God: A Nonbeliever's Search for the Truth about Everything* (New York: Grand Central Publishing, 2014), pp. 47-48.

[21] Ibid., p. 53.

[22] Reynolds Price, *Clear Pictures*. (New York: Scribner, 2009), pp. 234-235.

[23] Ibid., pp. 235-236.

[24] Ibid., pp. 234-235.

25 William Wordsworth, "Lines Written a Few Miles above Tintern Abbey," from William Wordsworth, Stephen Gill, ed., The Oxford Authors (Oxford and New York, Oxford University Press, 1984), p. 134.

[26] H. W. Piper, *The Active Universe: Pantheism and the Concept of Imagination in the English Romantic Poets* (London: University of London, Athlone Press, 1961), pp. 3-4.

It's worth noting, however, that Wordsworth shifted his beliefs late in life to adopt a much more conventional, dualistic Christian framework for perceiving God and nature.

[27] David Hinton, *Hunger Mountain* (Boulder, Colo.: Shambala, 2012), p. 9.

[28] Bhante Guranatana, "Mindfulness" in *Voices of Insight,* Sharon Salzberg, ed. (Boston and London: Shambhala, 2001), pp. 133-139.

[29] Joseph Goldstein, *The Experience of Insight: A Simple and Direct Guide to Buddhist Meditation* (Boston and London: Shambhala, 1987), pp. 20-21.

[30] Immanuel Kant, Critique of Pure Reason, Paul Guyer and Allen W. Wood, eds. (Cambridge: Cambridge University Press, 1999), pp. 338-345.

[31] John Banville, "A Beautiful and Closely Woven Tapestry," in *The New York Review of Books,* Vol. LXII, No. 17 (November 5, 2015), page 60.

[32] James Joyce, "The Dead" in *Dubliners* (New York: The Viking Press, Inc., 1967), p. 224.

[33] Augustine. *Confessions* (New York: New American Library, 1963), p. 149.

I've been intrigued for many years by how often this same phenomenon appears in the spiritual literature of many different traditions. Just one example: Augustine of Hippo writing in Book VII, Chapter 10, of *The Confessions*:

> I entered into the innermost part of myself... and I saw with my soul's eye (such as it was) an unchangeable light shining above this eye of my soul and above my mind. It was not the ordinary light which is visible to all flesh, nor something of the same sort, only bigger, as though it might be our ordinary light shining much more brightly and filling everything with greatness. No, it was not like that; it was different, entirely different from anything of the kind.

Bibliography

Albers, Jan. *Hands on the Land: A History of the Vermont Landscape.* Cambridge, Mass.: The MIT Press, 2002.

"Andersonville National Historic Site." Wikipedia. Accessed November 3, 2016.

https://en.wikipedia.org/wiki/Andersonville_National_Historic_Site

"Andersonville Prison Camp." HistoryNet.com. Accessed July 13, 2016.

http://www.historynet.com/andersonville-prison-camp

Augustine. *Confessions.* New York: New American Library, 1963.

"Balloon Framed Houses." HereAndThere.org. Accessed May 26, 2016.

http://www.hereandthere.org/oldhouse/balloon-framing.html

Banville, John. "A Beautiful and Closely Woven Tapestry," in *The New York Review of Books,* Vol. LXII, No. 17 (November 5, 2015).

Basho, Matsuo, tr. Robert Hass, in "Basho's Hokku," by David Landis Barnhill.

http://www.uwosh.edu/facstaff/barnhill/es-244-basho/bashos-hokku.pdf

Beadle, David and Seabrooke Leckie. *Peterson Field Guide to Moths of Northeastern North America.* New York: Houghton Mifflin Harcourt, 2012.

Bhadantácariya Buddhaghosa. "The Five Factors of the Resting Place" in *The Path of Purification (Visuddhimagga),* Bhikkhu Ñáóamoli, trans. Colombo, Sri Lanka: Buddhist Publication Society, 2010.

Bettelheim, Bruno. *The Uses of Enchantment: The Meaning and Importance of Fairy Tales.* New York: Vintage Books, 2010.

Births, Deaths, and Marriages—1857-1916. Unpublished records in the town hall archives for Washington, Vermont. Bonfield, Lynn A. and Mary C. Morrison.

Bonfield, Lynn A. and Mary C. Morrison. *Roxana's Children: The Biography of a Nineteenth-Century Vermont Family.* Amherst, Mass.: University of Massachusetts Pres, 1995.

Bowers, Edgar. "The Astronomers of Mont Blanc." *Collected Poems.* New York: Alfred A. Knopf, 1997.

Buson, Yosa. *Haiku Master Buson,* Yuki Sawa, tr.; Edith Siefert, ed. Torrance, California: Heian International, Inc., 1978.

"Butterfly as Christian Symbol." Catholic Saints Info online.

http://www.catholic-saints.info/catholic-symbols/butterfly-christian-symbol.htm

"Carbon Dioxide Emissions Rise to 2.4 Million Pounds Per Second." CBS News online. Accessed September 38, 2016.

http://www.cbsnews.com/news/carbon-dioxide-emissions-rise-to-24-million-pounds-per-second/

Carlsen, Spike. "Warming Up Fireplaces" in *The Family Handyman.* September, 1996. Vol. 46, Issue 8.

"Civil War Soldiers: Information about Soldiers from the Civil War." HistoryNet.com. Accessed July 8, 2016.

http://www.historynet.com/civil-war-soldiers.

"Climate Change." Environmental Protection Agency online. Accessed May 1, 2016. (The Trump administration now appears to have removed this page.)

http://www.epa.gov/climatechange/ghgemissions/global.html

Cooper, J. C. *An Illustrated Encyclopaedia of Traditional Symbols.* New York: Thames & Hudson, 1987.

Crapsey, Adelaide. *The Complete Poems and Collected Letters of Adelaide Crapsey,* Sutton Smith, Susan, ed. Albany, N.Y.: State University of New York Press, 1977.

Dante Alighieri. *Inferno.* Robert Hollander and Jean Hollander, trans. New York: Doubleday, 2000.

de la Mare, Walter. *Collected Poems 1901-1918.* [City unknown:] QontroClassic Books, 2010.

Dickinson, Emily. *The Complete Poems of Emily Dickinson,* Thomas H. Johnson, ed. New York: Little Brown and Company, 1961.

Dillard, Annie. *Holy the Firm.* New York: Harper & Row, 1977; HarperPerennial, 1988, 2003.

Egan, Charles, trans./ed. *Clouds Thick, Whereabouts Unknown: Poems by Zen Monks of China.* New York: Columbia University Press, 2010.

Ehrenreich, Barbara. *Living with a Wild God: A Nonbeliever's Search for the Truth about Everything.* New York: Grand Central Publishing, 2014.

The English Romantic Poets. London: University of London, Athlone Press, 1961.

"The Environment." Morsoe.com. Accessed July 10, 2018.

    https://morsoe.com/us/about-morsoe/the-environment

"Estimating Firewood from Standing Trees." The University of New Hampshire Cooperative Extension (PDF). Acessed August 23, 2016.

    https://extension.unh.edu/resources/files/Resource001044_Rep1200.pdf

"Johan Christian Fabricius." *Encyclopedia Britannica* online. Accessed July 14, 2018.

    https://www.britannica.com/biography/Johann-Christian-Fabricius

Freud, Sigmund. *A General Introduction to Psychoanalysis.* [City unknown:] Andesite Press, 2015.

Frost, Robert. "Mowing" in *Robert Frost: Collected Poems, Prose, and Plays,* Richard Poirier and Mark Richardson, eds. New York: Library of America, 1995.

———. *The Poetry of Robert Frost,* Edward Connery Lethem, ed. New York: Henry Holt and Company, 1969.

Gardner, John. *On Becoming a Novelist.* New York: Norton, 1999.

"Germany Runs Up Against the Limits of Renewables." MIT Technology Review online. Accessed May 23, 2016.

    https://www.technologyreview.com/s/601514/germany-runs-up-against-the-limits-of-renewables/

Gleason, Ben and Theresa, "Growing Wheat in Vermont" (PDF).

    http://northerngraingrowers.org/wp-content/uploads/Wheat-Gleason.pdf

"Glossary of Forest Terms in British Columbia." Ministry of Forest and Range online. Accessed July 9, 2016.

https://www.for.gov.bc.ca/hfd/library/documents/glossary/Glossary.pdf

Gold, Herbert. "Vladimir Nabokov, The Art of Fiction" in *The Paris Review.* Summer-Fall 1967.

Goldstein, Joseph. *The Experience of Insight: A Simple and Direct Guide to Buddhist Meditation.* Boston and London: Shambhala, 1987.

Guranatana, Bhante. "Mindfulness" in *Voices of Insight,* Sharon Salzberg, ed. Boston and London: Shambhala, 2001.

Hallgrímsson, Jónas. "Mowing Song" ("Sláttuvísa"). Accessed May 1, 2016.

http://www.library.wisc.edu/etext/jonas/Slattu/Slattu.html

Harrison, William Pogue. *Forests: The Shadow of Civilization.* Chicago: University of Chicago Press, 1993.

Hawthorne, Nathaniel. "Fire Worship" in *Mosses from an Old Manse.* Newcastle-upon-Tyne, U.K.: Cambridge Scholars Publishing, 2009.

———. *The Scarlet Letter.* New York: Penguin Classics, 1962, 2016.

Hazelrigg, Ann Ph.D. Personal correspondence.

Hinton, David. *Hunger Mountain.* Boulder, Colo.: Shambala, 2012.

Job 1:9, King James Version.

"John Ransom's *Andersonville Diary*" (book review), Kansas City Public Library online, " http://www.kclibrary.org/blog/kc-unbound/john-ransoms-andersonville-diary

Joyce, James. "The Dead" in *Dubliners.* New York: The Viking Press, Inc., 1967.

Jung, C. G. *Memories, Dreams, Reflections.* New York: Vintage, 1989.

———. The Red Book. New York: W. W. Norton & Co., 2009.

Kant, Immanuel. *Critique of Pure Reason,* Paul Guyer and Allen W. Wood, eds. Cambridge: Cambridge University Press, 1999.

Karlinsky, Simon ed. *The Nabokov-Wilson Letters, 1940-1971.* New York: Harper & Row, 1979.

Kornfield, Jack. "Natural Freedom of the Heart: The Teachings of Ajahn Chah" in *Voices of Insight*, Sharon Salzberg, ed. Boston and London: Shambhala, 2001.

"Life Expectancy by Age, 1850–2011." InfoPlease.com. Accessed April 3, 2016.

http://www.infoplease.com/ipa/A0005140.html

Lindblade, Eric. "The Newport Barracks"(blog). Accessed June 5, 2016.

http://newportbarracks.blogspot.com

Long, Stephen. *Thirty-eight: The Hurricane that Transformed New England*. New Haven: Yale University Press, 2017.

Longfellow, Henry Wadsworth. *Evangeline*. Mineola, N.Y.: Dover Publications, 1995.

Lowell, Amy. "The Pond" from *The Complete Poetical Works of Amy Lowell*. New York: Houghton Mifflin Company, 1955, 1983.

Martin, Richard. "Germany Runs up against the Limits of Renewables" in MIT Technology Review, May 24, 2016.

Matson, Tim. *Earth Ponds: The Country Pond Maker's Guide to Building, Maintenance, and Restoration*, 3rd ed. Woodstock, Vermont: Countryman Press, 2012.

McGrory Klyza, Christopher and Stephen C. Trombulak, *The Story of Vermont: A Natural and Cultural History*. Hanover, N.H., and London: University Press of New England, 2015.

Melville, Herman. *Moby-Dick; or, The Whale*. New York: Harper Perennial Classics, 2011.

Mertins, Louis. *Robert Frost: Life and Talks-Walking*. Norman, Oklahoma: University of Oklahoma Press, 1965.

Newman, Barry. "Who Needs a WeedWacker When You Can Use a Scythe?" *The Wall Street Journal* Online. June 29, 2012.

http://online.wsj.com/article/SB10001424052702304782404577490583379647566.html

Newman, Bruce. *A Beginner's Guide to Tibetan Buddhism*. Ithaca, New York: Snow Lion Publications, 2004.

New York Observer staff. "Radio Rudy vs. Ferret Man." *New York Observer* online. Accessed March 3, 2012.

http://www.observer.com/1999/08/radio-rudy-vs-ferret-man/

"Northern Spring Peeper—Pseudacris crucifer" in Animal Diversity online. Accessed July 14, 2018

http://animaldiversity.org/accounts/Pseudacris_crucifer/

Parini, Jay. *Robert Frost: A Life.* New York: Henry Holt and Company, 1999.

Piper, H. W. *The Active Universe: Pantheism and the Concept of Imagination.* London and New York: Bloomsbury Academic, 2014.

Pitzer, Sarah. "Growing Wheat of Your Own." *Mother Earth News* online. Accessed October 4, 2017.

http://www.motherearthnews.com/real-food/growing-wheat-zmaz10fmzraw?pageid=1#PageContent1

Poirier, Richard. *Robert Frost: The Work of Knowing.* Stanford, Calif.: Stanford University Press, 1977, 1990.

Premoli-Droulers, Francesca. *Writers' Houses.* New York: The Vendome Press, 1995.

Price, Reynolds. *Clear Pictures.* New York: Scribner, 2009.

"Products." Windhager.com. Accessed October 17, 2016.

http://www.windhager.com/int_en/

"Profile Analysis." U.S. Energy Information Administration. Accessed September 12, 2012.

http://www.eia.gov/state/analysis.cfm?sid=VT

"Revolutionary [War] Soldiers Buried in Washington, Vermont." Unpublished document in the archives of Calef Public Library, Washington, Vermont.

Richardson, Robert D. *Henry Thoreau: A Life of the Mind.* Berkeley: University of California Press, 1986.

Shapiro, Alan. "Why Write?" in *Best American Essays,* Robert Atwan, ed. New York: Mariner, 2006.

Shelley, Percy Bysshe. *The Complete Poems of Percy Bysshe Shelley.* New York: Modern Library, 1994.

Snodgrass, W. D., quoted in Jeffrey Meyers, *Robert Frost: A Biography.* Boston: Houghton Mifflin, 1996.

"Soldier's Record for Bohonan, Alvah," in Vermont in the Civil War online.

http://vermontcivilwar.org/get.php?input=9789

"Soviet Famine of 1932-33" in Wikipedia.

https://en.wikipedia.org/wiki/Soviet_famine_of_1932–33

Steckel, Richard. "The Health and Mortality of Women and Children, 1850-1860," in *The Journal of Economic History*, Vol. 48, No. 2, The Tasks of Economic History (June 1988).

Teague, Allison. "Vermonters Return to Wood Heat: It's Still the Way to Go." VermontWoman.com. Accessed August 16, 2016.

http://www.vermontwoman.com/articles/2015/0215/05-woodheat/woodheatarticle.html

Thurber, James. *Fables for Our Time*. New York: Harper Perennial; Harper Colophon, 1939; 1983.

Tolstoy, Leo. *Anna Karenina*, Richard Pevear and Larissa Volokhonsky, trans. New York: Penguin Classics, 2004.

Tresemer, David. *The Scythe Book: Mowing Hay, Cutting Weeds, and Harvesting Small Grains with Hand Tools*. Chambersburg, Penn.: Alan C. Hood & Company, Inc., 1981, 1996.

Trubek, Ann. *A Skeptic's Guide to Writers' Houses*. Philadelphia: University of Pennsylvania Press.

Tuten, Nancy Lewis and John Zubizarreta, The Robert Frost Encyclopedia Santa Barbara, Calif.: Greenwood Publishing, 2001.

United States Censuses for 1840, 1850, 1860, 1870, and 1880.

Vermont Agricultural Censuses for 1850, 1860, 1870, and 1880.: unpublished log books located at the Vermont State Library, Montpelier, Vermont.

"What is the Current Temperature of the Universe?" Reference.com. Accessed June 24, 2016.

https://www.reference.com/science/current-temperature-universe-9a4d7f89e72e21c3

William Wordsworth, "Lines Written a Few Miles above Tintern Abbey," in *William Wordsworth*, Stephen Gill, ed., in The Oxford Authors. Oxford and New York: Oxford University Press, 1984.

Wilson, Tracy V. "What's the Difference between Moths and Butterflies?" *How Stuff Works.* Accessed November 12, 2012.

    http://animals.howstuffworks.com/insects/moth-versus-butterfly.htm

"Wood Stoves and Wood-fired Central Heaters." Vermont Official State Website, Agency of Natural Resources, Department of Environmental Conservation. Accessed August 16, 2016.

    http://www.vtwoodsmoke.org/health.html

Woolf, Virginia. *Death of the Moth and Other Essays.* New York: Harcourt Brace and Jovanovich, 1974.

———. *A Room of One's Own.* New York: Harcourt Brace & Co., 1989

Zeller, Paul G. Personal correspondence with the author.

———. *The Ninth Vermont Infantry: A History and Roster.* Jefferson, North Carolina: McFarland & Company, 2008.

Acknowledgements

Above all, I want to thank Doris and Paul, our immediate predecessors on Whitcomb Hill, who made our presence here possible in the first place; and also Dianne DeLong, whose friendship and assistance have made our years here better, safer, and more enjoyable.

In addition, I owe deep thanks to many other friends who have contributed to my efforts to make sense of Whitcomb Hill and to make being here satisfying in so many ways:

Julie Albright (1947-2017)
Edie Almeleh
James Barszcz and Jane Seiden
Fred and Sylvie Blanchard
E. Bohonnon
Elizabeth Burnett and Larry Tamburri
Erika Butler and Tom Absher
Gary Carrier
Carol Davis
Jason and Jill Deberville
Anita Diamant and Jim Ball
Shawn Ecklund
Jolie Elan
Tamara Cohn Eskenazi
Steve Fedder and Patty McBride
Justine Gadd, PA-C
Steve Gilbert and Missy Gilbert
Laurie Sverdlove and Gregg McCurdy
Jonna Goulding and Marcus Coxon
Annette Hansen-Schmidt and Kate Salerno
Joanne Hardy
Ann Hazelrigg, Ph.D.

Kevin Kerin, M.D.
Rick LaCroix
Pat Leebens and Charlie Soulé
Marilyn Levy
Steve Long and Mary Hays
Marty and Amber Lambert
Monique Lonner
Nicole Lonner Dorfman
Burt Kimmelman and Diane Simmons
Susan Margin
Lenny McCarthy
Robert Miller
Jeff Moran
Lance Moran
Ernie Parrish
Harry Roush
Kalynn Roya
Charlie Sandlin and Jen Jolls
John Silbersack
Bram Starr, M.D.
Andy Sweet and Nancy Rainwater
Robert and Phyllis Schultz
Jonathan Strong and Scott Elledge
Laurance Thompson
Vince Vermette
Meredith Sue Willis
Paul G. Zeller
Tony and Debbie Ziter

These institutions provided information and assistance:

Bailey/Howe Library, University of Vermont
The Rutland Historical Society
Shelburne Farms
The Shelburne Museum
The University of Vermont Agricultural Extension
The Vermont Granite Museum
The Vermont Historical Society
The Vermont State Library
The Vermont State Archives

About the Author

Born in Denver and raised in Colorado, Mexico, and Peru, E. J. Myers attended Grinnell College and the University of Denver. He has worked in a wide variety of professions and trades, including inpatient health care, emergency medical services, carpentry, cabinetmaking, and publishing. He is the author of forty-two published books, most issued by mainstream companies, among them four novels (*The Mountain Made of Light, Fire and Ice, The Summit,* and *Last Things*); fourteen children's books; a well-received, much-reprinted book about bereavement, *When Parents Die: A Guide for Adults;* and over a dozen books co-authored or ghostwritten for clients or other authors. He lives with his wife in central Vermont.

For information about E. J. Myers, visit his Web site at:

www.edwardmyerswriter.net

About Montemayor Press

Montemayor Press is an independent publisher of literature for adults and children. To learn more about our books, visit:

www.MontemayorPress.com

or write for a catalogue at:

Montemayor Press
P. O. Box 546
Montpelier, VT 05601

www.ingramcontent.com/pod-product-compliance
Lightning Source LLC
Chambersburg PA
CBHW072343100426
42738CB00049B/1494